A MARMAC GUIDE TO

HOUSTON

• AND •
GALVESTON

Edited by
Syd Kearney

PELICAN PUBLISHING COMPANY
Gretna 2001

ISBN: 1-56554-710-1

The Marmac Guidebook series was created by Marge McDonald of Atlanta, Georgia. As owner of a convention and sightseeing service in Atlanta for fourteen years, she learned from visitors and those relocating to Atlanta what information was important to them. She also served as president and CEO of the Georgia Hospitality and Travel Association for four years and in 1978 was named Woman of the Year in Travel by the Travel Industry Association of America.

We would like to thank the Greater Houston Convention & Visitors Bureau, the City of Houston, the Galveston Island Convention and Visitors Bureau, the Greater Houston Partnership, the City of Houston Aviation Department, the Port of Houston, the Houston International Protocol Alliance, Dancie Perugini Ware Public Relations, the Houston Museum of Natural Science, the Houston Museum of Fine Arts, and the many restaurateurs, hoteliers, and public relations professionals who made this book possible.

Information in this guidebook is based on authoritative data available at the time of printing. Prices and hours of operation of businesses listed are subject to change without notice. Readers are asked to take this into account when consulting this guide.

Printed in Canada
Published by Pelican Publishing Company, Inc.
1000 Burmaster Street, Gretna, Louisiana 70053

CONTENTS

MAPS

KEY TO LETTER CODE

E	Expensive	CH	Entrance Charge
M	Moderately Expensive	NCH	No Charge
I	Inexpensive		

FOREWORD

The Marmac guidebooks are designed for the resident and traveler who seek comprehensive information in an easy-to-use format and who have a zest for the best in each city and area mentioned in this national series.

We have chosen to include only what we can recommend to you on the basis of our own research, experience, and judgment. Our inclusions are our reputation.

We first escort you into the city, introducing you or reacquainting you as we relate the history and folklore that is indigenous to it. Next we assist you in *learning the ropes*—the essentials of the community, necessary matters of fact, transportation systems, lodging and restaurants, nightlife and theater. Then we point you toward available activities—sightseeing, museums and galleries, shopping, sports, and excursions into the heart of the city and to its environs. And finally we salute the special needs of special people—the international traveler, senior citizens, the handicapped visitor, children, and students. New residents will discover a whole chapter of essential information just for them. A special feature is a detailed chapter on nearby Galveston.

The key area map is placed at the opening of the book, always at your fingertips for quick reference, the margin index, keyed 1-6 and A-F, provides the location code to each listing in the book. Subsidiary maps include a downtown street map keyed 7-12 and G-L, intown and out-of-town touring maps, and a Galveston map.

The Marmac guide serves as your scout in a new territory among new people or as a new friend among local residents. We are committed to a clear, bold, graphic format from our cover design to our contents, and through every chapter of the book. We will inform, advise, and be your companion in the exciting adventure of travel in the United States.

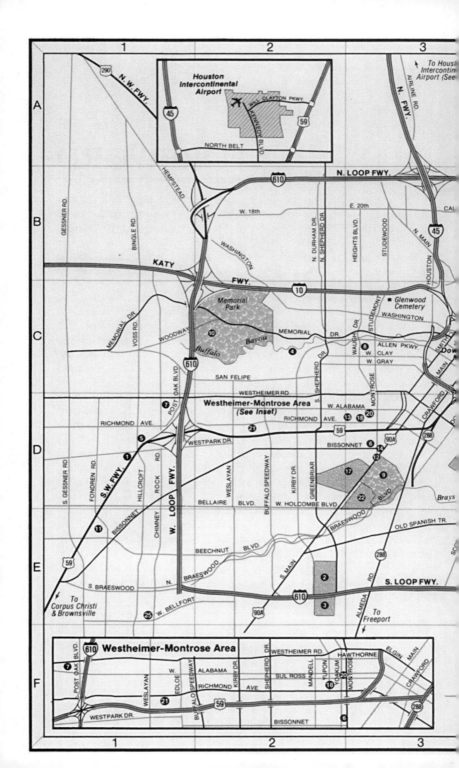

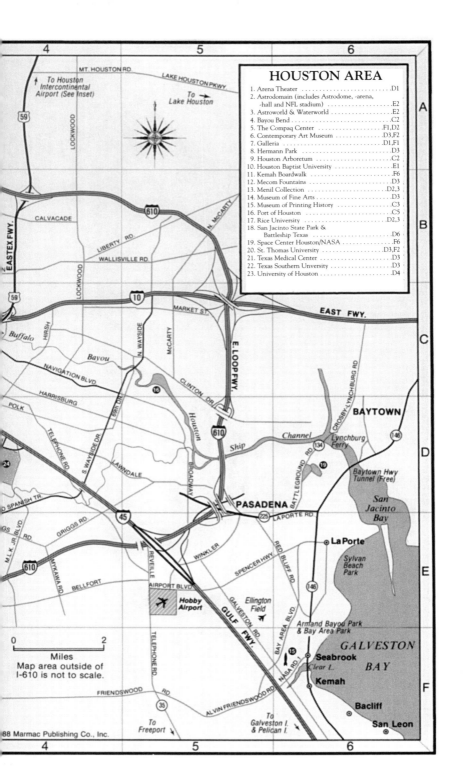

HOUSTON AREA

88 Marmac Publishing Co., Inc.

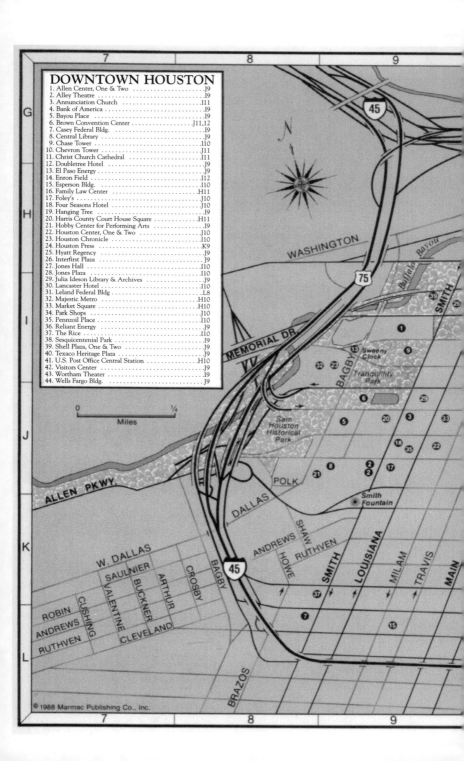

DOWNTOWN HOUSTON

© 1988 Marmac Publishing Co., Inc.

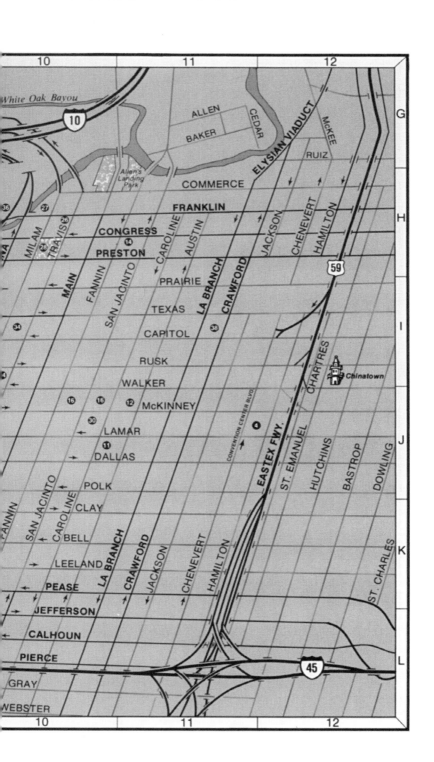

Sam Houston Statue   *Courtesy of Houston Convention & Visitors Bureau*

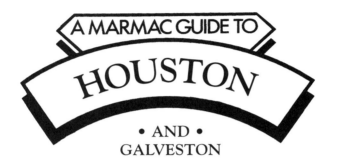

A MARMAC GUIDE TO

HOUSTON

• AND •
GALVESTON

HOUSTON PAST

The City's Namesake

The man for whom this city was named led a colorful life, at times defying reason, and often restless in his wanderings, but a born leader. A native of Virginia, Samuel Houston was a descendant of Sir Hugh of Padivan, the founder of Hughstown Castle of Scotland. Later the spelling changed and became Houston. During his lifetime Houston was governor of Tennessee and Texas, a U.S. Senator, signer of Texas' Declaration of Independence, twice president of the Republic of Texas, general in command of the troops that led Texas to victory in its war with Mexico, and an adopted Cherokee chief.

Houston's family had taken him to Tennessee at an early age where, living close to a neighboring Indian tribe, he became intrigued with its life and lore. He was later to marry Tiana, the daughter of the Cherokee chief, and great-aunt of Will Rogers. He practiced law and became governor of Tennessee. His future looked bright indeed, until suddenly his first wife, Eliza, left him; with that he resigned his post and elected to live with the Indians. Adopted as a son of the Supreme Chief, Oo-loo-te-ka, he served his tribe as an advisor. Later he was to move to Oklahoma where he continued to direct the affairs of the Cherokees. He had long nurtured a plan to emigrate to Texas, where the affairs of the American colonists in the Mexican state had captured his interest.

Working his way down through Arkansas, he arrived in Texas as settlers chafed under the bridle of edicts emanating from the government in Mexico City. The tall, vigorous politician from Tennessee captured the imagination of the colonists, and before long he was put in command of the cause for Texas independence.

Had he heeded the warnings of U.S. President Andrew Jackson, a good friend from his days in Congress, he never would have persisted in his resolve to free Texas from Mexico. Had he listened to his critics, Texas today might still be part of Mexico, and, most likely, so might much of the western United States. Had he listened, the United States might yet be confined to its eastern lands, deprived of the opportunity to exploit the vast resources and wide-open spaces of the West.

13

But Houston was determined that the small band of Texas heroes who had been wiped out while defending the Alamo at San Antonio had not died in vain. The battle cry, "Remember the Alamo!" was echoed as he positioned his small army at the San Jacinto peninsula. There he awaited the right moment to attack Gen. Antonio Lopez de Santa Anna's superior forces that had massed to put down the rebellious Texans. Houston had deployed between 700 and 800 men, clearly outnumbered by Santa Anna's 1,600.

On April 21, 1836, while the Mexican army was taking its "siesta," General Houston sounded the attack and in less than 20 minutes it was all over. Santa Anna was captured, the treaty of surrender was signed, and Texas was a free nation; the Republic of Texas was born.

This battle has been called the most decisive of our times, because just nine years later, Texans voted to join the Union, and the annexation by the United States precipitated the Mexican-American war. The United States won that war, along with much of what was to become the western half of our nation.

The City's Founders

With its independence, Texas saw the arrival of many pioneers and prospectors from the East seeking the good life in the new republic. Among them were two New York land speculators shopping Texas for an ideal interior location to establish a port city for trade with the outside world.

The brothers John and Augustus Allen had heard of a canal-like stream called Buffalo Bayou that merged with the San Jacinto River to the east and meandered toward fertile farms and cotton fields at its western extreme. Failing to acquire land at Harrisburg near the junction of that river and bayou, they followed the stream farther inland until they came upon its confluence with White Oak Bayou, a likely enough spot for vessels to turn around and head back out to sea. That spot, where they stepped ashore to found their townsite, is now Allen's Landing Park at the foot of Main Street in downtown Houston.

In August 1836, the brothers struck a deal, purchasing close to 7,000 acres from the widow of John Austin for a little more than $9,000 and, with a wise political gesture, named their town Houston, in honor of their friend and hero, General Sam.

Capital Gained

The Allens made another astute move when they talked the Texas congress into moving its headquarters from nearby Columbia to Houston. Thus, with their townsite as the capital of the new Republic of Texas, it follows that Gen. Sam Houston was soon named its president.

They advertised their city in newspapers in Texas and in the United States, boasting it would become a great commercial center and a leading world port.

The city fathers who followed the Allens imitated their lead with a spirit of boosterism, and down the line their prognostications proved right on target.

Seat of Government Lost

One of the few major goals that never came to fruition in Houston was the plan to make it the permanent seat of government. Actually, the Texas congressmen arrived from Columbia even before the Capitol building was begun, and they folded tents and headed for the hills of Austin before it was ever completed. Houston held on to its role as the capital only from 1837 to 1840 and again for a short span in 1842. For a while, then, it seemed founding the city had been a colossal mistake.

After Houston lost its coveted role in government, the value of Texas money took a nose dive, there was little trading, and the ravages of cholera and yellow fever nearly decimated the town. Things began to look bleak and there was even talk of abandoning Houston.

But the majority of settlers doggedly held on to the dream that one day the bayou could be developed into a major shipping lane. Progress was slow at first, because the land routes into the city were impassable during frequent monsoon-type rains that created such mud bogs even oxen sank helplessly up to their knees.

Rails Spur Shipping

But the coming of the railroads was the spur needed to boost progress along the bayou. Houston visionaries and power brokers wasted no time in connecting the rails at Houston with Galveston and all points into the interior. And it wasn't long before Houston was called "The City Where 17 Railroads Meet the Sea."

Port Dream Comes True

All this time the Port of Galveston held a strong lead in competition with Houston, but the idea of developing the bayou persisted. Off and on over the years Houstonians continued pressing for measures of improvement, widening and dredging Buffalo Bayou a little more each time.

Then, in 1900, Mother Nature dealt the island city of Galveston a devastating blow, which became known as one of the world's worst natural disasters. Islanders awakened early one September morning to a surprise hurricane and tidal wave of incredible force sweeping over the entire island, leaving up to 8,000 known dead in their wake. During the ensuing years, as Galveston worked to recover and rebuild, Houston was making headway toward the final phase of development of its port, and by 1914 it came of age. In that year President Woodrow Wilson pressed a button in the White House and, by remote control, fired a cannon that officially opened the Port of Houston to the world. As a feat of engineering, the port and the 50-mile ship channel that made it possible were such a marvel at the time that Will Rogers was prompted to say, "Houston is the only city that dared to dig a ditch to the sea."

Oil in Her Veins

A little more than a decade before this event, Houston had discovered oil in her veins. According to the *Guinness Book of World Records*, the world's greatest gusher was the Lucas well at Spindletop, about 90 miles east of the city. When it blew in, the gusher could be heard more than a mile away, and that mighty roar sent prospectors scurrying across Texas in hot pursuit of the "black gold." Many a fortune was made practically overnight, and thus the legend of the land of the "giants" and the big rich was born. Following Spindletop another huge discovery was made north of Houston at Humble. Those finds alone ultimately spewed forth two of the petroleum industry's top giants: Texaco and the Humble Oil & Refining Co. (later known as Exxon).

By the time oil was pouring in at record levels, Houston entrepreneurs were getting ready for the next move. Sinclair Oil was the first to build a major refinery here, and others followed, setting up along the banks of the bayou. In typical Houston fashion, business leaders saw to it the crude found its way from the fields through pipelines right into Bayou City refineries, where ships and rail cars lined up to take the byproducts out to waiting world markets.

Thus, drenched in oil, many Houstonians focused on other enterprises. Oil field tools and equipment were vital to the highly competitive drilling industry, and native sons such as Howard Hughes Sr. invented such things as the oval cone drill now in universal use. The multiplicity of these endeavors fixed Houston as the oil field equipment manufacturing capital of the world.

Diversification

During the two world wars, particularly the second, many new industries were introduced that became vitally important to Houston's economy. There were mass conversions of existing factories to wartime production, and still others opened. Steel manufacturing and ship-building became major industries as did plastics, synthetic rubber, and, using salt, gas, seawater, oil, and sulfur, explosives. The age of petro-chemicals had come into its own and, again, Houston took the lead as the world center for this new industry.

By the close of World War II, Houston had developed another rich resource—natural gas. It wasn't long before Easterners and Midwesterners became familiar with terms such as "Big Inch" and "Little Inch," which were pipelines that Houston-based Texas Eastern Transmission Corporation laid for transporting gas for heating wintry states in the north.

The People of Houston

From the beginning, Houston attracted foreign immigrants, pre-dominantly Germans and Bohemians (Czechs). The Mexicans were already here, and joining the waves of early immigrants were thousands of East Texas and Louisiana Acadians, who arrived to seek a better life in the oil fields and continue the age-old tradition of working area rice fields. Slavery was forbidden in Mexico, but many Texan colonists were involved in the illicit trade, and thus many blacks were brought in to work the rich cotton and farmlands along the Brazos River.

The majority of Houston's settlers, though, were Southern whites seeking a new life during the post-Civil War Reconstruction era. They brought their Old South ways with them, but because Houston strad-dles the gateway to the Southwest, Southern gentility often gave way to a harsher frontier spirit. Thus the newcomer will observe today that many native Houstonians seem a mixed breed of Southerners with out-going, robust Southwestern ways, influenced with an unusual blend of Mexican and Cajun "joie de vivre."

But in many other ways the Houstonian is a paradox, like Houston itself, resisting all attempts to be pinned with any label or description.

Houston is Houston. In some ways, it remains a self-centered youth with an unshakable faith in its own destiny, an undying belief in itself and in the idea that nearly anything is possible.

HOUSTON TODAY

A Lot Has Happened Since 1836 —————

Even the visionary Allen brothers who founded Houston would be astounded if they could return today to see what is happening to the bayou town they inaugurated in 1836.

These two New York land speculators promoted their new settlement with some fanciful claims, but even they couldn't possibly have foreseen that in just 160 years it would be the largest city in Texas and the fourth most populous center in the country with over 4.4 million inhabitants.

This gangly bayou town has come of age. The rawboned blue-collar kid has emerged a well-rounded, cosmopolitan center of commerce. And while with its miles of refineries and hundreds of other heavy industrial sites, Houston still wears her blue-collar label prominently, it has a new, dressier image. One that is broad enough to include space sciences, medical research, computer technology and the financial industry.

Houston's promising investment opportunities, minimum taxation, low cost of living, temperate climate, and overall potential have captured the imagination of the world, and immigrants continue to arrive daily.

Within the city limits sprawl 617 square miles of urban development and suburb linked by 570-plus miles of completed freeways and toll roads. Encompassed in that area are industrial sites, billion-dollar office parks, warehouse districts, shopping centers, condos, hotels, and subdivision housing.

All Around Town —————

Unlike many of the nation's cities, Houston has several major business districts. The oldest and largest is the downtown central business district, proclaimed by a magnificent futuristic skyline rooted primarily in finance and energy companies.

Uptown Houston boasts the tallest building in the nation outside of a central business district. The 65-floor, art-deco Williams Tower is the striking feature among hundreds of buildings constituting the Galleria/Post Oak area. The area concentrates elite shops, restaurants, hotels, and clubs together with office buildings and apartments.

The South Main corridor is the third key district, the site of the world-famous Astrodome and the renowned Texas Medical Center. Many medical support firms are in the area, along with the city's top museums and its premier park.

Outside these areas are many other major developments such as Greenway Plaza and the North Belt.

The Oil-Port Duo

The city continues to diversify into a much broader business base than one might expect, but the big bulge in the biceps continues to be energy in all its related forms. And any discussion of energy from oil should be in juxtaposition with shipping, because the exploration and refining industry practically grew up with the Port of Houston. Together they constitute the backbone of the city's economic base.

Before the great oil discoveries in the fields north and east of Houston, there was a concerted community effort to make good the founders' dream of developing a major world port. Eventually this was accomplished with the widening and dredging of Buffalo Bayou to accommodate every class of ocean-going vessel.

Who would have thought that the first steamboat, *Laura*, that made it up the twisting path of the sluggish bayou, would blaze the trail for the more than 5,000 ships a year that call on the Port today? And that the high banks' groves of cedar, pecan, magnolia and oak would be replaced with several major refineries and more than 150 other types of industrial plants stretching along the inner half of the 50-mile channel to the Gulf of Mexico?

Many of those companies manufacture such basic products as fertilizers, chemicals, plastics and synthetic rubber. But the Port handles a vast variety of other goods as well, including heavy machinery and oil tools, sand and gravel, steel, agricultural products, sulfur, paper and automobiles. Houston definitely has achieved its initial goal, for today the Port ranks first in the nation in international tonnage moved and second only to New York in total tonnage.

The Changing Profile

While much of the central spotlight remains on energy, there is growing diversity in other ventures entering the mainstream, making marked changes in the city's complexion.

A major shift in this direction occurred at the close of World War II, when city fathers foresaw the importance of establishing excellent medical care in a city even then experiencing a population explosion. In 1945 the Texas Medical Center was organized for the development and coordination of what has become one of the largest, if not the most mixed-use, medical facilities in the world. There are 41 different hospitals, schools, and other institutions, and the center is still expanding. It has gained greater renown in the prevention and treatment of children's diseases, cancer research and open-heart surgery. As a center of study, the complex draws more than 16,500 students annually from all parts of the globe, introducing a new kind of brain pool to Houston.

The Space Age

Another major image change took place in 1962, when the National Aeronautics and Space Administration opened its 1,620-acre training and flight-control center here. At the peak of the Mercury/Gemini/Apollo programs NASA employed more than 5,000, mostly white-collar personnel involved in space sciences and related industries.

It is noteworthy that more than 125 companies followed NASA to Houston. But even before that, the city had a standard-bearer in space-age pursuits at Rice University, the first to establish a curriculum in space sciences. That was followed by the implementation of similar programs at the University of Houston, which later opened a branch campus at Clear Lake, providing strong academic support for the space effort.

NASA virtually transformed what was once a cow pasture on the city's southeastern fringe. Today the growth continues all the way to Galveston Bay, where housing, hotels, shopping centers, low-rise office parks, and giant resort developments have been evolving.

The International Look

The best indicator of Houston's growth as an international city is George Bush/Intercontinental Airport, which several years ago added a fourth terminal. That facility is dedicated to international travelers, which number about 4.5 million each year. Bush/Intercontinental serves more than 31 million passengers annually, making it the twelfth-busiest airport in the nation.

The majority of foreign arrivals stem from international trade. Nearly 600 foreign companies have offices in Houston. And Houston-based firms account for more than 56 percent of Texas companies with offices abroad. Foreign interest is at such a peak there are now more than 70 nations with consular offices here.

The Convention and Visitor Trail

When Houston hosts a convention, and that happens an average of about 500 times per year, there is a trail of delegates from around the world.

Houston has long boasted more than 1.7 million square feet in exhibit halls situated mainly in three complexes, namely Reliant Park (formerly known as the Astrodomain), the George R. Brown Convention Center and Compaq Center (formerly known as The Summit). The largest at the moment is Astrodomain, anchored by the world-famous Astrodome and augmented by the Astrohall and the Astroarena. Second is the Brown Center, which contains about 500,000 square feet of exhibit space including a 6,600-seat arena, a 3,600-seat theater, a ballroom, and parking for 3,000 vehicles.

Compaq Center is one of the city's busiest venues, hosting more than 2 million guests to 220 events each year, including concerts and major touring shows. In addition, Compaq Center is home to four sports teams: the Rockets, two-time NBA champions; the Comets, three-time WNBA title winners; the Aeros, a minor-league hockey team that won the 1999 Turner Cup as champions of the International Hockey League; and the ThunderBears of the Arena Football League.

Other favorite venues of meeting planners include the Wortham Center, Jones Hall and the Aerial Theater, all within blocks of one another in the downtown Theater District.

And while conventioneers pour in from around the world, the Houston area hosts 14 million tourists each year.

Cognizant of this growing role in corporate, convention, and visitor business, the hotel industry is hitching its wagon to the Gulf Coast star. At this writing there are approximately 46,000 rooms in major Houston hotels and motels.

The Third Coast

In addition to promoting convention and visitor activity, the convention and visitors bureau is aggressively involved as liaison for

Houston with the motion picture industry. Texas has become known in the movie circles as the "Third Coast" in filming because of the its moderate weather and the breaks it gives moviemakers such as permit-free filming, and generous hotel and sales tax exemptions. It was the forerunner among Texas cities in establishing a sales staff to solicit films and the first to form a private motion picture council to better serve the industry. More than 120 projects, including three feature films, were completed here in 1999, generating $39 million in revenue.

The Entertainment World

As in its industrial circles, Houston has a broad mix in entertainment, ranging from country and western nightlife to esoteric dance programs, and from jazz to Gilbert and Sullivan. It is one of few cities in the country with its own grand opera, symphony, ballet, and professional theater, plus a Broadway musical production company.

The Academic Scene

Some of Houston's 48 colleges, universities and institutes are visitor attractions in themselves. Rice University, established in 1912 and arguably the flagship of Houston's excellence in science and engineering, is on South Main and boasts the only Ivy League-looking campus for miles.

The state's second-largest educational institution is the University of Houston, with a total enrollment of 33,000 on its five campuses. It is worth a stroll around the main campus just to see the numerous works of outdoor art and fine architecture. (See VISUAL ARTS.)

Texas Southern University opened in 1934 and is the state's largest predominantly black campus. The University of St. Thomas is Houston's largest Catholic school and was designed by the famous architect, Philip Johnson. Other institutions of higher learning include Houston Baptist University, the South Texas College of Law, University of Texas Health Science Center, Baylor College of Medicine, Prairie View A&M School of Nursing, and Texas Woman's University-Houston Center.

The Houston Independent School District is the nation's seventh-largest with more than 210,000 students.

Climate and Dress

At this point we would dispel all myths about Texans' boasts. We're not going to say come on down, the weather is great . . . we're simply going to say, y'all come but dress comfortably.

Here are the unvarnished facts: the average temperature year-round is 68.4 degrees Fahrenheit; while the average precipitation is 46 inches per year. As former Mayor Louie Welch once quipped, "If you don't like Houston's weather, just wait five minutes." He's the same source for the observation that "Houston has two seasons: summer and February." We can offer a dry run with afternoon temperatures in the high 90s in summer or a "blue norther" dipping overnight into the low teens during the brief winter months.

Yes, it's humid and it rains much of the year, but we can almost guarantee you'll never shovel snow, and about the only ice you'll see is at a skating rink. You can shed your winter wear from early March to early December and during that time should stick to cottons and other light-weights. But at times from early December through late February, you definitely should have a top coat, sweater and rain gear handy. But not to worry about summer or winter . . . Houston is climate-controlled with air conditioning everywhere, above ground, underground, and even outdoors in some spots.

This can be a dressy town, especially evenings at fine restaurants and chic parties. Otherwise it tends to be fairly casual, even at cultural events.

The most practical fabrics are cottons, linens, rayons, and silk for the summer and light woolen blends for winter. Houston men continue to stick with traditional conservative attire, especially those who are older and more professionally oriented. The young of both sexes lean toward jeans.

MATTERS OF FACT

There are many telephone numbers that you might need at your fingertips, whether you are a visitor here, a new resident, or even if you have lived in Houston a long time. Some of the contacts that might be of interest to you for more specific needs are already listed in chapters such as INTERNATIONAL TRAVELER, NEW RESIDENTS, TRANSPORTATION, and others.

The following list repeats a few of those numbers, but most fall under the heading of miscellaneous.

AAA—713-524-1851
Ambulance—Houston Fire Department
  dispatcher; 713-222-7644
American Red Cross—713-526-8300
Area Code—409, 713, 281 and 832
Automobile Registration License and
  Title—713-224-1919 (Harris County
  Tax Assessor/Collector's Office)
Better Business Bureau—713-868-9500
Chambers of Commerce—
  Greater Houston Partnership
  (Houston Chamber of Commerce);
  713-844-3600
  Acres Home; 713-692-7003
  Alvin/Manvel; 281-331-3944
  Baytown; 281-422-8359
  Clear Lake; 281-488-7676
  Conroe/Montgomery; 409-756-6644
  Crosby/Huffman; 281-328-6984
  Cy-Fair; 281-955-1100
  Deer Park; 281-479-1559
  East End; 713-926-3305
  Fort Bend County (Stafford, Missouri
  City, Sugar Land and First Colony);
  281-491-0800
  Friendswood; 281-482-3329
  Galena Park; 713-672-6443
  Galleria; 713-629-5555
  Galveston; 409-763-5326

Greater Heights Area; 713-861-6735
Greater Katy Area; 281-391-2422
Greater Southwest Houston;
713-666-1521
Houston Northwest; 281-440-4160
Houston West; 713-785-4922
Humble; 281-446-2128
La Porte/Bayshore; 281-471-1123
Magnolia; 281-356-1488
North Channel Area; 281-450-3600
North Forest; 281-449-3644
North Galveston County;
281-337-3434
North Houston/Greenspoint;
281-872-8700
Pasadena; 281-487-7871
Pearland; 281-485-3634
Rosenberg/Richmond; 281-342-5464
South Belt/Ellington; 281-481-5516
South Houston; 713-943-0244
Southeast Harris County;
713-473-7777
Texas City/La Marque; 409-935-1408
Tomball; 281-351-7222
Westchase; 713-780-9434
Woodlands/South Montgomery
County; 281-367-5777
City Hall—713-247-1000
  City Parks & Recreation (schedule of

events in public parks); 713-845-1000 or 713-845-1111.

Convention Center; 713-853-8000

Office of the Mayor; 713-247-2200

Climate—Annual averages (calculated over the past 50 years, according to the National Weather Service)

Rainfall: 46 inches (117 cm)

Snow or ice: almost zero

Normal summer maximum: 92° (33° C)

Normal winter maximum: 65° (18° C)

Driest month: March

Coldest month: January

Warmest month: July

Wind: South/southeast prevailing

Consumer Product Safety Commission—800-638-2772 (U.S. Govt.)

Consumer Services—Consumer Credit Counseling Service; 800-873-2227

Convention Sales & Services—

Clear Lake/NASA Area Convention & Visitors Bureau; 281-488-7676.

Galveston Island Convention & Visitors Bureau; 409-763-4311.

Greater Houston Convention & Visitors Bureau; 713-437-5200 or 800-446-8786.

Dentist—Dentist Referral Service; 713-961-4337

Doctor—Harris County Medical Society; 713-524-4267

Physician Referral Service; 713-942-7050

Texas Nurses Association; 713-523-3619

Emergency ambulance service; 911

Driver's License—Texas Department of Public Safety; 713-681-6187

Emergency/Crisis Counseling—

American Association for Lost Children; 713-466-1852

Child Abuse Hot Line; 800-252-5400

Children's Protective Services; 713-626-5701

City Wide Club; 713-523-1640

Crisis Hotline; 713-228-1505

Family Service Center; 713-861-4849

Food Bank; 713-223-3700

Houston Area Women's Center; 713-528-6798

Hunger Hotline; 713-680-9976

Interfaith Ministry of Greater Houston; 713-522-3955

Mental Health Association; 713-522-5161

Poison Control; 800-764-7661

Runaway Hotline; 800-392-3352

Emergency Rooms—

Bellaire Medical Center, 5314 Dashwood; 713-512-1500

Texas Children's Hospital, 6621 Fannin; 713-770-5454

Northside General Hospital, 2807 N. Little York; 713-697-7777

Hermann Hospital, 6411 Fannin; 713-704-4060

Ben Taub General, 1504 Taub Loop; 713-793-2000

Lyndon B. Johnson General, 5656 Kelley; 713-636-5000

Equal Employment Opportunity Commission—713-209-3320 (U.S. Govt.)

FBI—713-693-5000

Federal Information Center-800-688-9889 or TDD 800-326-2996

Fire—911 or 713-222-7643

Harris County—713-755-5000

Precinct 1; 713-755-6111

Precinct 2; 713-755-6220

Precinct 3; 713-755-6306

Precinct 4; 713-755-6444

County Judge: Harris County Judge Robert Eckels; 713-755-4000

Harris County Heritage Society—713-655-1912

Hospitals—Harris County Hospital District; 713-715-2800

Houston Independent School District—Information; 713-892-6390

Human Resources—Texas Department of Human Services; 713-692-1635

Institute of International Education—713-621-6300

IRS—800-829-1040

Lawyer—
Houston Bar Association;
713-7591133
Houston Lawyer Referral Service;
713-237-9429
Legal Aid—Gulf Coast Legal
Foundation; 713-652-0077
Library—Central Public Library;
713-236-1313
Local Laws—
Pertaining to alcohol sales and con-
sumption—Everyone must be 21 or
older to drink in public places in
Texas; liquor stores open 10 am-9 pm;
closed Sun and certain holidays; most
bars stay open until 2 am; no alco-
holic beverages sold on Sundays until
after noon. Even first offenders are
sentenced to jail for DWI. (See NEW
RESIDENTS chapter for details.)
Metropolitan Transit Authority—Route
information and schedules;
713-635-4000
Motorists Assistance Program—
713-225-5627
Newspapers—
Major dailies:
The Galveston *Daily News*;
281-488-1009 (Houston)
The Houston *Chronicle*; 713-220-7171
Passport Offices—713-209-3153
Pets—City of Houston Animal Control,
713-238-2170; Humane Society,
713-433-6421
Pharmacy (24-hour)—Eckerd Drugs;
713-660-8934
Randalls; 713-721-0052
Walgreens; 800-925-4733
Poison Control Center—800-764-7661
Police—Emergency; 911 or 713-222-3131
Population—About 1.9 million city; 4.4
million statistical region
Port of Houston—713-670-2400
Post Office—Central Station (H10), 401
Franklin; 713-227-1474
Radio Stations—
AM—
KBME (790) Top 40
KCOH (1430) Urban contemporary

KIKK (650) Business/talk
KILT (610) Sports
KJOJ (880) Christian
KMPQ (980) Tejano
KPRC (950) News/talk
KSEV (700) News/talk
KTEK (1110) Christian news, talk
KTRH (740) News/talk/sports
KYOK (1590) Disney
KYST (920) Spanish talk
FM—
KPVU (91.3) Jazz
KBXX (97.9) Urban contemporary
KHCB (105.7) Christian
KHMX (96.5) Adult contemporary
KTJM(98.5) Urban contemporary
KIKK (95.7) Country/Western
KILT (100.3) Country/Western
KKBQ (92.9) Country
KLOL (101.1) Album rock
KLTN (102.9) Spanish contemporary
KMJQ (102) Urban contemporary
KODA (99.1) Adult contemporary
KPFT (90.1) Alternative public access
KQQK (106.5) Bilingual Top 40/
Tex-Mex
KRBE (104.1) Top 40
KRTS (92.1) Classical
KOVE (100.7) Tejano
KUHF (88.7) Noncommercial classical;
National Public Radio
KLDE (107.5) Rock oldies
Sheriff's Office—Citizens complaints;
713-221-6000
Social Security—800-772-1213
Social Services—United Way Helpline;
713-957-4357
SPCA—713-869-8227
Television Stations—
KHOU-TV, Channel 11 (CBS);
713-526-1111.
KHSH-TV, Channel 67 (Home
Shopping Network); 281-331-8867
KHTV-TV, Channel 39 (Warner
Bros.); 713-781-3939
KNWS-TV, Channel 51
(Independent); 713-974-5151
KPRC-TV, Channel 2 (NBC);
713-222-2222

KRIV-TV, Channel 26 (Fox); 713-479-2600

KTMD-TV, Channel 48 (Telemundo); 713-974-4848

KTRK-TV, Channel 13 (ABC); 713-666-0713

KTXH-TV, Channel 20 (Paramount); 713-661-2020

KUHT-TV, Channel 8 (PBS); 713-748-8888

KXLN-TV, Channel 45 (Univision); 713-662-4545

Texas Alcoholic Beverage Commission—713-880-3003

Texas Medical Center—
Administration; 713-791-6454
Visitor Information; 713-797-0100

Texas Rangers—713-681-1761

Texas Workforce Commission—
800-832-9243

Tickets—
Front Row; 713-977-5555
Northside Tickets; 281-447-8833
Ticket Company; 713-629-4747
Ticket Connection; 713-524-3687
Ticketmaster; 713-629-3700

Time Zone—Central (on daylight-saving time April-October)

Traffic Laws—Seat belts, infant seats required by law. May turn right on red; may turn left on red when moving from one-way street onto another one-way. Consuming alcohol while driving is illegal. Maximum speed limit on freeways 70 mph. (See TRANSPORTATION.)

U.S. Customs—281-985-6700

Veteran's Administration—Benefit information and assistance; 800-827-1000

Weather—Forecast and local weather; 713-529-4444

TRANSPORTATION

With the existing variety of transportation systems including land, rail, air, and sea, getting to Houston is no problem.

But once you arrive, getting around Houston is problematic. A city of 617 square miles with nearly 3.6 million registered vehicles, Houston's only method of mass transit is a public bus system run by the Metropolitan Transit Authority (Metro). Metro hopes to have a light rail system up and running between downtown and the Astrodome area in 2004, but until then it is vital that visitors and newcomers be familiar with the alternatives for moving about in this highly mobile city.

TO HOUSTON

Air

Houston's two major commercial airports are Bush Intercontinental and William P. Hobby. Together, operating at nearly full capacity, they serve more than 40 million passengers annually. Combining the services at both airports, Houston has nonstop flights to 114 U.S. cities, plus 34 direct and nonstop destinations abroad, thus conveniently connecting Houston to more than 148 points around the globe.

Located 22 miles north of downtown, **Bush Intercontinental (IAH)** is the city's largest. Seventeen airlines serving more than 150 cities worldwide are spread out among its four terminals. Houston-based Continental schedules more than 500 flights per day from its IAH hub.

The similar design of all four terminals is as follows: the lower level is devoted to a subway route and pedestrian tunnel; the street level is for baggage claim, car/taxi/limo pickup, and auto rentals; and level three is primarily for enplaning, deplaning and people amenities. Ticket counters are on level three in all terminals except the international terminal, where they are at street level.

The Mickey Leland International Airlines Building (also known as Terminal D or IAB) handles all international arrivals and departures at

Bush Intercontinental. As the eighth-largest international passenger gateway in the nation, Bush's federal inspection service facilities can process arriving international passengers in 30 minutes or less.

Bush/IAH terminals have signage and audio assistance in English and Spanish; at Customs the directories are also in German, French, and Arabic. At IAB, passengers can exchange more than 74 currencies between 7:30 am and 9 pm, when all scheduled international flights arrive and depart. All the auto rental pick-up and drop-off points are located near the airport on Kennedy Boulevard and Will Clayton Parkway, with counters at the terminals.

Intercontinental Airport's four runways (6,000 ft., 9,400 ft., 10,000 ft., and 12,000 ft.) can serve any present or foreseeable aircraft in commercial use.

Hobby (HOU) was once the city's only airport but it is busier today than it ever was with nonstop or direct service to more than 65 domestic destinations. A recent multimillion-dollar expansion and renovation program has provided an additional concourse, an expanded baggage-claim area, renovated concourses, new dining and cocktail facilities, plus a new garage with covered parking for 3,500 vehicles.

Five major airlines, several commuters, and hundreds of private aircraft use Hobby, which has most of the conveniences and services found at Intercontinental. Many of Houston's frequent travelers appreciate the compact size (only 80 acres compared to IAH's 8,000) and its convenience (less than 10 miles from the central business district).

Airlines Serving Houston

Here are the airlines serving Bush Intercontinental's Terminals A, B, C, D, and Hobby Airport. Telephone numbers and Internet sites are for reservations and information.

Aeromexico
(Terminal D) 800-237-6639;
www.aeromexico.com.

Air Canada
(Terminal D) 800-776-3000;
www.aircanada.ca.

Air France
(Terminal D) 800-237-2747;
www.airfrance.com.

AirTran
(Hobby) 800-247-8726;
www.airtran.com.

America West
(Terminal B) 800-235-9292;
www.americawest.com.

American
(Terminal A and Hobby)
800-433-7300; www.aa.com.

American Eagle
(Hobby) 800-433-7300;
www.aa.com.

Atlantic Southeast Airlines
(Terminal A and Hobby)
800-282-3244; www.asa-air.com.

Aviacsa
(Terminal D) 800-237-6396
British Airways
(Terminal D) 800-247-9297;
www.british-airways.com.
Canadian Airlines
(Terminal A) 800-426-7000;
www.cdnair.ca.
Cayman Airways
(Terminal D) 800-422-9626;
www.caymanairways.com.
Comair
(Terminal A and Hobby) 800-
354-9822; www.fly-comair.com.
Continental
(Terminal B, C & D) 281-821-
2100; www.continental.com.
Continental Express
(Terminal B and Hobby) 281-
821-2100; www.continental.com.
Delta
(Terminal A & Hobby) 800-221-
1212; www.delta-air.com.
KLM
(Terminal D) 800-374-7747;
www.klm.com.

Lufthansa
(Terminal D) 800-645-3880;
www.lufthansa.com.
Northwest
(Terminal B and Hobby)
800-225-2525; www.nwa.com.
Southwest
(Terminal A & Hobby) 281-922-
1221; www.southwest.com.
Sun Country
(Terminal A) 800-752-1218;
www.suncountry.com.
TACA
(Terminal D) 800-535-8780;
www.grupotaca.com.
TWA
(Terminal A) 713-221-2000;
www.twa.com.
United
(Terminal A) 800-241-6522;
www.ual.com.
USAir
(Terminal A) 800-428-4322;
www.usairways.com.

Ground Services To and From Houston Airports

Buses and Vans. Airport Express provides motor-coach service
between the Bush and Hobby airports and various locales around the
city. Service is offered from downtown Houston, the Medical Center,
the Astrodome area, the Galleria, Greenway Plaza and Houston's west
side. Pick-up points change frequently; call 713-523-8888 for current
information, fares, and instructions. Be sure to allow 60 minutes travel
time to Bush and 40 minutes for Hobby. Passengers with more time
than money can save 50% or more over what a cab likely would cost,
but will require substantially more time and patience.

Some hotels and motels offer courtesy car service to/from Airport
Express stops if not the airport itself. Ask your hotel/motel management whether it offers such a service and at what, if any, price.

The **Metro public bus** system operates a varying schedule of buses
linking downtown with both airports.

The 50 Harrisburg-Airport route functions from early morning to late evening every day, taking passengers to/from Hobby in about 40 minutes for $1 (exact change).

The 102 Bush/IAH Express links downtown with Intercontinental airport early morning through late evening daily. The trip takes about an hour and costs $1.50 (exact change).

These are city buses with no special provision for luggage. Fares, routes, and stops can change with virtually no notice. For the best information on where, when, and how to catch these buses, call Metro at 713-635-4000, or see www.metro.com.

Taxis. At Intercontinental there are taxi dispatch offices just outside the South entrance of each terminal. By zone, the fares range from a low of $29 for downtown, up to $52 for the far East Side near NASA.

There are about 50 taxi companies in Houston. Because of its large fleet of over 1,500, **Yellow Cab,** 713-236-1111, is the most highly visible at the airports and around town.

One of Houston's best-kept transportation secrets is affiliated with Yellow Cab: **Towne Car,** 713-236-8877.

Towne Car service costs no more than regular cabs to or from airports, and is available by reservation or direct call, although mainly for longer or more involved hauls.

What makes Towne Car distinctive is also the source of its name: dark blue Lincoln Towne Cars subtly marked with Towne Car livery. The cars invariably offer sparkling clean, air-conditioned interiors, an ocean of clean trunk space, and the most conscientious and dependable drivers. One professional traveler has been using the same Towne Car and driver for nearly a decade and swears it's the only way to go to and from the airport.

Aircraft Rental and Charter

Two major fixed-base operators are located at Intercontinental Airport. They are **Garrett General Aviation Service Division,** 281-230-7800, and **Qualitron Aero Services,** 281-443-3434. The Garrett passenger terminal is at 17250 Chanute, and Qualitron is at 17725 Kennedy Blvd.

There are numerous fixed-base operators at Hobby. Check with Hobby Airport Operations, 713-640-3000, for a listing by ramps.

Automobile

Houston is at the junction of Interstate 10, crossing the country from east to west; I-45, originating at Galveston and terminating at

Dallas; and I-610, the "Loop" encircling the city. Another roadway, the Sam Houston Tollway/ Beltway 8, is located about 12 miles from the central business district and makes an 88-mile loop around the city.

Still another proposed superhighway is the Grand Parkway, which has been in the works since 1984. As proposed, the 170-mile road would link Chambers, Liberty, Harris, Montgomery, Fort Bend, Brazoria and Galveston counties. When completed it would be C-shaped, beginning at Texas 146 in Baytown and concluding at Texas 146 in Galveston County.

It is advisable to stop at a Texas Highway Department Information Center when coming into Texas or at a major gasoline station to pick up a map, and ask for assistance on getting into Houston. Once you are in town the **Greater Houston Convention & Visitors Bureau,** 901 Bagby, 713-437-5200, can assist. Ask your bell captain or car rental agent for directions on leaving the city.

Consider using the Sam Houston Tollway/Beltway 8 system, which flows freely even at rush hours and can save lots of time and aggravation—even if you must go a bit out of your way to use it. Tolls are payable at various segments, with the maximum payout about $8.

Bus

Greyhound/Coach USA has a terminal downtown at 2121 Main (L9), 800-231-2222.

Rail

AMTRAK, 713-224-1577. Amtrak has a passenger station downtown (H9) at 902 Washington Ave. The Sunset Limited, which runs between Los Angeles and Orlando, Fla., stops in Houston three times each week.

Package Tour

There is a trend in the United States for vacationers to take the simple route in holiday planning by paying a bottom-line price for a "package tour." This can include anything from the basic hotel room and ground transfer, to more extravagant offerings such as chauffeured limo, helicopter transfer, and champagne treatment all the way. These are priced accordingly from budget to luxury and are sold through travel clubs, hotels, travel agents, tour operators, and card-holder clubs.

Another type of package might be a "weekend special," which most lodgings put together themselves and, again, the offerings run the gamut. Check with your local travel agent or directly with the hotel of your choice.

AROUND HOUSTON

Bus Charters

Coach USA is the local leader in tour, charter and sight-seeing buses. Call 713-671-0991.

Public Transportation

Metropolitan Transit Authority (Metro) runs the public bus system, which operates more than 1,300 vehicles servicing 1,281 square miles. The fare on all local rides is $1. Metro also operates 28 Park N Ride routes; fares vary.

Exact change is required on all boardings, except passengers who have monthly passes or Stored Value Cards. Stored Value Cards, which work like debit cards, are issued in amounts starting at $15. The cards offer a savings for frequent riders in that each card has more value than its purchase price. For example, a $15 card will pay for $18.75 in fares.

Day and week bus passes also are available for $2 and $9, respectively.

Metro stops are easily identified with metal poles labeled "Bus Stop." Park N Ride lots are also marked. The average waiting time during peak periods is 10-15 minutes; during the normal time of the day, 20-30 minutes; during late night, early morning or weekends, 45-60 minutes.

Tickets, maps, and route and schedule information are available weekdays at Metro Ride Stores, which are downtown at 720 Main and 813 Dallas and at Sharpstown Mall. Information also is available by calling 713-635-4000. Metrolift offers curb-to-curb service for disabled or senior passengers; call 713-225-0119. www.ridemetro.com.

Taxi

Apart from the taxi operations at the airports there are stands at most major hotels and motor hotels. Taxis are permitted to cruise, and you may hail a cab, but it is best to call in advance with a specific address for pickup.

Port of Houston   *Courtesy of Greater Houston Convention & Visitors Bureau*

The city has structured taxi fares as follows: the flag drop charge is $1.50 for the first 1/10 mile, then it is 30¢ for each additional 1/5 mile; a mile ride costs about $3. Waiting charge is $18 an hour. Bear in mind that, depending on the size of the cab, four may ride for the price of one.

There are about 50 taxi companies in the Houston area; the largest is **Yellow Cab,** 713-236-1111. Several other choices may include **Liberty Cab,** 713-695-6700; **Square Deal Cab,** 713-659-7236; **United,** 713-699-0000; and **Fiesta Cab,** 713-236-9400 (bilingual drivers).

Auto Rentals

There are more than 100 companies involved in renting and leasing. Most of them rent by the day, week, or month. You should shop for the best deal, but here are a few suggestions: **Advantage,** 800-777-5500; **Alamo,** 800-327-9633; **Avis,** 800-331-1212; **Budget,** 800-527-0700; **Dollar-Rent-A-Car,** 800-800-4000; **Enterprise,** 800-736-8222; **Hertz,** 800-654-3131; **National,** 800-227-7368; and **Thrifty,** 800-367-2277.

Limousine Charters

More than 30 limousine companies operate in Houston. Two recommendations: **Action Limousines,** 713-781-5466; and **Ambiance Carriages,** 281-880-8696.

Private Car

When driving your own car be sure to plot your course with clear routing instructions.

Special Information on Major Thoroughfares

It should be helpful to the visitor and the newcomer to know that Houstonians refer to certain freeways and expressways in colloquial terms. It can be confusing, for example, when asking for directions to I-10 East and you are told to head out the Beaumont Highway. The following key is an attempt at clarification.

Interstate 45 North—North Freeway or Dallas Highway.

Interstate 45 South—Gulf Freeway or the road to Galveston (not to be confused with Old Galveston Road, which is not a freeway).

Interstate 610—The Loop (in all directions north, south, east and west).

U.S. 59 North—Eastex Freeway or Cleveland Highway.

U.S. 59 South—Southwest Freeway.

Interstate 10 East—East Freeway or Beaumont Highway.

Interstate 10 West—Katy Freeway or San Antonio Highway.

Highway 290—Northwest Freeway, the Austin Highway, or Hempstead Highway.

Highway 225 East-LaPorte Freeway.

Highway 3—Old Galveston Road.

Hempstead Highway—Old Katy Road.

Alternate 90—Old Spanish Trail and S. Wayside Drive.

Alternate 90 South—South Main.

Highway 90 North—McCarty St. or Old Beaumont Highway.

Highway 35—Telephone Road.

Highway 288—Almeda Road or the new South Freeway.

The principal through streets and avenues downtown are: Main Street, which runs generally north and south; Fannin runs parallel to Main and is a major artery going south; Texas Avenue, a crosstown street, becomes Harrisburg Boulevard toward the east; Prairie, a crosstown street, becomes Memorial Drive going west; Lamar, crosstown street, becomes Allen Parkway going west; Travis from downtown puts you on I-45 North; Milam from downtown to U.S. 59 South; Louisiana to I-10 West; Smith to U.S. 59 South; Chartres or Rusk from downtown to U.S. 59 North; Jefferson to I-45 South; Main to Alternate 90 South.

Speed limits vary, depending on the area and type of street. Freeways are posted with 70 mph maximum and 45 minimum. The speed limit on major streets is 35, which becomes 40-45 in outlying areas. Residential streets usually are 30 mph, and in school zones it's a heavily enforced 20 mph at posted times on school days.

IMPORTANT: Do NOT pass a stopped school bus when its stoplights are flashing, regardless of the direction of your approach and regardless of the impatience of drivers behind you. Police can *arrest* you.

In Texas it is permissible to turn right at a red light unless otherwise posted, but you must first come to a complete stop and look in both directions before moving on. You may also turn left on red if turning from a one-way street onto another one-way. Again, stop and look before proceeding.

During rush hours all major freeways have a contra-flow HOV (high-occupancy vehicle) lane. Anyone driving in the closely monitored HOV without at least one passenger will be stopped and ticketed. At peak drive times, HOV lanes might require three people per vehicle minimum.

The following are some helpful driving hints. Remember that Houston, like other major cities, is moving fast. Entry ramps onto the freeways tend to be short, so be careful to ease over to allow people in. Use the maps at the beginning of this book, which are clear and easy to read. Or have a map beside you in the car, your route boldly and clearly highlighted in advance.

Never leave anything of value in a vehicle or trailer, even when locked, overnight.

In warmer months, never leave children or pets in a closed vehicle. Even when the vehicle is vacant, leave a window slightly open to prevent windows from shattering under intense heat. Interior temperatures can rise to well over 100 degrees F in a matter of minutes.

In case of emergencies or in need of other auto assistance: **AAA** (D2), 3000 Southwest Freeway; 713-521-0211. **City of Houston Police,** 713-222-3131 or 911 for emergencies only; 713-308-3500 for auto theft; TTY/TTD for deaf community only 713-224-0675. **Houston Fire Departmment or Paramedics Ambulance,** 911 for emergencies only; or 713-224-2663 (deaf community only).

Tours

More than a score of companies offer a variety of tour programs, some scheduled and others by special arrangement, and ranging from aerial to ground to sea, both in Houston and Galveston. There also are foreign language and industrial tours by special arrangement.

For a complete list of sightseeing companies, contact the **Greater Houston Convention & Visitors Bureau** at 713-437-5200.

Here are some recommended tour companies:

Gray Line Tours of Houston (C4), 713-671-0991, offers several comprehensive sightseeing tours daily. Hotel pickup can be arranged.

Discover Houston Tours, 713-222-9255, offers daily downtown guided walking tours, which originate at the CVB's visitors center within City Hall, 901 Bagby. It specializes in walking tours of Houston's tunnel system, as well as heritage and restaurant tours.

Tourworks of Houston, 281-320-0713, offers outings to NASA, Old Town Spring and the San Jacinto Monument, as well as a eight-hour grand tour of the city. Hotel pickup can be arranged.

Houston Tours, 713-988-5900; www.houstontours.com, offers custom tours as well as three-hour city tours and guided excursions to Galveston and Space Center Houston.

Walking

Downtown sidewalks are generally wide and clean and certain

streets lend themselves to window shopping, having points of architectural interest and historical and cultural attractions.The downtown
pedestrian tunnel system is especially interesting and comfortably air-
conditioned. For a quick look at the system, go underground at the
Hyatt Regency Houston Hotel and walk northeast one block to the
mall under the 1100 Milam Building. (A DOWNTOWN WALKING
TOUR is included under SELF-GUIDED CITY TOURS.)

Just west of the downtown area is Buffalo Bayou Park with hike-and-
bike trails on both sides along Memorial and Allen Parkway. (See
SIGHTS and SPORTS.)

LODGING

With more than 46,000 rooms, there is hardly a quadrant in the city that doesn't have its share of fine lodging, with the greatest concentration in The Galleria/Post Oak and the North Belt areas near Bush-Intercontinental Airport.

There is a hotel, inn, or resort to suit nearly every traveler's needs, budget, or taste.

The following selection of hotels, motor hotels, campgrounds, and resorts is keyed to maps at the beginning of the book. If a restaurant, pool, or lounge is outstanding, it will be singled out, and unless otherwise stated nearly all hotels have these features.

The following key is used at the end of each listing.

BF—Barrier-free from the front door throughout, including guest rooms and public space. Increasingly, telephones and water fountains are at correct levels for the handicapped, as are elevator buttons, frequently also in braille. (All hotels might not meet the standards of "barrier-free," but nearly all have handicap-accessible rooms available. Features and quantity will vary.)

FL—Some foreign language personnel at key positions.

PA—Pets allowed. If there are size restrictions, we will advise. (Many hotels will require a refundable deposit to assure against damage caused by a pet; others might charge a cleaning fee. In all cases, hotels request that pets not be left alone in rooms, kept out of pool areas and be leashed when in other public spaces.)

Be aware that while hotels have rack rates that might be categorized as expensive, moderate or inexpensive, they frequently offer discounts or weekend specials that could fall into a cheaper category. Also, rates fluctuate periodically and what might be inexpensive during one quarter might become moderate the next. Be sure to check with the lodging of your choice to determine whether you qualify for a special discount or whether a package rate is available at the time you plan to check in.

And don't forget to budget for the hotel tax. Houston's seventeen percent hotel/motel tax is one of the steepest in the country and most hotels quote rates that do not include tax. Seven percent of the collected taxes goes to maintenance of convention/tourism facilities and marketing; two percent goes for Astrodomain expansion; two percent goes to the Harris County-Houston Sports Authority, which is charged with building sport facilities such as Enron Field and the new domed football stadium; and six percent goes to the state.

E	Expensive, $100 and up for a double room;
M	Moderate, $70-$100 for a double room;
I	Inexpensive, less than $70 for a double room.

Finally, be aware that amenities, décor, facilities, accessibility, courtesy transportation and specialized services—just like ownership, management, name, and rates—are subject to change without notice. Inquire about requisite amenities when making a reservation.

HOTEL SAFETY

Without being alarmist, staying in a hotel requires diligence when it comes to safety.

When checking in, make sure your room number is not revealed to other guests. Most clerks will write down your room number at check-in. If they say the number aloud in front of other guests, ask for another room. Women traveling solo might want to register using only their last name and first initial.

Request a room that is not adjacent to stairwells. Insist on a well-lit corridor. Second-floor rooms near the lobby are desirable.

Never open your door to a stranger. Have hotel employees and room service staff slip their IDs under the door before opening it.

Use in-room safes for valuables. If an in-room safe is unavailable, inquire about other options.

As a public-safety service, we include the following guidance in case of a hotel fire. All information is taken from a publication of the National Safety Council.

Preliminary precautions start after you check into your hotel. Check the exits and fire alarms on your floor, count the doorways between your room and the exit, keep your key close to your bed. In case smoke blocks your exit, check the window latches and any adjoining buildings or decks for low-level escape.

In case of fire, *crawl* to the door. Don't stand; smoke and deadly gases rise.

If the doorknob is hot—*do not open*—stay in your room. Then open the window, phone for help and hang a sheet from the window to signal for help. Turn on the bathroom fan. Fill the tub with water to wet towels and sheets to put around doors if smoke seeps in. Make a tent over your head with a blanket at a partially opened window to get fresh air.

If the doorknob is *not* hot, leave, close the door to your room, proceed to the exit, counting doorways in the dark, and walk down to ground level. If blocked at lower levels, turn around, walk up to the roof and keep the roof door open to vent stairwell. Wait for help on the roof. **Do not use elevators. Remember to stay low to avoid smoke and gases.**

HOTELS AND MOTELS

ADAM'S MARK HOTEL (D1) 2900 Briarpark Dr.; 713-978-7400. *E*. This 600-plus-room property is a big-city, upbeat hotel with enough amenities on premises and nearby to keep the whole family entertained. Swim outdoor to indoor, then enjoy a workout, sauna or whirlpool. Free parking. Also large exhibit center and meeting space. Nationwide reservations: 800-444-2326. Internet: www.adamsmark.com. *FL*.

ALLEN PARK INN (C3), 2121 Allen Parkway; 713-521-9321. M. This comfortable motel is convenient to downtown in a quiet location overlooking Buffalo Bayou Park. It is a corporate inn with ballroom, meeting rooms and suites, 24-hour room and telephone answering service. Features include health club, free parking, some kitchenettes, and special rates for extended periods of stay. Internet: www.allenparkinn.com.

ASTRODOMAIN HOTELS (E2), Kirby at I-610. This complex is made up of four hotels with a total of more than 1,000 rooms and suites. Hotels are convenient to the Astrodomain and Six Flags Astroworld. Note that although these hotels are adjacent to these attractions, they might require long walks across steamy parking lots to reach them. The complex includes **Holiday Inn Astrodome,** M, 713-790-1900; **Sheraton Astrodome Hotel,** M, 713-748-3221; **Radisson Suite Hotel Astrodome,** M-E, 713-796-1000; and **Days Inn Astrodome,** I, 713-796-8383.

BEST WESTERN. Independently owned and operated properties are reasonably priced, but can vary wildly in style and amenities. Generally they have free parking and pools. Restaurants nearby. Nationwide reservations: 800-528-1234. Internet: www.bestwestern.com. *I*.
Best Western Greenspoint (A1), 14753 I-45 North; 281-873-7575. Opened in January 2000. Seven miles from Bush-Intercontinental Airport.
Best Western Greenway Plaza (F1), 2929 U.S. 59 South; 713-528-6161. Recently renovated high-rise. Meeting space available. Convenient central location. *PA*.
Best Western Hobby Airport Inn (E5), 8600 I-45 South; 713-910-8600. A half-mile from the airport; courtesy shuttle available.
Best Western Houston East, 15919 I-10 East in Channelview; 713-452-1000.

Best Western Houston West, 22455 I-10 West in Katy; 281-392-9800. Complimentary continental breakfast and newspaper. *PA.*

COMFORT INNS & SUITES. Good choice for travelers on a budget but looking for more than bare-bones experience. Properties offer large rooms, complimentary continental breakfasts and morning newspapers. Lack restaurants and lounges. Part of the Choice Hotel family. Nationwide reservations: 800-424-6423. Internet: www.choice-hotels.com. *I-M.*

Comfort Inn Brookhollow (A1), 4760 Sherwood Lane; 713-686-5525.

Comfort Inn East Houston (C6), 1016 Maxey Road; 713-455-8888.

Comfort Inn Hobby Airport (E5), 9000 Airport Blvd.; 713-943-0035. Located 1.3 miles from Hobby Airport.

Comfort Inn NASA (F6), 750 W. Nasa Road 1; 281-332-1001.

Comfort Inn West, 22025 I-10 West; 281-392-8700.

Comfort Suites Galleria (C1), 6221 Richmond; 713-787-0004.

Comfort Suites Intercontinental, 15555 JFK Blvd.; 281-442-0600. Located one mile from Bush-Intercontinental Airport; courtesy shuttle available.

Comfort Suites North, 150 Overland Trail; 281-440-4448.

DAYS INN OF AMERICA. These motels, designed for the budget-minded family traveler, maintain a high standard of management. Two double beds per room, free parking. *BF, PA (CH).* Nationwide reservations: 800-329-7466. Internet: www.daysinn.com. *I.*

Days Inn Astrodome (E2), 8500 Kirby; 713-796-8383. Convenient to Astrodome and theme parks.

Days Inn Galleria/Westchase (C1), 9041 Westheimer; 713-783-1400.

Days Inn Greenspoint (F1), 12500 I-45 North; 281-820-1500. Convenient to Bush-Intercontinental Airport.

Days Inn Hobby Airport (E5), 1505 College; 713-946-5900. Courtesy shuttle to airport.

Days Inn Medical Center (D3), 4640 Main; 713-523-3777. Free shuttle service to medical center and downtown.

Days Inn Northwest, 12170 Highway 290; 713-688-4888.

Days Inn Wayside (D4), 2200 S. Wayside; 713-928-2800.

DOUBLETREE HOTELS. This upscale chain offers spacious, comfortable accommodations without a lot of fuss. Public spaces are particularly inviting. Restaurants, lounges, and fitness facilities are standard. And you always get freshly-baked chocolate-chip cookies. Doubletree Guest Suites feature separate living rooms and bedrooms with refrigerator and wet bar; Doubletree Club Hotels cater to the business traveler with conference rooms and self-service business centers. Nationwide reservations: 800-222-8733. Internet: www.doubletreehotels.com. *E.*

Doubletree Allen Center (J9), 400 Dallas; 713-759-0202. An elegant downtown hotel with 341 deluxe rooms. Lobby bar overlooking the lovely fountain gardens of the Allen Center. Concierge, meeting facilities and a full-service business center.

Doubletree Club Hotel (D1), 2828 U.S. 59 South; 713-942-2111.

Doubletree Guest Suites (C1), 5353 Westheimer; 713-961-9000. A high-rise hotel overlooking The Galleria.

Doubletree Post Oak (C1), 2001 Post Oak; 713-961-9300. An elegant international hotel designed by the world-famous architect, I. M. Pei. Convenient to the Galleria/Post Oak shopping district. Balconies offer superb views of Houston skyline.

ECONO LODGE. Another in the Choice Hotel family, this chain provides clean, budget-friendly accommodations. Targets the senior traveler by providing specially equipped rooms with amenities such large-button telephones with volume control, large-button TV remotes, brighter lighting and grab bars in shower and bath. Nationwide reservations: 800-553-2666. Internet: www.econolodge.com. *I.*

Econo Lodge Brookhollow (A1), 6630 Hoover; 713-956-2828.

Econo Lodge Medical Center (D3), 7905 S. Main; 713-667-8200. Free shuttle to medical center.

Econo Lodge North, 7447 I-45 North; 713-699-3800.

FOUR SEASONS HOTEL (J10-11), 1300 Lamar; 713-650-1300. *E.* One of Houston's finest downtown deluxe hotels offers elegance in an art nouveau ambience. A full-service corporate and convention facility. Spacious and beautifully landscaped multilevel lobby features bar and terrace with light meals and entertainment. The *De Ville* is one of Houston's best restaurants. Adjacent to downtown's only shopping mall. Heated pool with terraced gardens. Special room services include robe, shoeshine, newspapers and turn-down service. Courtesy shuttle limo anywhere downtown. *FL, BF, PA.* Nationwide reservations: 800-332-3442. Internet: www.fourseasons.com.

HILTON HOTELS. There are several Hilton hotels and inns in Houston, situated in strategic sectors throughout the city. This premier international company offers luxury accommodations in each location. Nationwide reservations: 800-445-8667. Internet: www.hilton.com. *M-I.*

Hilton Hobby Airport (E5), 8181 Airport Blvd.; 713-645-3000. Across the street from Hobby Airport, this high-rise hotel has 305 rooms and features suites with Jacuzzis. Also swimming pool, two restaurants and shuttle service to the airport. Ballroom, meeting space. *BF, FL, PA.*

Hilton Inn Houston West, 12401 I-10 West; 281-496-9090. Situated on the city's booming West Side, this 162-room hotel is oriented to corporate business. Free parking. Meeting rooms. *BF.*

Hilton Southwest (D1), 6780 U.S. 59 South; 713-977-7911. M. A high-rise, full-service hotel. Ballroom and meeting rooms. Heated pool and fitness center. Car rental and airline desks. Free parking. *BF, FL, PA (deposit)*.

Houston Plaza Hilton (D2), 6633 Travis; 713-313-4000. E. An 18-story luxury hotel featuring 181 rooms and suites complete with wet bar and refrigerator. Also health club that includes a pool, running track, saunas and weight room. A restaurant and lounge.

University Hilton (D4), 4800 Calhoun; 713-741-2447. This 86-room hotel is unique within this famous chain. Located on the central campus of the University of Houston, it is a training facility for the 900 students of the Conrad N. Hilton College of Hotel and Restaurant Management. Renovated in 2000, the hotel offers 45,000 square feet of meeting and conference space, as well as an excellent restaurant. Overseen by chef Cesar Rodriguez, Eric's is earning rave reviews for its intriguing international cuisine. Guests will find the latest innovations in the hospitality industry as Hilton frequently uses this hotel to test gadgets and room-design prototypes. The campus also is convenient to Hobby Airport, downtown and excursions south. *FL, PA.*

Westchase Hilton and Towers (D1), 9999 Westheimer; 713-974-1000. A deluxe hotel located on the fashionable West Side next to the Carillon Shopping Center. Ballroom and fully equipped meeting rooms. Run by the city's most acclaimed chef, Robert Del Grande, the striking Rio Ranch restaurant serves a mighty fine chicken-fried steak. *FL, PA.*

HOLIDAY INNS. The world-famous Holiday Inn green logo can be seen in almost every section of the city, offering its traditional service to America's travelers, whether on business or pleasure. Most offer the same range of services and amenities. *FL, PA,* free parking and ample meeting facilities. Nationwide reservations: 800-465-4329. Internet: www.holiday-inn.com. *I-E.*

Holiday Inn Airport-Intercontinental, 15222 JFK Blvd.; 281-449-2311. Complimentary shuttle service to airport. *PA.*

Holiday Inn Astrodome (E2), 8111 Kirby; 713-790-1900. Within walking distance to the Astrodome, this 242-room property caters to the business traveler and vacationing families. Convenient to medical center.

Holiday Inn Crowne Plaza (C1), 2222 I-610 South; 713-961-7272. Large, bustling hotel located in heart of The Galleria/Post Oak shopping district with free shuttle to shopping.

Holiday Inn Galleria (C1), 7787 I-10 West; 713-681-5000. *PA (small).*

Holiday Inn Houston East (C6), 15157 I-10 East; 713-452-7304.

Holiday Inn Houston North, 16510 I-45 North; 281-821-2570.

Holiday Inn Medical Center (D2), 6800 S. Main; 713-528-7744. On-site car rental and airline desk. Twelfth-floor fitness center offers fabulous views of downtown Houston.

Holiday Inn NASA (F6), 1300 NASA Rd. 1; 281-333-2500.

Holiday Inn Northwest, 14996 Northwest Freeway; 713-939-9955.

Holiday Inn Select Greenway Plaza (F2), 2712 U.S. 59 South; 713-523-8448. *PA.*

Holiday Inn Select Houston/Park I-10 West, 14703 Park Row, 281-558-5580. *PA.*

Holiday Inn Southwest (E1), 11160 U.S. 59 South; 281-530-1400.

HOTEL SOFITEL (A1), 425 N. Sam Houston Parkway East; 281-445-9000. *E.* This $30 million hotel/restaurant complex close to Bush-Intercontinental Airport is one of the first of this French chain of hotels to be constructed in the U.S. French cuisine and rooms featuring European period reproduction furnishings. Perfumed soaps and shampoos, turn-down service, special hangers, and theatrical lighting in baths. Features 24-hour concierge. Meeting and convention facilities. Indoor heated pool with garden terrace. Outdoor tropical pool and gazebo bar. Fitness room with massage available. Courtesy van to and from Bush-Intercontinental Airport and to Greenspoint Mall. Free parking. *BF, FL, PA.* Nationwide reservations: 800-763-4835. Internet: www.sofitel.com.

HOWARD JOHNSON. For traveling Americans, this pioneer of the motor lodge concept offers a dependable standard of accommodation and dining. Nationwide reservations: 800-446-4656. Internet: www.hojo.com. *I-M.*

Howard Johnson Astrodome/Medical Center (D3), 9604 S. Main; 713-666-1411. Renovated in 2000.

Howard Johnson Express Inn (C2), 4602 I-10; 713-861-9000. Central location makes hotel convenient to downtown, The Galleria area and museum district.

Howard Johnson Express Inn Airport, 13611 Rankin Circle W.; 281-821-0410. Shuttle service available to Bush-Intercontinental Airport.

Howard Johnson Hotel (E5), 7777 Airport Blvd.; 713-644-1261. Convenient to Hobby Airport with courtesy shuttle.

Howard Johnson Plaza Hotel, 702 N. Sam Houston Parkway East; 281-999-9942. Shuttle service available to Bush-Intercontinental Airport.

HYATT. This chain is known for its high standards in comfort and guest services. Expect superior amenities and eager-to-please staff. Nationwide reservations: 800-233-1234. Internet: www.hyatt.com. *E.*

Hyatt Regency Houston (J9), 1200 Louisiana; 713-654-1234. This downtown hotel completed a $15 million renovation in 2000, upgrading meeting rooms, guest rooms and its 30-story atrium. Two bars and three eateries, including the city's only revolving restaurant. *The Spindletop* offers dramatic and romantic views of the city skyline. Connected to Houston's downtown tunnel system. Airline and car rental desks. *FL, BF.*

Hyatt Regency Houston Airport, 15747 JFK Blvd.; 281-987-1234. Luxury 314-room hotel catering to the business traveler. Meeting rooms and high-tech amphitheater. Pool, fitness room and close to golf. Five minutes from Bush-Intercontinental Airport. Complimentary airport shuttle. *FL.*

LA COLOMBE D'OR (F2), 3410 Montrose Blvd.; 713-524-7999. *E.* This Old World type hostelry with only five suites, a penthouse and a French restaurant, was cited by *Esquire* magazine in a feature titled, "One of the Six Best Small Big City Hotels." It is located in one of the few remaining mansions along the once fashionable Montrose Boulevard. The home was built in 1923 by Walter Fondren, one of the principals in the founding of Exxon. All of the original parquet floors, wood paneling, and decorative friezes have been restored. The suites and penthouse are appointed in fine antiques and decorative arts. The original library is a quiet corner for reading or conversation before an elegant meal in one of Houston's best restaurants, La Colombe d'Or's own dining room. Overnight guests get the real VIP treatment and can have dinner in their own private dining room.

THE LANCASTER (I10), 701 Texas Ave. at Louisiana; 713-228-9500. *E.* A downtown historic landmark, the Lancaster is as close as Houston gets to a boutique hotel. It is located in the heart of the city's Theater District and is steps from dozens of outstanding restaurants and nightclubs. The 93-room hotel has been renovated to unprecedented grandeur. There are only nine rooms on each floor, and they feature custom-made furniture and Italian-marble baths, and each room has VCR and CD players. This is a traditional Old World hotel with all brass hardware, a doorman, a concierge desk and valet parking. Member of Small Luxury Hotels of the World. Internet: www.lancaster.com/hotel.

LA QUINTA INNS & SUITES. This San Antonio-based chain operates several Houston-area properties. Dependable service and accommodations. All have pools. Complimentary services include continental breakfast, local calls, and cribs. Meeting room often available. No onsite restaurants, but always located along major highways or near business or entertainment centers. *PA (small)*. Nationwide reservations: 800-531-5900. Internet: www.laquinta.com. *I-M*.

La Quinta Astrodome (E2), 9911 Buffalo Speedway; 713-668-8082.

La Quinta Baytown, 4911 E. I-10; 281-421-5566.

La Quinta Brookhollow (B1), 11002 Highway 290; 713-688-2581. Convenient to downtown and The Galleria/Post Oak district.

La Quinta Galleria (C1), 1625 W. Loop South; 713-355-3440.

La Quinta Greenway Plaza (F1), 4015 U.S. 59 South; 713-623-4750. *I*. Close to Compaq Center.

La Quinta Hobby Airport (E5), 9902 I-45 South; 713-941-0900.

La Quinta Intercontinental (A1), 6 N. Belt East; 281-447-6888. *I*. Courtesy car for Bush-Intercontinental Airport.

La Quinta North, 17111 I-45 North; 281-444-7500.

La Quinta Park 10, 15225 I-10 West; 281-646-9200.

La Quinta Southwest (E1), 8201 U.S. 59 South; 713-772-3626. Convenient to Memorial Hospital and Sharpstown Center.

La Quinta Sugar Land, 12727 U.S. 59 South; 281-240-2300.

La Quinta Wilcrest (B1), 11113 I-10 West; 713-932-0808. Convenient to Town & Country Village and Memorial Center.

La Quinta Wirt Road (B1), 8017 I-10 West; 713-688-8941. Near The Galleria/Post Oak shopping district.

La Quinta Woodlands, 28673 I-45 North; 281-367-7722.

MARRIOTT HOTELS. This upscale chain's Houston-area hotels all adhere to the quality and service that has given the Marriott an excellent reputation around the world, promoting a dedicated following of business and family travelers. The chain's Courtyard by Marriott properties are geared to the business traveler with rooms featuring large work desks, voice mail and comfortable seating areas. Nationwide reservations: 800-228-9290. Internet: www.marriott.com. *E*.

Houston Marriott Westside, 13210 I-10 West; 281-558-8338. A 400-room leisure and corporate hotel on the city's west side. A specialty restaurant plus lounges. Overlooks a three-acre lake with tributary extending into an atrium lobby. Special rooms equipped for business guests. Amenities include health club on premises and close access to Bear Creek Golf World. *FL, PA*.

J.W. Marriott Hotel (F1), 5150 Westheimer; 713-961-1500. This hotel across the street from The Galleria, has 518 rooms, plus a 20,000-square-foot exhibit center. Other features include a 24-hour room service and secretarial service, indoor-outdoor pool and fully equipped health club. *BF, FL*.

Marriott Houston Airport (A2); 281-443-2310. A full-service hotel catering to the business traveler. More than 200 of its 560 rooms boast specially equipped workspace. Abundant meeting space plus a large ballroom. Features 2 fine restaurants, one a revolving rooftop dinner spot. Hotel between IAH Terminals B & C connects to the free subway train linking all four terminals at the airport.

Marriott Medical Center Houston (D2), 6580 Fannin; 713-796-0080. This 386-room high-rise hotel caters to Texas Medical Center visitors as well as corporate, convention, and tourist business. *FL, PA*.

Marriott North at Greenspoint (A1), 255 N. Sam Houston Parkway East; 713-875-4000. *E*. Near Bush-Intercontinental Airport and adjacent to Greenspoint Mall. Free parking. Features 400 rooms plus indoor/outdoor pool, saunas, and exercise room. Ballroom and meeting rooms. *FL*.

Courtyard by Marriot Brookhollow (A1), 2504 N. Loop West; 713-688-7711. Convenient to downtown and Memorial Park. Restaurant, pool and self-service laundry.

Courtyard by Marriot Galleria (F1), 3131 I-610 South; 713-961-1640. Surrounded by great shopping. Restaurant, pool and self-service laundry.

Courtyard by Marriot Hobby Airport (E5), 9190 I-45 South; 713-910-1700. Lounge, but no restaurant. Pool and self-service laundry.

MOTEL 6. This no-frills chain boasts a devoted following. Folks who appreciate the little things such as free local calls, free parking and swimming pools. Restaurants nearby. *PA (small)*. Nationwide reservations: 800-466-8356. Internet: www.motel6.com. *I*.

Motel 6 Astrodome (E2), 3223 S. Loop West; 713-664-6425.

Motel 6 Baytown, 8911 Highway 146; 281-576-5777.

Motel 6 Clear Lake (F6), 1001 W. Nasa Road 1; 281-332-4581.

Motel 6 Hobby Airport (E5), 8800 Airport Blvd.; 713-941-0990.

Motel 6 Jersey Village, 16884 Hwy 290; 713-937-7056.

Motel 6 Katy, 14833 Katy Freeway.; 281-497-5000.

Motel 6 Northwest, 5555 W. Thirty-fourth St.; 713-682-8588.

Motel 6 Southwest (E1), 9638 Plainfield; 713-778-0008.

Motel 6 Spring, 19696 Cypresswood; 281-350-6400.

Motel 6 West, 2900 W. Sam Houston Parkway; 713-334-9188.

OMNI HOUSTON HOTEL (C1), Four Riverway; 713-871-8181. *E*. This delightful hotel is in the center of the West Side commercial center, close to The Galleria, but so hidden away in the woods along Buffalo Bayou that it almost lends itself to being an exclusive resort. This is pure elegance in beautiful surroundings with rustic bike trails and a sparkling manmade lake off the main lobby. There are four bars and restaurants, fitness center, tennis courts and two pools, three-mile jogging course, conference/meeting rooms and an English-style pub. Valet parking (CH); also free self-parking in garage. *BF, FL.* Nationwide reservations: 800-843-6664. Internet: www.omnihotels.com.

PARK PLAZA WARWICK HOTEL, (D3)5701 Main; 713-526-1991. *E.* A luxury property since its debut in 1926, the grande dame of Houston hotels recently enjoyed a much-needed face lift. The 308-room hotel has perhaps the best address in town. Located in the Museum District, it is steps from four major museums, as well as all the attractions of beautiful Hermann Park. Nationwide reservations: 800-670-7275. Internet: www.parkhtls.com.

RADISSON. Consistently well-managed, well-located properties. All are good, some exceptional. Excellent values on weekends. Nationwide reservations: 800-333-3333. Internet: www.radisson.com. *M-E.*

Radisson Hotel-Astrodome (E2), 1400 Old Spanish Trail; 713-796-1000 This 630-room full-service property features the city's largest ballroom, a steakhouse, two swimming pools, fitness center and game room. Located across the street from the Astrodomain and near the Texas Medical Center. The penthouse floor of this hotel once was the most expensive hotel room in the world. It is now used for private functions.

Radisson Hotel-Hobby Airport (E5), 9100 I-45 South; 713-943-7979. A 288-room hotel with two restaurants, meeting space, pool, and fitness room. Complimentary transportation to airport and golf course. *PA.*

Radisson Suites Houston West, 10655 I-10 West; 713-461-6000. *I-E.* High-rise hotel in Town & Country Village. Function rooms. Well-regarded restaurant.

RAMADA INNS. Situated in outlying areas of the city, these hotels offer good value and service. Special rooms for the business traveler include complimentary breakfast, in-room work desk with data port, voice mail, free local calls and other upgraded amenities. Ramada Limited properties offer continental breakfast, but no restaurant or lounge. Nationwide reservations: 800-228-2828. Internet: www.ramada.com. *M-E.*

Ramada Inn-Hobby (E5), 8611 Airport; 713-947-0000. Complimentary breakfast and airport shuttle. Restaurant, fitness room and outdoor pool.

Ramada Inn-NASA (F6), 1301 NASA Rd. 1; 281-488-0220. *M-E.* Two blocks from Space Center Houston and convenient to Galveston and Kemah. Offers 198 rooms and meeting space. *PA.*

Ramada Limited-Intercontinental Airport, 15350 JFK Blvd.;

281-442-1830. Complimentary executive breakfast and airport shuttle. Fitness room with sauna and outdoor pool with Jacuzzi.

Ramada Limited-Sharpstown (D1), 6885 U.S. 59 South; 713-981-6885. M. This property is a high-rise, convenient to Sharpstown Center and surrounding corporate offices. Complimentary continental breakfast.

Ramada Plaza (B1), 7611 I-10; 713-688-2222. This 250-room hotel with conference facilities and business center is centrally located. Appealing to both the business traveler and families. Full-service restaurant and outdoor pool. Courtesy transportation within five-mile radius. *PA.*

RENAISSANCE HOTEL (F1), Six Greenway Plaza East; 713-629-1200. E. This is an award-winning hotel in the heart of the Greenway Plaza corporate and entertainment complex that includes Compaq Center. Offering 389 deluxe rooms, as well as 22 meeting rooms. A twentieth-floor lounge offers great views of Houston; a sports bar sees plenty of action before and after Compaq Center events. Poolside service for beverages. The hotel also features a fitness room. Nationwide reservations: 800-468-3571. Internet: www.renaissancehotels.com. *BF, FL, PA.*

THE ST. REGIS (C2), 1919 Briar Oaks Lane off San Felipe; 713-840-7600. E. Marble fireplaces, dramatic floral arrangements, custom wood molding, objets d'art and fine furnishings make this hotel one of Houston's most luxurious. Formerly the Ritz-Carlton, this 12-story hotel recently completed a $6.2 million renovation. Geared to corporate executives and distinguished social activities. Features include a fully equipped business travelers' center, health club and an outdoor swimming pool. Valet parking and complimentary car service. Part of the Starwood Collection. Internet: www.luxurycollection.com. *FL, PA.*

SHERATON HOTELS. This chain, also part of the Starwood family, has an international reputation for service and special amenities. Caters to the business and leisure traveler, without shortchanging either. Expect to find good restaurants and swimming pools, along with personal attention. Nationwide reservations: 800-325-3535. Internet: www.sheraton.com. *M-E.*

Sheraton Brookhollow (A1), 3000 N. Loop West; 713-688-0100. This 382-room hotel is convenient to The Galleria/Post Oak area. Meeting and banquet rooms; fitness center and heated pool. *PA (small only).*

Sheraton North Houston, 15700 JFK Blvd.; 281-442-5100. A major hotel that recently was renovated. Boasts 420 rooms, health club and indoor and outdoor pools. Oriented to business traveler with 248-seat, fixed-stage amphitheater, large ballroom and 22 meeting rooms.

Courtesy car for Bush-Intercontinental Airport. Free parking. *BF, PA (small only).*

Sheraton Suites (C1), 2400 I-610 South; 713-586-2444. Opened in 2000, this 286-room property is within walking distance of The Galleria and Houston's premier shopping district. Features restaurant, outdoor pool, hot tub, and fitness center. Meeting space and business services available. *BF.*

SUPER 8. Travel guru Arthur Frommer calls this 1,900-property chain the "McDonald's of motels." Excellent value for folks who require few frills. Nationwide reservations: 800-800-8000. Internet: www.super8.com. *I.*

Super 8 (E5), 6711 Telephone Rd.; 713-645-7666. Free shuttle to Hobby Airport.

Super 8, 4045 I-45 North; 713-691-6671.

Super 8, 15615 I-10 East; 281-452-0719.

Super 8, 8888 I-45 South; 713-910-8888. Convenient to Hobby Airport.

WESTIN. Upscale hotel chain that prides itself on service. Its two hotels here are connected to the Galleria shopping mall (F1) and draw a large international clientele. Nationwide reservations: 800-937-8461. Internet: www.westin.com. *E.*

Westin Galleria, 5060 W. Alabama; 713-960-8100. This deluxe establishment anchors the southwest end of The Galleria. Hotel's Italian bistro, Delmonico's, is extremely popular. Valet parking (CH). *FL.*

Westin Oaks, 5011 Westheimer; 713-623-4300. At the east end of The Galleria, this luxury property offers 406 spacious rooms and suites plus ballroom and meeting facilities. A sidewalk-style cafe and deli overlooks The Galleria ice rink. This hotel has consistently won AAA's Four Diamond Award for years. It features traditional design and European service, and includes full concierge and valet parking (CH). Jogging track and health club. *FL.*

WYNDHAM GREENSPOINT HOTEL (A2), 12400 Greenspoint Dr.; 281-875-2222. *E.* Emphasizing convenience and full service for the business traveler, this striking modern Gothic hotel features tastefully appointed guest rooms and meeting space including a 15,200-square-foot ballroom. Also a recreational center, outdoor pool, sauna and athletic club nearby. Free shuttle service to Bush-Intercontinental Airport. Nationwide reservations: 800-822-4200. Internet: www.wyndham.com.

Resorts

THE HOUSTONIAN, HOTEL, CLUB AND SPA (C1), 111 N.

Post Oak Lane; 713-680-2626. E. In the heart of Houston is this modern retreat where the hustle and noise of city life is softened by a buffer zone of heavily wooded acreage meandering along Buffalo Bayou. This ultra-exclusive hotel was George Bush's official Texas residence during his term as president. Full-service spa and new golf club with (off-site) 18-hole championship course designed by Rees Jones. Dramatic public areas include three restaurants, two lounges, and two swimming pools (one heated). Business travelers will find this property, with its fully equipped meeting rooms and private dining rooms, ideal. Internet: www.houstonian.com.

MOODY GARDENS HOTEL, Seven Hope Blvd., in Galveston; 888-388-8484. E. Lushly landscaped grounds and its proximity to Moody Gardens attractions (See GALVESTON chapter.) add to the appeal of this 300-room convention hotel. Full-service spa, indoor/outdoor pool, jogging track and beach. Three bars and two restaurants, including a posh, ninth-floor dining room with outstanding island views. Internet: www.moodygardens.org.

SAN LUIS RESORT & CONFERENCE CENTER, Fifty-third and Seawall Blvd. in Galveston; 800-445-0090. E. This four-diamond hotel offers 243 rooms, all with balconies overlooking the Gulf of Mexico. Also a tropical garden with heated pool, swim-up bar and waterfall. New spa offers full range of body treatments. Treasure Island Kids Club offers supervised fun for ages 4-12. Lighted tennis courts. Restaurants include an award-winning steakhouse. Internet: www.sanluisresort.com.

SOUTH SHORE HARBOR (F1), 2500 South Shore Harbor in League City; 281-334-1000. E. Get away without going too far. This waterfront resort offers terrific views of Clear Lake and Galveston Bay. Three solarium rooms boast full-size, room-for-a-crowd Jacuzzis with fantastic bay views. Two-floor, three-bedroom penthouse suites accommodate family gatherings or couples who value their space. Complimentary shuttle service to Hobby Airport. Internet: www.sshr.com.

THE WOODLANDS EXECUTIVE CONFERENCE CENTER & RESORT, 2301 N. Millbend Dr.; 281-367-1100; E. This resort caters to the business traveler and corporate groups in an idyllic setting, with resort atmosphere and fine recreational outlets—all just 25 minutes from downtown Houston via I-45 North to The Woodlands' 25,000 acres of forests, fine homes and great weekend resort activities. This is the home of the world-famous Shell Houston Open golf tournament, and there are two championship courses on the premises, full-service spa and fitness center, indoor/outdoor racket courts, and miles of bike trails. Arrangements available for water sports, including boating and fishing on nearby lakes. Meeting rooms and about 360 guest rooms. Internet: www.woodlandresort.com.

Bed and Breakfast

While not as abundant as in tourist-oriented cities such as San Antonio and Fredericksburg, bed and breakfast establishments can be found in Houston. Amenities vary widely. Special needs or requests should be addressed at the time you make your reservation.

A good source for bed and breakfast information is Historic and Hospitality Accommodations of Texas (HAT), whose members must satisfy high standards of excellence. Call 800-428-0368. Internet: www.hat.org.

Here are four we can recommend:

ANGEL ARBOR BED & BREAKFAST INN (B3), 848 Heights Blvd; 800-722-8788. M-E. Yes, the five guest rooms have angelical names such as Raphael and Michael, but we think this bed and breakfast takes its name from innkeeper Marguerite Swanson's scrumptious breakfasts. Cranberry scones, strawberry cinnamon bread and bacon muffins are reasons to get out of bed. Nice in-room amenities and inviting public areas. Internet: www.angelarbor.com.

LOVETT INN (C3), 501 Lovett Blvd; 713-522-5224. M-E. A terrific Montrose location makes this eight-room inn convenient for exploring downtown and the Museum District. Interesting variety of restaurants and shopping within walking distance. Lovely pool and gardens. Internet: www.lovettinn.com.

PATRICIAN BED & BREAKFAST (D3), 1200 Southmore; 713-523-1114. M. Large, homey rooms in a 1919 mansion, located in the Museum District. Convenient to downtown and the medical center.

SARA'S BED & BREAKFAST INN (B3), 941 Heights Blvd.; 713-868-1130. M-E. Well-established Heights inn features 13 cheery rooms with Texas-proud names such as Dallas, Fort Worth and Fredericksburg. Looking for romance? Take the Austin Suite with its four-poster bed and claw-foot bathtub. Internet: www.saras.com.

DINING

Decisions! Decisions! If dining out in Houston poses a problem, choosing a restaurant is it. Eight thousand eating establishments, plus scores of cuisines and culinary styles, can make a decision overwhelming. Fun and delightful, but overwhelming.

Our aim herein is to assist the traveler, the newcomer, and even the native Houstonian in sorting out what's available, what to expect, and where to find it.

With our proximity to the Gulf of Mexico and Galveston Bay, seafood and fish of every description top many menus. Because history has stirred Texas and Mexico together so thoroughly, our kitchens continue to share many influences, loading plates with food specialties ranging from pure Mexican to the happy hybrid called Tex-Mex.

Harris County has a long history as cattle country, and today it still ranks near the top in Texas in cattle production. So, completing a visit to what you might call the "cow-pital" of Harris County—Houston—means corraling a dee-licious, nutritious, Texas-size steak. To eat more exotically, enjoy the world of ethnic and foreign influences evident in the great variety of cafés, restaurants, and other establishments, large and small, plain and fancy, throughout the city.

Houston continues its phenomenal growth as a dining-out town and readily seems to absorb all comers and newcomers.

But here we must serve a warning.

Many establishments grow into local institutions, but the restaurant business in Houston can be as fickle as anywhere else. Some come, some go. Specialties and menus change periodically, and so do entire themes. Even restaurants categorized by specialties tend to mix menus, such as seafood and steaks, or Italian and American, or Vietnamese and Chinese.

Prices are volatile and subject to frequent, unpredictable change. They can make an unwitting liar of the most diligent guidebook.

We have done our best to make this chapter as accurate and timely as possible, while at the same time informative. Still, the nature of this type of information, coupled with a lot of necessarily subjective judgment, requires us to remind you to consider it as guideline, not gospel. Our cost categories based on an appetizer, entree, and dessert remain:

E   Expensive, more than $20 per person.
M   Moderate, $10-$20 per person.
I   Inexpensive, less than $10 per person.

The following compendium should give you not only a good idea of the huge variety Houston offers restaurant-goers, but also lots of specific ideas about where to satisfy your appetite and your curiosity.

So, take your pick. Have a seat. And enjoy!

RESTAURANTS BY AREA

DOWNTOWN

Angelika Café & Bar, *American,* M.
Benihana, *Asian,* M-E.
Brennan's, *French/Continental,* E.
Buca di Baco, *Italian,* M-E.
China Garden, *Asian,* I.
Clive's, *French/Continental,* E.
Daily Review Café, *American,* M.
DeVille, *French/Continental,* E.
Dong Ting, *Asian,* M-E.
Fusion Café, *Soul Food,* I.
Hard Rock Café, *Burgers,* M.
Kim Son, *Asian,* I-M.
Liberty Noodle, *Asian,* E.
Longhorn Saloon, *Burgers,* I.
Market Square Bar & Grill,
    Burgers, I.
Remington Grill, *American,* E.
Ruggles Latino, *Latin American,* E.
Sake Lounge, *Asian,* M-E.
Sambuca, *Mediterranean,* E.
Solero, *Spanish,* M.
Tasca, *Spanish,* M-E.
This Is It, *Soul Food,* I.
Treebeard's, *Cajun,* I.
Zydeco Louisiana Kitchen, *Cajun,* I.

MONTROSE

Baba Yega, *Burgers,* I.
Blue Agave, *Mexican/Tex-Mex,* M.
Boulevard Bistrot,
    French/Continental, M-E.
Café Noche, *Mexican/Tex-Mex,* M.

Darby's, *German/Austrian,* E.
Empire Café, *American,* I.
Fox Diner, *American,* M.
La Colombe d'Or,
    French/Continental, E.
La Mora, *Italian,* M-E.
Mark's, *French/Continental,* E.
Ming's Café, *Asian,* I.
Niko Niko, *Mediterranean,* I.
Nino's, *Italian,* M-E.
Nippon, *Asian,* M.
River Café, *American,* M-E.
Ruggles, *American,* E.
Sierra Grille, *American,* E.
Tony Ruppe's, *American,* E.

THE GALLERIA/POST OAK

America's, *Latin American,* E.
Anthony's, *French/Continental,* E.
Café Annie, *American,* E.
Delmonico, *French/Continental,* E.
Masraff's, *French/Continental,* E.
McCormick & Schmick's,
    Seafood, E.
Post Oak Grill,
    French/Continental, E.
Ruggles 5115, *American,* E.
Tony's, *French/Continental,* E.

RICE VILLAGE

Benjy's, *American,* E.
Collina's, *Italian,* I.
Mi Luna, *Spanish,* M.

Prego, *Italian,* M.

COMPAQ CENTER AREA

Goode Company, *Barbecue,* I-M.
Hobbit Café, *Vegetarian,* I-M.
Khyber North Indian Grill, *Indian,* M-E.
Maxim's, *French/Continental,* E.
Ragin' Cajun, *Cajun,* M.
Vietopia, *Asian,* E.

RIVER OAKS AREA

Backstreet Café, *American,* M-E.
Beck's Prime, *Burgers,* I.
Churrasco's, *Latin American,* E.
Confederate House, *American,* E.
Hunan River, *Asian,* M.
La Griglia, *Italian,* M-E.
A Moveable Feast, *Vegetarian,* I-M
Otto's, *Barbecue,* I.
Ouisie's Table, *American,* E.
Rainbow Lodge, *American,* E.
Taco Milagro, *Mexican/Tex-Mex,* I-M.
Tony Mandola's Gulf Coast Kitchen, *Seafood,* M-E.

RICHMOND STRIP

Bombay Brasserie, *Indian,* M.
King Fish Market, *Seafood,* M-E.
Rivoli, *French/Continental,* E.

UPPER WESTHEIMER

Beck's Prime, *Burgers,* I.
Benihana, *Asian,* M-E.
Mama's, *Burgers.* I-M.
The Palm, *Steak,* E.
Rio Ranch, *American,* M.
Rodizio, *Latin American,* M.

POINTS WEST

Ashiana, *Indian,* M.
Droubi's, *Mediterranean,* I.
Fuzzy's, *Pizza,* I.
La Reserve, *French/Continental,* E.
Las Alamedas, *Mexican/Tex-Mex,* M-E.
Lynn's Steakhouse, *Steak,* E.
Old Heidelberg, *German/Austrian,* M.
Rotisserie for Beef & Bird, *American,* E.
Rudi Lechner's, *German/Austrian,* M.
Scott Chen's, *Asian,* E.
Taste of Texas, *Steak,* E.
Vargo's, *American,* E.

HARRISBURG GULF FREEWAY-EAST END

Eric's, *American,* E.
Ninfa's, *Mexican/Tex-Mex,* I-M.
Shanghai Red's & Brady's Landing, *American,* M-E.
Taj Mahal, *Indian,* M.

RESTAURANTS

American

Angelika Café & Bar (I9), 510 Texas at Bayou Place; 713-225-1609. M. Creative pastas, sandwiches and salads are the foundation of the Angelika, which is located within the confines of downtown's only movie theater. The restaurant is noted for its Cajun-style fried oyster sandwich and linguine with ancho-marinated grilled chicken. Open daily.

Backstreet Café (C2), 1103 S. Shepherd; 713-521-2239. M-E. Located in a large, old house, this café draws crowds with its garden patio and menu items such as its famous Meatloaf Tower, an elevated edible of juicy meatloaf, garlicky mashed potatoes, wilted spinach and mushroom gravy. Open daily.

Benjy's (D2), 2424 Dunstan; 713-522-7602. E. Superbly prepared seafood and excellent pizzas are trademarks of this cutting-edge restaurant. Draws a California-dreaming clientele. Closed Mondays. Reservations advised.

Café Annie (F1), 1728 Post Oak; 713-840-1111. E, very. Houston's award-winning restaurant and not without reason. Chef/owner Robert Del Grande's dining room is exquisite with high ceilings and rich leather banquettes. Signature dishes include Wood-grilled Shrimp with Avocado Relish and Pheasant Roasted with Cinnamon, Applewood and Smoked Bacon served with Peach and Mustard Marmalade. Closed Sundays. Reservations and jackets strongly recommended. Internet: www.cafe-express.com.

Confederate House (C2), 2925 Weslayan; 713-622-1936. E, very. This dinosaur of the dining scene recently got a more modern menu that takes it into the Twenty-first century without alienating its older clientele. Try the Crabmeat Monte Cristo or Quail with Veal Ravioli. Extensive wine list. Closed Sundays. Reservations advised. Jackets are not required, but in this clubby atmosphere you'd be more comfortable with one.

Daily Review Café (D3), 3412 W. Lamar; 713-520-9217. M. A hip crowd fills this sleek restaurant with garden patio and herb garden. A changing seasonal menu offers treats such as Chicken Pot Pie with Fennel; Smoked Duck Confit Spring Rolls; Baked Goat Cheese Salad; and Pecan-crusted Chile Relleno. Closed Mondays. Reservations only for parties of five or more.

Empire Café (D3), 1732 Westheimer; 713-528-5282. I. This Montrose café in a converted gas station draws an eclectic crowd that tends to linger over their lattés. The menu is weighted with focaccia sandwiches and pizza. Sunday breakfast service features innovative treats such as Gingerbread Waffles and Hot Polenta With Honey Cream and Toasted Almonds. Open daily.

Eric's Restaurant (D4), 4800 Calhoun; 713-743-2513 E. Located in the Hilton Hotel on the University of Houston campus, this innovative restaurant turns out some interesting Latin-inspired cuisine. What is special about this place is that patrons are lab rats, of sorts. The staff here are students of UH's college of hotel and restaurant management. The dining room itself is less than inspiring, but the entrees including veal rack and pork roast, are quite good. Open daily.

Fox Diner (C3), 2815 S. Shepherd; 713-523-5369. M. This tiny place is a charmer: whimsical art, a paint-splattered floor, an open kitchen just inside the front door and chef/owner Tom Williams' welcoming smile. The menu is New South: Fried Green Tomato Salad; Shrimp and Grits with Tasso Red-Eye Gravy; King Ranch Casserole and Real Texas Frito Chili Pie. Williams' tiny Jalapeno-cheese Corn Muffins are cute and tasty. Open daily.

Ouisie's Table (C2), 3939 San Felipe; 713-528-2264. *E.* Stylish, yet comfortable restaurant with intimate garden rooms. A blackboard menu entices with upscale comfort food such as Shrimp and Cheese Grits; Sautéed Wild Mushrooms; Roasted Mashed Sweet Potatoes; and Ouisie's Spud, a baked potato with sour cream, caviar, scallions, garlic olive oil and fresh dill. Closed Sundays and Mondays. Internet: www.ouisiestable.com.

Rainbow Lodge (C2), One Birdsall; 713-861-8666. *E.* On the banks of Buffalo Bayou, this wonderful old 1935 house was converted to a convincingly authentic hunting lodge resort complete with trophies, and huge plate-glass windows overlooking rustic woods and landscaped grounds. Specialties include numerous game dishes, including pheasant, duck, elk and deer, as well as seafood. Closed Mondays. Internet: www.rainbow-lodge.com.

Remington Grill (F1), 1919 Briar Oaks Lane in the St. Regis Hotel; 713-403-2631. *E, very.* An expensive hotel requires a fine restaurant and this is it. Plush décor with mahogany walls and colorful artwork. Terrific appetizers such Oyster Stew and Seared Calamari and Garlic Toast could make you forgo the main course. Open daily. Reservations advisable on weekends.

Rio Ranch (D1), 9999 Westheimer at Westchase Hilton; 713-952-5000. *M.* Having graduated beyond its original "campfire cuisine" concept, this gorgeous dining room with its Western motif is offering sophisticated fare such as Chilean Sea Bass and Atlantic Salmon with Soy Ginger Glaze. Of course, you can still get an artery-clogging chicken-fried steak served with mammoth biscuits. Open daily. Reservations advised. Dress runs the gamut from casual to formal. Internet: www.cafe-express.com.

River Café (F3), 3615 Montrose; 713-529-0088. *M-E.* A fashionably elegant dining room overlooking Montrose Boulevard with sidewalk café tables so popular along this street. The menu features pastas, veal, chicken, steak and seafood specialties. The brick walls are lined with changing exhibits of paintings by local artists. Open daily.

Rotisserie for Beef & Bird, 2200 Wilcrest; 713-977-9524. *E.* One of Houston's culinary institutions almost since the day owner-chef Joe Mannke opened it, American food with continental flair dominates a menu of excellent beef, poultry and game dishes. Poultry entrees include Roast Meaty Cackle Bird (an originally female capon),

Mesquite-grilled Partridge, Hickory Smoked Duckling, and from the rotisserie, Roast Duckling with Orange Sauce. Closed Sundays. Reservations advised. Elegant casual to dressy. Internet: www.rotisserie-beef-bird.com.

Ruggles Grill (F3), 903 Westheimer; 713-524-3839. *E*. Ruggles is a familiar name among theater-going Houstonians since the Westheimer location not only serves consistently fine food but is one of relatively few places catering to late-night crowds. Menu includes a number of vegetarian specialties. Casual atmosphere and live musical frequently. Closed Mondays. Reservations advised.

Ruggles 5115 (F1), 5115 Westheimer in Saks Fifth Avenue/The Galleria; 713-963-8067. *E, very*. This restaurant with its pretty and bright dining room is a favorite of the fashionable set who suspend their Galleria shopping expeditions only long enough to enjoy dishes such as Goat Cheese-Poblano-Chicken Quesadillas and Australian Lamb Chops Rubbed in Chipotle. Save room for the White Chocolate Bread Pudding. Closed Sundays.

Sierra Grille (D3), 4704 Montrose; 713-942-7757. *M-E*. A split-level dining room done up in elegant Southwestern style suits the relaxing style of chef/owner Charlie Watkins' menu, which is heavy on exotic game such as wild boar and ostrich. Watkins takes Texas favorites and gives them an upscale twist such as his Salmon Tacos with grilled salmon, marinated ginger, jicama and a creamy habanero sauce. Live music most nights. Reservations suggested. Internet: www.sierra1.com.

Shanghai Red's and **Brady's Landing** are right next to each other in the middle of the Houston Ship Channel on Brady Island; (D5), 8501 Cypress St.; 713-926-6666 (Shanghai Red's) and 713-928-9921 (Brady's). *M-E*. Shanghai Red's is in a rusty, mineshaft-looking building with junk Model-T cars in front. Enjoy cocktails in the dance hall section overlooking the banks of the Ship Channel. Many cozy seating areas tucked away on different levels, all overlooking the water. Features seafood. Open daily. Casual. The newer sister restaurant, Brady's, is more contemporary with floor-to-ceiling fireplaces, a sunken dining room, and a music bar. Brady's is popular with the business crowd and features beef, prime rib, and steaks. Open daily.

Tony Ruppe's (D3), 3939 Montrose Blvd.; 713-852-0852. *E*. Sophisticated Montrose restaurant is turning out some of the most imaginative cuisine in town. Consider the Wok-seared Hoisin Beef Summer Rolls, Crab and Shrimp Relleno with Goat Cheese or the Duck Enchiladas. Closed Sundays. Reservations advised.

Vargo's (C1), 2401 Fondren Road; 713-782-3888. *E*. Just off the bright and bustling Westheimer, you come to a winding drive with a white picket fence—follow it to the end to an unbelievably serene, country-club setting. Printed menu has replaced the verbal menu of earlier days, but at lunch, dinner, and Sunday brunch, the tradition of serving vegetables family style and a complimentary relish tray continues. Traditional steak and seafood favorites now share the much broader menu. After your meal, waddle out to the swinging bridge over the lagoon leading to trails along Lake Vargo for a little exercise. Open daily. Reservations advised. Coat and tie preferred, but not required.

ASIAN

It is difficult to tag new Asian restaurants with labels such as Chinese, Thai, Japanese etc., as many reach across borders for their inspiration and ingredients.

Benihana of Tokyo (J9), 1318 Louisiana; 713-659-8231. (D1), 9707 Westheimer; 713-789-4962. *M-E.* Japanese showchefship at its sharpest as knife-wielding whizzes put sizzle into steak, chicken, shrimp, scallops, or lobster together with fresh vegetables. Soft music and oriental décor conducive to conversation, whether on business or pleasure. Open daily.

China Garden (K11), 1602 Leeland; 713-652-0745. *I.* One of Houston's most popular, well-rounded Chinese menus, and offering an unbelievable array of 85 dishes ranging from Cantonese to Sichuan to Mandarin. Here you will find your favorite vegetables with chicken, sirloin, pork, shrimp, squid, or just plain. Open daily.

Dong Ting (F3), 611 Stuart; 713-527-0005. *M-E.* This promises the finest and most authentic Hunan Province specialties in town. Dishes include Spicy Squids and Hot Sauce Shrimp or you can try other delicacies such as Steamed Fish. A relaxing and rewarding experience. Open daily.

Hunan River (C2), 2015 W. Gray; 713-527-0200. *M.* A modern presentation of fine Chinese country cooking. This small, serene dining room brings the best in Hunan to fashionable River Oaks. No preservatives, artificial ingredients, or frozen foods go into the more than 70 entrees. The owners trace their recipes back to the classical form of cooking for Chinese dynasties. Hunan is synonymous with hot, but here the chef prepares your choice to the degree of spice you tolerate. Open daily.

Kim Son (J12), 300 Milam, 713-222-2789. Three other locations. *I-M.* Houston has one of the largest Vietnamese communities in the country, and, therefore, enjoys the wealth of authentic dining establishments that come with it. Perhaps the best known of them is Kim Son, where patrons feast on Vietnamese, Chinese or hybrid specialties, including various noodles, rices, and other dishes that fit or defy nearly any description. Many items come served with fresh cilantro, mint and bean sprouts as standard issue. Fresh gulf crabs, prepared with black pepper sauce or ginger and green onion, are more than delicious enough to justify the mess they generate. The menu is ponderous. Open daily.

Liberty Noodle (I10), 909 Texas; 713-222-2695. *M-E*. The small dining room at this stylish eatery is augmented by an appealing sidewalk patio. You'll want to sit there so everyone walking downtown knows how much you are willing to spend on noodles. Executive chef Annie Wong's inspired dishes are a tasty fusion of Asian inspiration (Korean barbecue, Vietnamese duck, Chinese dumplings) and plated with artistic flair. Oh, but those steep prices. Closed Sunday. Reservations recommended.

Ming's Café (D3), 2703 Montrose Blvd.; 713-529-7888. I. OK, the setting—a veritable shack with deck—doesn't inspire confidence. But the food comes quickly and is remarkably good. Alongside standard Chinese fare, the blackboard menu offers surprising specials such as Sea Bass with Japanese Crumbs, Crawfish Fried Rice, and Mushroom Chicken with Black Bean Sauce. Excellent vegetarian selections. Open daily.

Morningside Thai (D2), 6710 Morningside; 713-661-4400. *M-E*. In a former home in this residential area, you'll feel right at home with friendly attentive service willing to assist with your perusal of the menu. Tiny finger-size freshly cooked egg rolls are good starters. Another great appetizer is Shrimp Toast, or sample the variety tray. Seafood is the specialty, but there also are meats. Especially delicious is Whole Snapper in Plum Sauce. Reservations suggested. Open daily.

Nippon (F3), 3939 Montrose; 713-523-3939. *M*. This bright, modern, two-level sushi house is family-run with great taste. The interior is accented with original art of warriors and geishas. Upstairs is devoted to a teppanyaki grill; downstairs is the sushi bar. Appetizers include aged tofu and softshell crab. Entrees include sushi or sashimi with tuna, salmon, octopus, and yellow tail, or you might prefer a substantial shrimp tempura or sukiyaki, or traditional beef and chicken preparations such as shabu-shabu and Chicken Teriyaki. Open daily. Reservations required.

Sake Lounge (I9), 550 Texas in Bayou Place; 713-228-7253. *M-E*. Downtown crowds get their sushi fix at this attractive restaurant, which wraps around a prominent corner of Bayou Place. Particularly popular are the hand rolls stuffed with crab and octopus. Open daily. Reservations only for large parties.

Scott Chen's (C1), 6540 San Felipe; 713-789-4484. *E, very.* Pricy French-Asian fusion dishes that could be classified as edible art. But this sleek restaurant is at the crossroads of a culinary wasteland. Go for one of Chen's clever salads (the Caesar dressing is memorable) and the

Roasted Boneless Duck with Five-spice Brown Sauce. Extensive wine list, heavy on California and French vintages. Closed Sundays. Reservations advisable. Jacket preferred, but not required.

Vietopia (D2), 5176 Buffalo Speedway; 713-664-7303. *E.* A diva of a dining room deserves a marquee kitchen. Applause for both. Order the enormous appetizer, *Goi Do Bien Ngo Sen* or "seafood delight." It is. Also good are the Vietnamese eggrolls and beef with black pepper sauce. Open daily. Reservations a must on weekends.

BARBECUE

Goode Company Texas Barbecue, 5109 Kirby, 713-522-2530; 8911 Katy Freeway, 713-464-1901. *I-M.* In terms of flavor and quality, Goode Company arguably smokes up some of the best and most interesting barbecue in Houston, and maybe even in all of Texas. Standards such as beef (sliced brisket or chopped), chicken, ribs, pork, and link sausage are all gloriously available, but so, too, are such succulent innovations as a special, spicy barbecued pork, yummy barbecued sweetwater duck, and a spectacular jalapeno sausage. Marvelous tangy-sweet sauce. Outstanding barbecue beans (some of the best anywhere ever). And portions that could give you a hernia. Open daily.

Old Hickory Inn Barbeque, 8338 I-59 South; 713-271-8610. 5427 S. Braeswood; 713-723-8908. *I.* Very good and very reasonably priced barbecue beef, chicken, ribs, and sausage. Good side dishes include tasty barbecue beans and a sweet-sour, vinegar-dressed (no mayonnaise) cole slaw. Simple and casual. Open daily.

Otto's (C2), 5502 Memorial Dr.; 713-864-2573. *I.* Downtown workers and West Siders descend at lunchtime on this small establishment which has become a tradition for hamburgers and barbecue ribs, links, ham, or beef. This the Otto's that gained fame as the preferred purveyor of barbecue for former President George Bush. Orders to go. Closed Sundays.

BURGERS

Baba Yega (D3), 2607 Grant; 713-522-0042. *I.* Burgers are the specialty of this popular Montrose hangout. Good selection of vegetarian entrees. Open daily.

Beck's Prime, 2902 Kirby; 713-524-7085. 2615 Augusta; 713-266-9901. 11000 Westheimer; 713-952-2325. Also in Memorial Park. *I.* Bright and cheery, Beck's specializes in hamburgers, big, juicy, yummy, mesquite-grilled hamburgers that bump the ceiling on quality and flavor. Grilled onions make great even better at no extra charge. Fries? Onion rings? Of course! And hot dogs for frank-o-philes. Seriously good grilled swordfish sandwich. Grilled vegetables and salads. Open daily.

The Hard Rock Café (D2), 502 Texas in Bayou Place; 281-479-7025. M. Houston's outpost of this famous café recently joined the downtown party, setting up shop in Bayou Place after years on an un-hip spot of Kirby Drive. Just look for the 30-foot, neon guitar, a tribute to Texas blues legend Stevie Ray Vaughan. Much of the restaurant's famous music memorabilia collection centers on Texas rock 'n' roll stars, including Buddy Holly, Roy Orbison, Selena, ZZ Top and Janis Joplin. The relics aren't limited to Lone Star legends. You'll also see guitars belonging to the Grateful Dead's Bob Weir, Prince, Bob Dylan and The Who's Pete Townshend. Family friendly menu is heavy on burgers. A fun spot to grab a bite before heading to a game at Enron Field. Open daily. Reservations suggested for large parties.

Longhorn Café (I10), 509 Louisiana, downtown; 713-225-1015. I. Wood floors, brass foot rail at the bar, neon beer signs, boots 'n jeans and a wailin', twangin' jukebox let you know in a hurry this is authentic Texas country. The menu explains the makings of a chicken-fried steak. All "Frieds" served with homemade cream gravy. Then there's regular steak and chicken fingers, Texas three-alarm chili and deep-fried potato skins. Closed Sundays.

Mama's Café (C1), 6019 Westheimer, "Restaurant Row"; 713-266-8514. I-M. This place looks like an old-timey Sinclair filling station with art-deco tiles and benches out front, concrete floor, enamel-painted walls and shelves lined with license plates, vintage Texas postcards, and hundreds of local and imported beer cans, plus country antiques and plants. Whether for full meals or a proverbial bite, extremely popular with all kinds of folks. Huge weekend crowds for breakfast. This also is one of the few places you can get a burger late. Open to 4 am on Fridays and Saturdays. Daily specials announced on blackboard. Excellent fried catfish and Broccoli-Rice Casserole. Homemade pies and cakes. Open daily.

Market Square Bar & Grill (H10), 311 Travis, 713-224-0088. I. When the downtown scene seems too hectic and hip, we duck into this comfortable joint. We find high ceilings, a long bar and a patio that's right out of New Orleans. Great burgers include the Mushroom Blue Cheese Burger and the McCool, a veggie sandwich featuring a meaty portobello mushroom. And the roasted potatoes are an elegant touch. Closed Sundays.

CAJUN

Ragin' Cajun (E5), 4302 Richmond; 713-623-6321. M. On Friday and Saturday nights, the line at this counter-service restaurant often runs out the door. Buckets of mudbugs are consumed at the picnic tables inside the rowdy dining room festooned with Cajun-pride posters, neon beer signs and Louisiana sports memorabilia. We go for crawfish pie, oyster po'boys and sharply seasoned fried crawfish. Closed Sundays. Extremely casual.

Treebeard's (H10), 315 Travis; 713-228-2622. I. Sitting at the tables along the sidewalk at this popular spot facing historic Market Square you can enjoy a heaping platter of shrimp étouffee or red beans and rice. The duck gumbo and mustard greens with shrimp are just a few of the other standout items on the Cajun- and Creole-inspired menu. Cafeteria-style service. Closed Sundays.

Zydeco Louisiana Diner (K10), 1119 Pease; 713-759-2001. I. No ambience, just some of the best Cajun cuisine in town. Service is cafeteria-style but there's not a disappointment on the menu: oyster loaf, chicken jambalaya, red beans and rice and, arguably, the best gumbo in town. Open weekdays for lunch, except during crawfish season (February through May) when the Louisiana-born chef keeps the boilers going three nights a week.

CHAIN GANG

You don't have to be in town long to become familiar with the Houston's heavy hitters in the restaurant industry. Several large chains have roots here and command a loyal following. In most cases, you can't go wrong in stopping for lunch or dinner. Most feature reasonable prices and Texas-size portions. Here are a few. Check local listings for the nearest restaurant.

Galveston native Tilman Fertitta heads the **Landry's Seafood** Restaurants, a family that includes **Joe's Crab Shack, The Crab House, Cadillac Bar** and **Willie G.'s Seafood and Steakhouse.** You'll see outposts of these restaurants everywhere. All are family-friendly.

James Coney Island has been a Houston tradition since 1923. You'll find these extremely casual restaurants throughout Houston. The menu: Texas chili, cheese fries and hotdogs. A good value.

Enormous portions and reasonable prices are a trademark of the Pappas family restaurant chain. Among the family's restaurants are **Pappas Seafood House, Pappas Brisket House, Pappadeaux Seafood Kitchen** and **Pappasito's Cantina.** They also operate the **Pappas Brother Steakhouse.**

Hungry but low on cash? Seek out an **Antone's.** The specialty is po'boys. You can have meat, extra meat, tuna, turkey or a piggie (don't even ask). A recent addition to this traditional line is the Country Boy, a cool veggie sandwich with taboulleh and feta. Good selection of imported olives and other nibbles.

Another fixture on the Houston dining scene is **Café Express.** These upscale cafés feature counter service, giant bowls of pasta and plate-sized sandwiches. This is fast food for folks who wouldn't be caught dead at McDonald's.

FRENCH/CONTINENTAL

Anthony's, 4007 Westheimer; 713-961-0552. *E*. This is a smaller, more casual version of the world-famous Tony's on Post Oak with an incredibly creative menu, emphasizing Italian/French/Continental specialties that could spur even a confirmed anorexic down the road to temptation. Linguine with crawfish and shrimp, mushrooms, scallions, roasted pearl onions, and lobster cognac sauce. Crab, shrimp, and smoked salmon salad with tangerine and mint vinaigrette. Sliced beefsteak tomatoes, crumbled roquefort drizzled with a cabernet vinaigrette. A peppered chateaubriand of tuna for two. Whole hearth-roasted duckling with wild rice and mango-apricot or fresh raspberry sauce. Get the picture? Reservations strongly suggested. Elegantly casual to dressy attire.

Boulevard Bistro (D3), 4319 Montrose; 713-524-6922. *M-E*. Foodies flock to this intimate restaurant for chef/owner Monica Pope's flavorful concoctions such as Orange Chili Noodles and Mushroom-glazed Ahi with Sticky Rice. Closed Sundays. Reservations advised. (Pope, one of Houston's most celebrated chefs, recently opened a French fast-food post, 43 Brasserie, two doors down.)

Brennan's (F3), 3300 Smith St.; 713-522-9711. *E*. Relax in this old New Orleans garden atmosphere in the Brennan's tradition in this wonderful, treasured restaurant. Gaslights, louvered windows, lattice and palms set the right Old South mood for exquisite dining with your choice of famous Brennan's recipes, some of them American culinary classics. Sunday brunch, stretching the tradition of breakfast at Brennan's across the solar meridian, can start with a longtime favorite Turtle Soup with sherry, continue with Poached Eggs Creole or Eggs Scrambled with Beef Tenderloin, Roasted Peppers and Cheese, then finish with Creole bread pudding or Brennan's classic Bananas Foster. Dinner can begin auspiciously with Gulf of Mexico crab cakes or Texas Creole Barbecue Shrimp, proceed to Soups 1-1-1 (demitasse of turtle soup, gumbo and soup du jour), and one of several salads. Continue with Grilled Filet of Beef finished with a raisin peppercorn sauce or Grilled

Shrimp and Lump Crabmeat with Champagne sauce, then cap the whole experience with a slab of Peanut Butter Fudge Pie or a Praline Parfait. Fantastic food aside, the special touch on Sundays is Brennan's brunch is a "Jazz Brunch" featuring a live, New Orleans jazz band. Open daily. Reservations a must. Jacket required and tie requested.

Chez Nous, 217 South Ave. G in Humble; 281-446-6717. *E.* Located in a former Pentecostal church, this has become of Houston's favorite "special occasion" restaurants. The classic French fare, the extraordinary wine list and the impeccable service make birthdays, anniversaries and engagements even more memorable. Closed Sundays. Reservations advised.

Clive's (I10), 517 Louisiana; 713-224-4438. *E.* Power lunches or pre-theater noshing are this clubby restaurant's bread and butter. Favorites here are the Smothered Pork Chops with Mashed Potatoes and the Pan-seared Snapper with Crabmeat and Chardonnay Butter. The wine cellar is one of the Smart Set's favorite party rooms. Closed Sundays. Reservations required. Jackets recommended. Internet: www.clives.com.

Delmonico's (F1), 5060 W. Alabama; 713-960-6558. *E.* This is the Westin Galleria Hotel's gourmet dining room, named after New York's landmark restaurant. For the discriminating diner, a full range of entrees is offered as well vintage wines. Open daily. Reservations recommended.

DeVille (J11), 1300 Lamar; 713-652-6250. *E.* Located in the luxurious Four Seasons Hotel, this highly regarded restaurant offers modern French food. Executive chef Timothy Keating is turning out culinary masterpieces such as Sorghum-Glazed Atlantic Salmon with Horseradish Yukon Gold Potatoes and Grilled Caramelized Veal Chop with Wild Mushroom Crepe. A lunch menu offers great deals for budget-minded folks who want to sample some of the city's best cuisine. Sunday brunch also is popular. Reservations recommended.

La Colombe d'Or (F2), 3410 Montrose Blvd.; 713-524-7999. *E.* One of Houston's all-time finest restaurants set in perhaps the city's smallest, most unusual luxury hotel. Everything about this erstwhile mansion has been lovingly restored by active proprietor Stephen Zimmerman, who has catalyzed and supervised the menus since he opened La Colombe d'Or in 1980. Patrons dine on a refreshingly different menu based on the finest and freshest of seafoods, meats, poultry and vegetables. The cozy library offers an outstanding collection of vintage ports and cognacs. Open daily. Reservations recommended. While La Colombe d'Or is casual and relaxing, gentlemen should don a coat and tie for dinner.

La Reserve (C1), Four Riverway; 713-871-8181. *E.* This is the formal dining room in the deluxe Omni Hotel on the city's fashionable

West Side. An unforgettable gourmet dining experience where French chefs present six courses chosen nightly for your enjoyment. Closed Sundays. Reservations required, as is coat and tie.

La Tour d'Argent (B2), 2011 Ella Blvd.; 713-864-9864. *E*. In an unlikely setting in an early log cabin overlooking White Oak Bayou, La Tour d'Argent offers excellent French cuisine and a superior wine list. One of the city's most romantic restaurants. The service is excellent. Closed Sundays. Reservations suggested. Coat and tie required.

Mark's (D3), 1658 Westheimer; 713-523-3800. *E*. This elegant dining room is in an old church, which is appropriate considering the praise chef/owner Mark Cox gets for his "New American" menu. Try the Scottish Seawild Salmon Cheesecake with Mustard-Dill Vinaigrette or the Roast Corn Chowder with Smoked Apple Bacon. Open daily. Reservations advisable.

Masraff's (C1), 1025 S. Post Oak Lane; 713-355-1975. *E*. Here is hoping the "in" spot of the moment may outlast the hype. The odds are good thanks to the dramatic but warm dining room and the modern French fare of Tony Masraff, formerly of New York's Tavern on the Green and Windows on the World. Consider the Crisp Duck Fritters Pastilla; Wild Mushroom Ravioli with White Truffle Broth; and the Texas Quail with Caramelized Tarragon Sauce. Closed Sundays. Reservations recommended.

Maxim's (F1), 3755 Richmond; 713-877-8899. *E*. This is another of Houston's most famous, award-winning restaurants with a long tradition of great dining and fine French cuisine. Owner Camille Berman and son Ron's impressive establishment features a large central dining room with fine paintings, Italian glass chandelier, marble floors and perfect place settings, inviting you to a memorable experience. Friendly, expert waiters attend to your every need. Don't miss the lamb shank at lunch . . . otherwise you can count on their recommendations—the fresh Gulf seafood is excellent and Chicken Camille is exceptional, with the Creme Brulee a perfect finishing touch. Closed Sundays. Reservations advisable. Coat and tie recommended.

Post Oak Grill, 1415 S. Post Oak Lane; 713-993-9966. *E*. Presented by one of Houston's best and best-known restaurateurs, Manfred Jachmich, this high-profile and high-quality American-Continental restaurant entices fashionable diners with such creative offerings as Honey-chipotle Glazed Salmon with Roasted Corn Risotto; Warm Grilled Chicken Salad with Apples, Pecans, Grapes and Roquefort; Grilled Wild Boar Chop with Honey-chili Ancho Sauce; or Shrimp Pasta Diablo. Save room for dessert. Open daily. Reservations a must. Dressy casual to dressy.

The Rivoli (D1), 5636 Richmond Ave; 713-789-1900. *E*. The recipient of many awards for food and service, this classy East Coast-style restaurant is on the Houston celebrity circuit. Divided into several intimate and richly appointed dining areas by latticework and planters. The Rivoli boasts an extensive wine list and at tableside you have a selection of five flambees. Closed Sundays. Reservations recommended. Coat and tie requested for dinner.

Tony's (C1), 1801 Post Oak Blvd.; 713-622-6778. *E, very*. It is hard to determine what is better at this Houston institution: Tony Vallone's French-Italian fare, the attentive and gracious wait staff or the people-watching. This crimson-colored dining room is where Houston's smart set and visiting VIPs gather to be indulged and indulge in foie gras, rack of lamb and sinfully rich souffles. Reservations a must. Jacket required.

GERMAN/AUSTRIAN

Darby's (C3), 3322 D'Amico; 713-522-5305. *E*. Salzburg-born owner Hans Mair offers sophisticated Austrian fare not easily found in Texas. Try the hearty and authentic Wiener Schnitzel, Osso Buco or Calf's Liver with Apples. The Austrian apple strudel is to die for. This out-of-the-way bistro presents live music some nights. Closed Sundays.

Old Heidelberg Inn (C1), 1810 Fountainview at San Felipe; 713-781-3581. *M*. Heavy, high-beamed ceilings, stained glass and a piano bar accordionist playing all kinds of music, including old-time German favorites, create the right atmosphere for robust dining. Wash down your sauerkraut with German beer and join the fun at this family-friendly joint. Closed Sundays.

Rudi Lechner's, 2503 S. Gessner, 713-782-1180. *M*. An oompah band whips up the crowds at this boisterous and popular restaurant. Wear your stretchy pants and order the all-you-can-eat Heritage Dinner, a feast of roast pork loin, wiener schnitzel, sauerbraten, roasted chicken, red cabbage, sauerkraut and potatoes. Open daily. Reservations advised for weekends. Internet: www.rudilechners.com.

INDIAN

Ashiana, 12610 Briar Forest; 281-679-5555. *M*. Traditional Northern Indian cuisine with complex flavors is served in this airy yet elegant dining room in west Houston. Specialties include Fish Curry; Eggplant with Onions and Green Chilies; and Tandoori Leg of Lamb. Lunch buffet. Open daily. Reservations for dinner recommended.

Bombay Brasserie (C1), 5160 Richmond; 713-355-2000. *M*. A pretty dining room in an otherwise desolate strip center offers tasty Indian fare. The lunch buffet is particularly pleasant and convenient for visitors making The Galleria/Post Oak shopping scene. Good vegetarian fare. Open daily.

Khyber North Indian Grill (D2), 2510 Richmond; 713-942-9424. *I-M*. Char-grilled marinated meat and kebabs offer a tasty introduction to Indian fare for those with a timid palate. Open daily.

Taj Mahal (E5), 8328 Gulf Freeway; 713-649-2818. M. This fascinating restaurant is richly decorated with tapestries, rugs, brass trays and lamps. A glassed-in main dining area allows guests to watch the process of charcoal broiling various meats on skewers in the barrel-shaped pit ovens called tandoors. This restaurant in particular takes heed of the American taste and serves mild Indian dishes. Perhaps that is why it has been in business for more than 20 years. Closed Mondays.

ITALIAN

Buca Di Bacco (I10), 700 Milam; 713-224-2426. *M-E*. A favorite of the theater crowd, Buca Di Bacco dishes out home-style southern Italian fare in an unremarkable setting. Among the popular dishes is the Straw & Hay Chicken, a pasta dish with grilled chicken and tossed in a light, spicy sauce. Reservations required for dinner.

Collina's (D2), 2400 Times; 713-526-4499. *I*. Casual, family-friendly café that offers excellent pizzas and other light Italian fare. Closed Sundays. Other outposts are near Compaq Center and Memorial Shopping Center.

Damian's Cucina Italiana (C3), 3011 Smith; 713-522-0439. *E*. Step into the warm and aromatic dining room for a true Italian feast of antipasto, pasta, soup and salad, and an intriguing entree. The pasta list is especially pleasing with a range of linguine, fettuccine, tortellini and cannelloni. Entrees vary from fish and seafood to chicken breast stuffed with sausage and spinach. Closed Sundays.

La Griglia (C2), 2002 W. Gray; 713-526-4700. *M-E*. Ladies who lunch prefer this gem in the Tony Vallone's restaurant empire. Lean and eager to be seen, they lap up seafood salad and the attention of a fawning staff. And if nobody is looking, they pig out on the Snickers Frozen White Chocolate Mousse. Oh, the decadence. Open daily. Reservations advised.

La Mora Cucina Toscana (D3), 912 Lovett; 713-522-7410. *M-E*. Romance reigns at this candlelit Montrose cottage. The menu features earthy Italian fare such as roast pork and Cacciucco (seafood soup). Portions are ponderous, but you'll hate yourself if you don't try the Tiramisu. Closed Sundays. Reservations advised. Internet: www.lamora.com.

Prego (D2), 2520 Amherst; 713-529-2420. M. This trattoria in trendy Rice Village draws an attractive, yet casually clad clientele. The menu is winning, and so is the wine list, which has been singled out for its excellence by The Wine Spectator in 1998 and 1999. Open daily. Reservations recommended. Internet: www.pregohouston.com.

Nino's (C3), 2817 W. Dallas; 713-522-5120. M-E. For more than 20 years, Houstonians have been filling up on traditional lasagna, pizza and veal at this homey, well-respected restaurant. Closed Sundays. Reservations recommended. (Next door is Nino's sister—make that brother—operation. Vincent's is just a wee bit more casual and offers a lighter menu.)

LATIN AMERICAN

America's (C1), 1800 Post Oak Blvd.; 713-961-1492. E, very. The swanky dining room, a modern bat cave with psychedelic touches, is reason enough to visit this Post Oak restaurant. Isn't it nice that the food is terrific too? Chef/owner Michael Cordua's menu features adventurous pairings of grilled meats and sauces inspired by his Nicaraguan homeland. Closed Sundays. Reservations strongly advised. Internet: www.americas.com.

Churrasco's (D2), 2055 Westheimer; 713-527-8300. Another Cordua production. Large man-friendly dining room with hearty man-friendly fare such as Grilled Beef Tenderloin Basted with Garlic-parsley Chimichurri and Plaintain-crusted chicken. Service with a flourish. Open daily. Reservations strongly advised. Internet: www.churrascos.com. Other locations in West Houston and in the Clear Lake area.

Rodizio Grill (C1), 5851 Westheimer; 713-334-7400. M. Carnivores get their fill at this Brazilian beef bar. Colorfully clad waiters snake through the sleek dining room with skewers of meat, slicing grilled beef, poultry and pork right onto waiting plates. A great place to take out-of-town guests for a unique experience. Open daily. Internet: www.rodiziogrill.com.

Ruggles Latino (I10), 711 Main; 713-227-9141. E. You'll recognize the components—guava, black beans, mango—but be surprised at the innovative use in dishes such as lamb empanadas, crab quesadillas and smoked pork sandwiches. This Havana-inspired dining room, like other Ruggles eateries, can be crowded and loud. It also is plagued by notoriously long waits for a table. Music many nights. Closed Mondays and Sundays. Reservations recommended.

MEDITERRANEAN

Droubi's Bakery (D1), 7333 Hillcroft; 713-988-5897. I. This Middle Eastern market and bakery has a few tables for diners, but we think this is a terrific place to fill a picnic basket and then head for the shade of a tree. The pita bread is still warm from the oven. The olives and cheese are piquant. The hummus and baba ghanoush are about the best in town. Excellent falafel, too. Open daily.

Niko Nikos (D3), 2520 Montrose; 713-528-1308. *I*. Located in the heart of funky Montrose, this neighborhood café serves filling classics such as gyros, spinach pie, falafel sandwiches and stuffed cabbage rolls. Excellent Greek Salad. Open daily.

Sambuca (I10), 909 Texas; 713-224-5299. *E*. You will have to push your way past the crowded bar scene to get to a table at this dramatically designed restaurant. Your reward is Lobster Stuffed Filet Mignon; and Penne Pompeii, which is tossed with red grapes, Gorgonzola and roasted walnuts. Yum. Open daily. Live music nightly. Internet: www.sambucajazzcafe.com.

MEXICAN/TEX-MEX

Blue Agave (D3), 1340 W. Gray; 713-520-9696. *M*. Even when there is not a parking space to be had, there's plenty of room inside this popular restaurant. The bar area is cavernous, handling huge congregations of folks more interested in margaritas than the Tex-Mex fare served here. Persevere. Take a table up front (one is always open) and dig into chef/owner Charlie Watkins' baby-back ribs, exquisitely fried calamari and spinach and artichoke enchiladas. Open daily. Very casual.

Café Noche (D3), 2409 Montrose; 713-529-2409. *M*. This stark dining room can get a little loud on the weekends, but who needs to talk when you're shoveling it in. Among the highlights are tender cabrito and rich tortilla soup. The bar draws an eclectic cast of characters. Open daily. Internet: www.cafenoche.com.

Las Alamedas (B1), 8615 I-10; 713-461-1503. *M-E*. In a beautiful nineteenth-century-style hacienda filled with gorgeous Mexican antiques, this sybaritic retreat offers unusual Mexican dishes. The menu also provides for local Mexican favorites as well. Open daily. Reservations advised for Friday and Saturday nights. Dressier than most restaurants in this category.

Merida Restaurant (C4), 2509 Navigation; 713-227-0260. *I-M*. Authentic Mexican-American surroundings at a large, bright and colorful establishment, with menu offering traditional Mexican and Tex-Mex dishes, but highlighting Yucatan specialties (Merida, the restaurant's namesake, is the capital of the Mexican State of Yucatan). Mexican breakfasts are *especialamente* worth trying—especially the Huevos a la Mexicana (eggs coarsely scrambled with chopped onion, tomato, and serrano pepper). Open daily. Casual. Open seven days.

Ninfa's (C4), 2704 Navigation; 713-228-1175. M. This is the original location of Houston's most famous restaurant chain. Mama Ninfa Laurenzo, who opened this restaurant decades ago in the back of her home, is credited with igniting the fajita craze. And it still sizzles here. Terrific enchiladas too. Try a Ninfarita, the house version of a margarita. Open daily.

Pico's, 5941 Bellaire; 713-662-8383. M. Don't call this Tex-Mex. At this boisterous southwest restaurant, the fare is Mex-Mex. That translates to rich mole sauces and fresh fish. Try the Chiles en Nogada, which are roasted peppers stuffed with pork and covered with a cold creamy walnut sauce. Ole. But watch out for those margaritas. They are bucket-sized and brain-deadening. Open daily.

Taco Milagro (C2), 2555 Kirby; 713-522-1999. I-M. Taquerias are ubiquitous in Mexico. They offer tacos fast and cheap. Taco Milagro is Houston celebrity chef Robert Del Grande's version of a taqueria. A decidedly upscale version that attracts yuppies like flies to watermelon. Try the shrimp/bacon taco, the beefsteak enchiladas and the flavorful tamales. A salsa bar with a half-dozen spicy options invites experimentation. Open daily. Very casual.

PIZZA

Fuzzy's (C1), 823 Antoine; 713-682-8836. Several other locations. I. Neighborhood cafés draw families and postgame softball teams with their huge pies. Choose from deep or thin crust, both boast a mountain of cheese. Open daily.

Star Pizza (F2), 2111 Norfolk, 713-523-0800; (C3) 140 S. Heights, 713-869-1241. I. Nothing to brag about at these casual joints except really great pizzas, all made to order. You can do your own thing and create your pizza fantasy with over 20 extras from anchovies to fresh garlic to jalapenos to zucchini. They make their own sauce and dough (from unbleached, untreated flour) fresh daily. Other items on the menu include an Italian sausage sandwich, antipasto salad, and several pastas. Deliveries too. Open daily.

SEAFOOD

King Fish Market (D1), 6356 Richmond; 713-974-3474. M-E. We enjoy the handsome dining room with its colorful mural and blond woods. We like the eager-to-please youngsters that make up the waitstaff. But we love the work of the kitchen: Paneed oysters swimming in a spicy barbecue sauce, crispy coated catfish and pastas topped with crab and calamari. Open daily.

Kemah Boardwalk, Texas 146 at Kemah. M-E. It seems only right that not far from NASA is a skyrocketing project known as the Kemah Boardwalk. Once a handful of independently owned seafood restaurants overlooking Galveston Bay, this deliriously popular dining/entertainment center is now a six-pack of seafood restaurants (along with a Mexican eatery) sitting side by side. They are all owned by one company and are linked by an inviting boardwalk, complete with carnival games and rides. The seafood restaurants are: Joe's Crab Shack, Landry's Seafood House, The Crab House, The Flying Dutchman, Willie G.'s Seafood and Steakhouse and the Aquarium. On busy days, waits can be long, particularly for the upscale and eye-catching Aquarium. Our suggestion is to put your name on the list at the restaurant with the shortest wait and enjoy a drink at the Aquarium's bar. Any restaurant will do; they all offer similar fare, service and tariffs. Open daily. Internet: www.kemahboardwalk.com.

McCormick & Schmick's (C1), 1151 Uptown Park Blvd.; 713-840-7900. E. Located in a new upscale shopping center, this outpost of the Portland, Oregon-based chain is attracting a loyal clientele with its clubby atmosphere and super-fresh (and super-pricey) fish. Open daily. Reservations advised.

Tony Mandola's Gulf Coast Kitchen (C2), 1962 W. Gray; 713-528-3474. M-E. Whether you call it Italian-inspired or Cajun-flavored, this is just great seafood. Fried soft-shell crabs, slabs of fried catfish and oyster-festooned pasta. The dining room is casual, yet soothingly adult. Open daily. Reservations advised.

SOUL FOOD

Fusion Café (D3), 3722 Main St.; 713-874-1116. I. Don't be put off by the counter service and the small nondescript dining room. This is some of the best food in town. It borrows flavors from New Orleans and Jamaica with spicy jerk chicken, jazzed-up dirty rice, peppered shrimp with rice and slow-cooked oxtail. Don't skip the desserts: sweet potato pie and an extra-moist bread pudding. Closed Sundays.

This Is It (C3), 239 W. Gray; 713-523-5319. I. Situated at the edge of downtown, this place is usually packed with denizens of the historic old, predominantly black Fourth Ward, together with weekday visits by downtown business types. Arrive hungry and be prepared for Texas-size portions of soul food from the steam table. Your choice of ox tails, hocks, chitterlings, baked chicken, smothered steak, cabbage, cornbread dressing, yams, peas, rice, and pintos, plus other down-home dishes. Open daily.

SPANISH/TAPAS

Mi Luna (D2), 2441 University; 713-520-5025. M. This tapas bar overcomes its barnlike setting with tasty tidbits such as mussels marinated in sherry and olive oil and sprinkled with capers; baked goat cheese in a tomato basil sauce; and grilled lamb with couscous. The paella, an intoxicating mix of seafood, chorizo and chicken, is outstanding. Open daily.

Solero (I10), 910 Prairie; 713-227-2665. M. Despite growing competition, Houston's first tapas restaurant continues to attract the young and hip with bite-size servings of ceviche, snapper cakes, calamari and beef empanadas. Located in the 1882 Henry Brashear Building. Closed Sunday. Reservations advised.

Tasca (I10), 908 Congress; 713-225-9100. M-E. This gorgeous dining room and inventive kitchen were an immediate hit when Tasca opened in the summer of 1998. And the tapas bar's celebrity hasn't waned. Don't miss the fried calamari with peppery aioli and the escargot-and-cheese ravioli. Closed Sundays. Reservations recommended.

STEAK

Lynn's Steakhouse, 955 Dairy Ashford; 281-870-0807. E. This steakhouse in the far west part of town has a devoted following who are convinced you don't have to go into the city for a premium slab of meat. Excellent side dishes such as creamed spinach and broccoli. Closed Sundays. Reservations advised.

The Palm (D1), 6100 Westheimer; 713-977-2544. E. The granddaddy of steakhouses is committed to serving the perfect steak—and a pretty good Chilean sea bass. The clubby dining room belies the restaurant's strip-center address. Open daily. Reservations recommended.

Ruth's Chris Steak House (D1), 6213 Richmond; 713-789-2333. E. Of Louisiana fame, Ruth's Chris specializes in legendary, corn-fed U.S. Prime beef, and offers as well select seafood, veal, chicken and lamb. Steaks served sizzling in butter (optional), cut and cooked to your preference. Petite filet, filet, ribeye, New York Strip, Porterhouse or t-bone. From the list of nine spud options, select potatoes lyonnaise sautéed with onions or mashed with a touch of roasted garlic. Atmosphere is urban club—wood paneling, candle-lit tables/booths, upscale furnishings. Open daily. Reservations advised. Classy casual attire.

Taste of Texas, 10505 Katy Freeway; 713-932-6901. M-E. Owners Edd and Nina Hendee, along with special deputies, feverishly patrol their superior, superb and otherwise superlative steakhouse to make absolutely sure everything is to everybody's satisfaction. They needn't worry, although perhaps because they do, satisfaction rules. Said satisfaction sizzles to juicy perfection in 100 percent certified Angus steaks, from the petite filet mignon to the 32-ounce porterhouse. En route to the salad bar, customers select steaks (or whole lobsters) from a huge working display case. If you don't see a steak you want, more are cheerfully and voluntarily produced. Each steak gets a number, each customer a matching tag. Taste of Texas is so meticulous about quality, they will replace a steak and/or knock it off a bill without being asked—occasionally even after being asked not to. Unless you eat early or late, long lines are inevitable, but ameliorated with complimentary chips, salsa, and soft drinks in a waiting lounge. Most of all, those long lines are justified by the flavor and quality of the entire Taste of Texas repertoire. Open daily.

Vegetarian

The Hobbit Café (F2), 2243 Richmond; 713-526-5460. *I*-M. Part of the Houston dining scene for more than 25 years, this restaurant features a variety of vegetarian sandwiches on homemade bread, and quiches and salads. Carnivores will find grilled fish and chicken specials. Open daily.

A Moveable Feast (C3), 2202 W. Alabama; 713-528-3585. *I*-M. Taking its name from the Ernest Hemingway classic, this café features meatless versions of barbecue, enchiladas, fajitas and Reuben sandwiches. The café takes pride in its smoothies and fruit juices. After your meal, you can shop for organic produce, herbs, and all-natural beauty products. Closed Sundays.

THE PERFORMING ARTS

There is rarely a dark night on Houston stages, where scores of local performing arts groups delight audiences with every conceivable form of entertainment.

This is one of the few cities in the nation to boast major professional resident performing arts companies plus its own Broadway musical production group. The big four—Houston Grand Opera, Houston Ballet, Houston Symphony and the Alley Theatre—combined are currently presenting more than 1,000 performances a year, here and all over the world.

Visitors not only have a choice from among an impressive slate of events in the fall and winter, but are treated to fine outdoor performances in the spring and summer as well. A bonus is that many of the latter are free.

Thus the visitor and newcomer are promised bountiful opportunities to witness a wide range of programs from traditional to contemporary theater, from folkloric dance to full classical ballet, and from Bach to pop.

Good sources for current events listings and performance schedules are the Houston Press and Houston Chronicle. Look in particular in the Chronicle's Sunday Zest and Thursday Preview sections.

DANCE

Many Houstonians are traditionally as enthusiastic about the dance as they are about their favorite sports teams. And to satisfy this demand dozens of dance companies stomp and strut here.

The **Houston Ballet** leads this list. Started in 1968, it already has reached a widely proclaimed pinnacle of success, both in the United States and abroad. While it enjoys a fine reputation as a classical company, it is equally aggressive in developing a blend of contemporary works. Under the direction of Ben Stevenson, it ranks as one of the nation's largest dance companies, with 47 dancers, 10 soloists, and 9 principals. Its backup is drawn from an enrollment of some 450 students in the Houston Ballet Academy.

The ballet presents more than 80 performances a year in Houston, in addition to a score of programs on the road. The company has performed in China, Spain, Italy, France, Luxembourg, Switzerland, Monaco, Indonesia, and Scandinavia.

The Ballet performs its regular season in Wortham Theater Center (I9), 501 Texas, from September to June. It also performs annually at Miller Outdoor Theater (D3) in Hermann Park and the Woodlands Pavilion in The Woodlands.

Information: 713-523-6300; www.houstonballet.org. CH.

Here are some of the companies that keep Houston's toes tapping all year 'round:

Alien Nation, 713-223-8346. CH. Contemporary dance, often with mixed media. Performs at the Winter Street Art Center (C3), 2123 Winter St.

Chrysalis Dance Company, 713-661-9855. CH. Contemporary dance, often featuring regional choreographers. Performance venues vary.

City Ballet of Houston, 713-468-3670. CH. Chartered in 1958, this company maintains a well-rounded repertory of classical, contemporary, and some original works. Performs at the Grand 1894 Post Office in Galveston and Heinen Theater (D3), 3517 Austin.

Clear Lake Metropolitan Ballet, 281-480-1617; www.clmb.org. CH. In addition to a regular schedule of classical performances, this 25-year-old company reaches out to the community with demonstrations and lectures. Performs at the Bayou Theater on the University of Houston-Clear Lake campus (E6), 2700 Bay Area Blvd.

Colombian Folkloric Ballet, 713-799-2381. CH. Troupe was founded in 1983 to promote and preserve Colombian culture among Houston youth. Performance venues vary.

Dance Salad, 713-464-0162. CH. An annual program of eclectic contemporary dance with changing themes. Performed at the Wortham Theater Center (I9), 501 Texas.

Fly Dance Company, 713-521-4560. CH. An all-male dance company known for its acrobatics and hip-hop choreography. Performance venues vary.

Houston Metropolitan Dance Company, 713-522-6375. CH. Modern dance with ambitious programs. Performs at Heinen Theater (D3), 3517 Austin.

Isadora's Dish, 713-228-0914. CH. Contemporary dance with a feminist twist. Performance venues vary.

Kuumba House Dance Theatre, 713-524-1079; www.kuumbahouse.org.

CH. Founded in 1982, this energetic group takes a fresh and compelling approach to African dance. Performance venues vary.

Psophonia Dance Company, 713-716-4261. CH. Small contemporary dance troupe. Performance venues vary.

Sandra Organ Dance Company, 713-520-9876. CH. Contemporary troupe founded by the Houston Ballet's first African-American dancer. Performance venues vary.

Several Dancers Core, 713-862-5530. CH. Innovative Houston-based touring troupe, founded in 1980, that regularly sponsors workshops on classical, contemporary and ethnic dance. Performance venues vary.

Society for the Performing Arts, 713-227-4772; www.spahouston.org. CH. Sponsors visits by national touring dance companies several times a year. Performance venues vary.

Suchu Dance Company, 713-523-0679; www.suchudance.org. CH. Company's works are famous for their physicality and humor. Performance venues vary.

Texas Tap Ensemble, 713-686-9184. CH. Award-winning troupe of young dancers specializing in tap, jazz and modern works. Performance venues vary.

Weave Dance Company, 713-522-6217. CH. Five-member modern dance troupe with inventive choreography. Performance venues vary.

MUSIC

Classical

Since 1913, Houston has sought out symphony, even when it was performed in a vaudeville house.

The city provided more suitable surroundings with its City Auditorium, where early Houstonians flocked to see such illustrious immortals as Paderewski and Caruso. Years later, this hallowed old structure gave way to the **Jones Hall for the Performing Arts** (I10), 615 Louisiana. The $7.5 million Continental-style hall is a multipurpose, multiform facility with four separate seating arrangements, ranging from the capacity 3,000 to 1,800 for more intimate audiences.

Today the **Houston Symphony** presents more than 200 concerts each year, the bulk of which are performed at Jones Hall. Houstonians also look forward to the symphony's annual outdoor shows at the Woodlands Pavilion in the Woodlands and the Miller Theater in Hermann Park.

The 97-piece symphony boasts an annual budget of more than $19 million, allowing it to sponsor 300 educational and community out-reach performances each year.

Information: 713-224-7575; www.houstonsymphony.org. *CH.*

Other classical music programs:

Clear Lake Symphony, 713-639-0702. *CH.* Community orchestra offers six programs each year, as well as an annual Christmas "Pops" concert. Performance venues vary.

Houston Civic Symphony, 713-747-0018. *NCH.* This longstand-ing community orchestra performs free concerts at churches, schools and museums.

Houston Friends of Music, 713-285-5400. *CH.* Brings outstanding chamber ensembles to Houston from around the world. Performances at Stude Concert Hall at Rice University (D3), on campus.

Houston Youth Symphony & Ballet, 713-785-2422. *CH.* The country's oldest youth orchestra performs a half-dozen formal concerts each year, as well as entertains thousands of local schoolchildren.

Orchestra X, 713-225-6729; www.orchestrax.org. *CH.* This cut-ting-edge group combines classical music with young ideas such as self-expressive movement and interaction with the audience. Performance venues vary.

Virtuosi of Houston, 713-721-0312. *CH.* A chamber orchestra that provides training for gifted young musicians. Performance venues vary.

Opera

Interfaced with the long list of music ensembles in Houston is an equally large and varied list of choral groups ranging from barbershop quartets to Gregorian, and from gospel to grand opera. The latter is the granddaddy of them all.

Houston Grand Opera has achieved meteoric fame and has been widely acclaimed for its broad innovative repertoire that has included 24 world premieres. The 45-year-old company, which performs in Wortham Theater Center (I9), 501 Texas, is the only one in the world to have won a Tony, two Grammy and two Emmy awards.

It has an outstanding reputation for its staging of traditional operas in their original languages plus English-language programs, but the company also performs many works by American composers. Among its U.S. and world premieres, it has gained greatest renown for its revi-sionist treatment of such works as *Tremonisha* and *The Lady of the Lake*, which, until the HGO revived it in 1981, had not been seen in 150 years. Other imaginative productions have been Tod Machover and

Laura Harrington's *Resurrection* and the 2000 world premiere of *Cold Sassy Tree* by Carlisle Floyd.

Rated one of the top opera companies in America, HGO has two branches working in conjunction with the main company. They are **Opera New World** and **Houston Opera Studio.** Opera New World was founded by HGO director David Gockley in 1990 to commission and produce works that would appeal to a non-traditional audience. Houston Opera Studio, begun in 1977 by Gockley and composer Carlisle Floyd, is a training and performance program for young artists interested in music theater.

One of HGO's most popular events each year is its Plazacast, a free outdoor telecast of a live opera. Bleachers are set up on the plaza outside Wortham Theater and spectators are encouraged to bring blankets, lawn chairs, and picnic baskets.

Information: 713-227-2787; www.hgo.com. CH.

Other opera groups include:

Gilbert & Sullivan Society, 713-627-3570. CH. This group performs light opera in an annual series in July in Wortham Theater Center.

Opera in the Heights, 713-861-5303. CH. Intimate setting enhances the performances of this small but confident company presenting fully staged operas. Performances in historic Lambert Hall (B3), 1703 Heights.

Opera To Go, 713-546-0231. CH. This Houston-based group takes opera to Houston's schoolchildren. These "portable" operas come complete with costumes and sets. Frequently works with Houston Grand Opera. Performance venues vary.

Specialty

Bach Society, 713-523-2864. CH. Presents baroque music in concert and vespers setting. Performances at Christ the King Lutheran Church (D2), 2353 Rice Blvd.

Context, 713-665-2620. CH. Chamber music ensemble. Performances at Alice Pratt Brown Hall at Rice University (D3), on campus.

Da Camera, 713-524-5050; www.dacamera.com. CH. Offers an exciting and diverse schedule that includes jazz, contemporary and chamber music programs. Also known for its free lunchtime concerts and innovative educational programs. Performance venues vary.

Houston Blues Society, 713-942-9427. CH. Sponsors and schedules traditional blues concerts. Performance venues vary.

Houston Early Music, 713-432-1744. CH. Unique concerts that present music written and instruments used before 1800. Performance venues vary.

Houston Ebony Music Society, 713-529-7664. CH. Specializes in opera, traditional spirituals and classical music. Performance venues vary.

Society for the Performing Arts, 713-227-4772; www.spahouston.org. CH. Sponsors visits by national touring music groups, ranging from classical to jazz. Performance venues vary.

Choral

Bay Area Chorus. This group has performed for 17 years in the area doing traditional choral music. They usually perform two or three concerts a year. Performance venues vary. CH. Information: 281-335-7777.

Houston Boy Choir, 713-743-3398. CH. Associated with the University of Houston Moores School of Music, this 40-year-old choir performs with national and international symphonies and orchestras. Performance venues vary.

Houston Chamber Choir, 713-224-5566. CH. Houston's only professional concert choir often performs *a cappella*, as well as presenting works by Texas composers. Performance venues vary.

Houston Masterworks Chorus, 713-529-8900. CH. Houston's largest independent chorus presents works ranging from classical to contemporary. Performance venues vary.

Statesmen Chorus, 281-379-1460. CH. For 20 years, this chorus has been delivering *a cappella* performances. Venues vary.

THEATER

Cinema

In the past several years, new theaters have been popping up all over the greater Houston area. Most of these new movie palaces feature comfortable stadium seating with plush rocker seats and excellent sight lines.

The city has three "art house" theaters that specialize in foreign and independent films:

The **Landmark River Oaks** (C3), 2009 W. Gray, is the oldest of these three. This attractive old cinema has three screens: a large theater downstairs and two upstairs. The two second-floor screening rooms are as uncomfortable as they are small and only for the most earnest of film fans. Information: 713-524-2175.

The underutilized **Landmark Greenway Plaza** (F1), Five Greenway Plaza, also has three screens. Information: 713-626-0402.

New to the scene is the **Angelika Film Center,** (I9), 510 Texas in Bayou Place. This theater was a welcome addition to downtown when opened a few years back. Shows some mainstream movies, but mostly foreign and independent films. Café and bar. Information: 713-225-5232.

Here is a cross section of theaters that show first-run films. A number following a theater name generally implies the number of screens available:

Bay Area (F6), I-45 at Nasa Road; 281-554-5563.
Cinemark Katy, I-10 at Grand Parkway; 281-371-6000.
Commerce Park 8, I-45 N. at Richey Road; 281-319-4262.
Deerbrook Mall 24, FM 1960 at US 59 North; 281-319-4262.
Easton Commons, Hwy 6 at Hwy 290; 281-550-3966.
First Colony 24, I-59 at Sugar Land; 281-319-4262.
Fountains, I-59 at Kirkwood; 281-240-1175
Grand Palace Stadium 24 (F1), I-59 at Weslayan; 713-871-8880.
Gulf Point 30, I-45 South at Beltway 8; 281-319-4262.
Hollywood 20, Beltway 8 at Pasadena Boulevard.; 713-475-0081.
Katy Mills 20, I-10 at Pin Oak Road; 281-319-4262.
Magic Johnson Theater (A3), I-45 at Crosstimbers; 713-692-4600.
Marq*E Stadium 23 & IMAX (B1), Katy Freeway at Silber Road; 713-263-0808.
Memorial City Mall (B1), I-10 at Gessner; 713-467-5639.
Meyerland Plaza (D1), Loop 610 at Beechnut; 713-333-3456.
Meyer Park 16 (E1), S. Post Oak at Bellfort; 281-319-4262.
River Oaks Plaza W. Gray at Waugh; 713-524-8781.
Spectrum 9 (C1), Augusta at Westheimer; 713-781-3233.
Spring, I-45 at Holzworth; 281-288-7200.
Studio 30 (C1), Dunvale at Westheimer; 281-319-4262.
Tinseltown at 290, Hwy 290 at Northwest 100; 713-329-9975.
Tinseltown Westchase, Beltway 8 at Richmond; 713-952-1881.
Tinseltown Woodlands, I-45 at Lake Robbins; 281-364-0600.
West Oaks Mall 7, Hwy 6 at Westheimer; 281-493-9703.
Willowbrook 24, Hwy 149 at FM 1960; 281-319-4262.

Professional and Semi-Professional Theater

There is such an abundance of new talent on the boards in Houston that even many of the locals are not fully aware of the array of theatrical events available.

The anchor establishment has been and is today the world-famous **Alley Theatre** (I9-10), 615 Texas Ave., one of the oldest resident theaters in the United States.

Since its humble beginnings in 1947 in an 87-seat theater converted from a dance studio at the end of an alley (hence the name), this center has emerged as one of the leading theatrical production and training facilities in the world.

Regular season is from October through June, and the Alley enjoys strong support from a subscription audience of more than 35,000.

It is Houston's only professional resident repertory theater and has attracted guest directors from New York, Canada and the former Soviet Union. The Alley does hundreds of performances a year, divided between the regular season and summer productions, plus such special productions and programs as children's plays. The Alley has two theaters: one is a proscenium arch stage with seating for more than 800, and the other is the Neuhaus Arena for 300.

This theater is dedicated to plays of literary merit and brings to Houston a broad spectrum of classical and contemporary works by world-famous playwrights.

Information: 713-228-8421; www.alleytheatre.com. *CH.*

The **Ensemble** (F3), 3535 Main; 713-520-0055. *CH.* This 200-seat theater is the oldest African-American theater in the Southwest. This professional company's productions range from comedy to mystery, from musicals to drama, primarily by black playwrights.

Main Street Theater (D2), 2540 Times Blvd. in the Village; 713-524-6706. *CH.* Founded in 1975, this theater produces works of intellectual appeal as well as pure entertainment. Also offers children's theater.

Stages (C3), 3201 Allen Parkway; 713-527-8243; www.stagestheatre. *CH.* This is a repertory theater and the second-largest in Houston. It is home of the Texas Playwright's Festival and the Early Stages Children's Theatre. Concentrates on contemporary plays, musicals, and new and innovative works. There are two stages, the larger seating 250 and a more intimate one for 195. The large resident professional company rounds out its season with a revival of an American masterpiece or a world classic.

Theatre Under the Stars, 800-678-5440; www.tuts.com. *CH.* Founded in 1968, this is Houston's own Broadway musical production company, offering more than 200 performances each year.

In July of each year TUTS produces an extravaganza musical open free to the public in popular Miller Outdoor Theater (D3) in Hermann Park. (Please see SIGHTS chapter.) In past years, hundreds of thousands of Houstonians have flocked to see elaborate musicals such as such *Carnival, Grease* and *Fiddler on the Roof.*

Dancing Girl in front of Jones Hall facing the Alley Theatre   *Courtesy of Dale Young*

TUTS also provides instruction and stage experience to more than 600 students annually through its Humphreys School of Musical Theater.

Presently, TUTS productions are staged at the Wortham Theater Center (I9), 501 Texas, and Arena Theater (D1), 7324 SW Freeway. The production company will move into the spanking new Hobby Center for the Performing Arts, downtown Bagby at Walker, when it opens in 2002. The Hobby Center will feature two state-of-the-art performance halls: one seating 2,650 and one accommodating 500 patrons.

University and Amateur Theaters ————

Surprisingly good productions are found throughout the city in campus theaters and neighborhood little theaters.

Among them are several major university and high school drama department companies such as the **High School for the Performing and Visual Arts,** 713-942-1960; the **University of Houston,** 713-743-1000; and the **University of St. Thomas,** 713-522-7911. It does not have a drama department, but Rice University is the home of the **Rice Players,** the city's oldest collegiate theatrical company. Rice University; 713-527-4040.

Other theater companies include:

Actors Theater of Houston (D2), 2506 South Blvd.; 713-529-6606.
A.D. Players (D2), 2710 W. Alabama; 713-526-2721.
Bill & Tek's Excellent Theatre (E1), 2922 Fondren; 713-975-1881.
The Company on Stage (E1), 536 Westbury; 713-726-1219.
Country Playhouse, 12802 Queensbury; 713-467-4497.
Infernal Bridegroom Productions, P.O. Box 131644; 713-522-8443.
Interactive Theatre Company (B3), 1703 Heights Blvd.; 713-862-7112.
Litte Room Downstairs (E2), 2326 Bissonnet; 713-523-0791.
Masquerade Theatre (B2), 1537 N. Shepherd; 713-861-7045.
Pasadena Little Theater (D5), 4318 Allen-Genoa in Pasadena; 713-941-4636.
Playhouse 1960, 6814 Gant; 281-587-8243.
Theater Lab Houston, 1706 Alamo; 713-868-7516.
Theater Lenz & Company, 3337 FM 1960; 281-397-9067.
Theatre Southwest (D1), 8944 Clarkcrest; 713-977-6028.
Theatre Suburbia (B2), 1410 West Forty-third; 713-682-3525.

NIGHTLIFE

With a strong shot of adrenaline and plenty of stamina, one can nightclub hop across Houston, mixing it up with a little bit of country, jazz, opera, rock, reggae and salsa all in one night. You could go out every evening of the year and never backtrack in this swinging metropolis of thousands of watering holes.

At many places, the scene begins with happy hour and usually doesn't let up until 2 am; some clubs may stay open later but can't serve alcohol after hours. Some neighborhood bars are open and jumping by 8 am, and others save their big bash for Sunday jam sessions and jazz brunches.

Regardless of your mood, you can find the right setting here, where the dress codes run the gamut from extremely casual to coat required. But one restriction is you can't enter an establishment where food is served unless you are wearing shoes and a shirt, and Texas law says you must be 21 to belly up to the bar. If you are underage, you can enter a bar only if accompanied by parent or legal guardian.

A note about drinking and driving in Texas: The state recently lowered the level at which it considers a person legally intoxicated from a blood-alcohol level of 0.10 to 0.08. In practice that would mean a 170-pound man who consumes five beers in two hours could be considered drunk. Driving under the influence charges are serious in Houston and could land you in jail. If in doubt, have someone call you a cab.

BARS & NIGHTCLUBS

Cabo Mix-Mex Grill (I-10), 419 Travis; 713-225-2060. If you just judged food by the crowds, this chrome-and-neon bar could claim the Fish Taco title. Lunching office workers test the kitchen, but after 5 P.M., this place serves more margaritas than munchies.

Cadillac Bar (C2), 1802 Shepherd; 713-862-2020. Unpretentious and outrageous, this place is totally Houston. Lovely young ladies packing shot glasses strapped across their chests serve toxic tonics called Mexican shooters. Good margaritas and decent enchiladas. Be prepared to shout your order in this extremely loud watering hole. Open daily.

Dean's (I10), 316 Main; 713-227-3326. Trendy downtown spot housed in an old clothing store. Look for the neon sign flashing "home of easy credit."

La Carafe (H10), 813 Congress; 713-229-9399. Housed in the city's oldest commercial building, this popular spot oozes character. Very romantic after the happy hour crowds disperse. Worth a stop just to check out its jukebox lineup.

Last Concert Café (H10), 1403 Nance; 713-226-8563. Tex-Mex food and song nourish the clientele of this café on the fringe of downtown. The door is always open, but only to those who know to knock.

Marfreless (C2), 2006 Peden (entrance on McDuffie); 713-528-0083. Every town has a neat bar tucked away from the roar of the crowd, but this one is so tucked there are no signs and the entrance could dub for deliveries. This is a surprise pub, usually packed in spite of its secrecy, with mostly youngish to older college crowds conversing in the good-vibes atmosphere with low-key classical background music. Lots of smooching on the bar's second level.

Slick Willies (I9), 550 Texas at Bayou Place; 713-225-1277. Upscale pool hall with outstanding views of the bustling theater district. Several other locations in Houston.

Spindletop (J9), at the top of the Hyatt Regency Houston Hotel, 1200 Louisiana; 713-654-1234. While the world turns below on the frenzied "Spaghetti Bowl" traffic circles, you may enjoy a turn around downtown in this revolving club with soft stereo music for your relaxation. Lunch and dinner served. A splendid view of the city and one of the few from this level. No jeans or sneakers please.

Spy (H10), 112 Travis; 713-225-2229. This club made downtown cool again. Every one is thin, pretty, and well-dressed. Lavish outdoor patio.

State Bar (I10), 909 Texas; 713-229-8888. Decidedly upscale bar located in the renovated Rice Hotel building. The original State Bar was popular with journalists and politicians. This new version, with its manly décor and $8 martinis draws a more attractive and better-dressed crowd. Terrific patio. Dress code.

Swank Lounge (I10), 910 Prairie; 713-227-0459. Located above Solero restaurant, this intimate spot has a loyal, good-looking following. Want to blend in? Dress entirely in black.

CABARETS AND SUPPER CLUBS

Great Caruso, 10001 Westheimer; 713-780-4900. The only other place like this is the Petite Caruso in Paris. A great showplace with an array of continuous entertainment. Opera, Broadway tunes, and popular ballads brighten the atmosphere while you dine on gourmet cuisine in an Old World opera house setting. A marvelous collection of European antiques makes up the decor in this sensational club. Dress code.

Magic Island (D2), 2215 Southwest Freeway; 713-526-2442. It's not often one finds a massive Egyptian monument on the side of a busy freeway but . . . shazam . . . there's Magic Island. This beautiful modern Egyptian edifice is a $3 million replica of ancient desert splendor with many rooms to explore and to wonder at the hocus pocus going on inside. Each room features different acts of magic and stand-up comedy. There is also dancing and regal dining. Continental cuisine. Dress code.

Sambuca Jazz Café (I10), 909 Texas; 713-224-5299. Interesting menu and dramatic décor draw a crowd with attitude, style, and fat wallets. Jazz and swing bands keep toes tapping and the small dance floor delightfully jammed.

MUSIC FOR LISTENING AND DANCING

Anderson Fair (C3), 2007 Grant; 713-528-8576. The regulars—and everyone in this hard-to-find venue is a regular—love to tell how Lyle Lovett played here before he got the big hair. Regional singer-songwriters are this tiny club's specialty.

Big Easy Social & Pleasure Club (D2), 5731 Kirby; 713-523-9999. Blues, jazz and zydeco reign at this Rice Village club.

Billy Blues Bar & Grill (D1), 6025 Richmond; 713-266-9294. The outrageously priced barbecue and steep cover charges bug us, but this Richmond Strip club consistently books the best blues acts.

Cezanne (D3), 4100 Montrose; 713-522-9621. Intimate room features exceptional jazz vocalists and bands. The perfect accompaniment to a romantic evening.

Cody's (D2), 2540 University; 713-520-5660. After years in charming digs on a Montrose rooftop, this jazz club headed for the tonier life in the Rice Village. Known for presenting the locally grown jazz groups.

Fabulous Satellite Lounge (C3), 3616 Washington, 713-869-2665. Small room, big sound and lively bar make this optimal setting for catching local and regional acts of every variety.

Fitzgerald's (B3), 2706 White Oak; 713-862-3838. Don't worry if it looks like the building is about to fall down. That's the way it looked 20 years ago when our parents partied here. Rock rules a calendar loaded with punk, metal and alternative groups. Extremely casual.

Mary Jane's (C3), 4216 Washington; 713-869-5263. This scruffy club spotlights an eclectic mix of touring bands.

McGonigel's Mucky Duck (D2), 2425 Norfolk; 713-528-5999. Acoustic stars, regional rockers, bluegrass bands and Celtic crooners grace the small bandstand at this family-run pub. Reserve a table or listen from the patio out back. Some no-smoking shows.

Rudyard's Pub (C3), 2010 Waugh; 713-521-0521. One of the last great rooms for cutting-edge rock. See the bands here before they get big.

Scott Gertner's Skybar (F2), 3400 Montrose; 713-520-9688. Contemporary and Latin-infused jazz are staples of this penthouse club offering spectacular views of downtown Houston.

Shakespeare Pub, 14129 Memorial; 281-497-4625. Steep cover charges give you the blues? Try this far west end pub known for its rhythm and blues and reasonable admission fees.

COMEDY CLUBS

Comedy Showcase, 12547 Gulf Freeway; 281-481-1188. This large club often features national acts and its South Houston location draws folks who never would venture into the big city.

ComedySportz (B3), 1703 Heights Blvd. in Lambert Hall; 713-868-1444. Improvisational comedy teams compete for laughs while interacting with audience. A real hoot and family-friendly show.

Just Joking Comedy Café (D1), 9344 Richmond; 713-975-7262. Located in a west-end strip center, this club often spotlights nationally known black comics.

Laff Stop (C2), 1952 West Gray; 713-524-2333. City's premier comedy club brings professional stand-up comedians direct from New York, Las Vegas and Hollywood with a new show every week.

Radio Music Theater (D2), 2623 Colquitt; 713-522-7722. Intimate productions often feature the misadventures of the fictitious Fertle family of Dumpster, Texas. Shows have loyal following; reservations a must.

KARAOKE

And you thought this craze begun 20 years ago in Japan was dead? Think again. Dozens of clubs and bars have designated nights for the sing-alongs, but here are clubs that offer karaoke nightly:

Cork Club, 9425 Country Creek; 713-981-8171.

Reno's, 20814 Gulf Freeway; 281-316-2235.

Spotlight Karaoke (D1), 5901 Westheimer; 713-266-7768.

The Running Board, 9509 FM 1960 W.; 281-469-1500.

SPORTS BARS

For many fans, a great sports bar is better than the bleachers. So when the game is sold out or the home team is on the road, Houstonians flock to their favorite sports bar to catch all the action. Here are some we like:

Al's Sports Bar & Grill, 3838 S. Dairy Ashford; 281-493-3838. You gotta love a place where the bartenders will watch your pitcher if you have to run an errand during the seventh-inning stretch. They'll even renew the plastic bag of ice that keeps your pitcher chilled. Limited menu.

Big John's, 6150 S. Wilcrest; 281-498-3499. Draws sports fans and a colorful cast of regulars. Good spot to watch international sporting events such as rugby, soccer, and cricket.

Bubba's Sports Bar & Grill (C2), 6225 Washington; 713-861-7161. Absent the bells and whistles of the big places, this neighborhood sports bar is a place where patrons can concentrate on games and grub. Family-friendly with a breakfast buffet on weekends. Very casual.

Champs Americana (C1), 1121 Uptown Park; 713-627-2333. This upscale sports bar focuses more on the food, which is excellent, than on the games. It's difficult to follow the action on the screens from some tables, but the hip crowds that flock here don't seem to mind.

Dave & Busters (D1), 6010 Richmond; 713-952-2233. This adult playground features the latest in video arcade hits, virtual reality games, a classy pool hall, restaurant and two bars. Dozens of TVs make this a great place to catch the big game.

Grif's (F3), 3416 Roseland; 713-528-9912. This Montrose neighborhood bar is a haven for Houston sports fans—at least the ones lucky enough to find a parking spot. Outdoor patios are hopping after 5 P.M. with downtown crowds; inside you'll find sports fans that are passionate and well-informed. The food is what you'll find at the ballpark—burgers and beer.

Forgetta 'Bout It, 13245 Jones Road; 281-807-4116. More than 50 televisions, a beyond-the-basics menu and a super-friendly staff make us root for this place.

SRO Sports Bar & Café (D1), 2517 S. Gessner. Arena layout and barn-size wall of screens make for great sightlines. A game room features the latest in video arcade games as well as pool tables. Menu emphasizes finger foods. Can get crowded during football season and major events. Sister operations include SRO Sports Bar & Café, 6892 FM 1960 W. and SRO Too, 2517 Mangum.

PUBS & BREW PUBS

Ale House (D2), 2425 W. Alabama; 713-521-2333. Terrific selection of draft and bottled beer at this popular watering hole. Pretty garden seating. Limited menu.

Bank Draft (D2), 2424 Dunstan; 713-522-6258. This small neighborhood joint in the Rice Village takes its brews seriously.

Black Labrador Pub (D3), 4100 Montrose; 713-529-1199. Warm atmosphere and cold beer are trademarks of this too-airy-to-be-authentic pub. Try the bangers and mash or a shepherd's pie on a rainy day. Patio seating available.

Brewery Tap (H10), 717 Franklin; 713-237-1537. A veteran of the downtown scene, this pub features more than 30 taps and a colorful clientele. Located in an old bottle shop of long-gone Magnolia Brewery.

Gingerman (D2), 5607 Morningside; 713-526-2770. This extremely popular Rice Village pub is famous for its wall of taps, which dispense as many as 70 exotic brews. Congenial crowds pack the patio, but parking can be a pain. Internet: www.gingermanpub.com.

The Harp (D3), 1625 Richmond; 713-528-7827. Unpretentious neighborhood pub with darts, patio and bar staff that appreciates the art of a Guinness pour.

Kenneally's Irish Pub (C2), 2111 S. Shepherd; 713-630-0486. Fun-loving Irish-flavored bar that knows how to celebrate St. Patrick's Day and home-team championships. Arguably the best pizza in town.

Mercantile Brewery (I10), 1010 Prairie; 713-224-2337. Houston's newest brew pub produces its own ales and pours another 40 guest brews. Housed in the former Isis Theater, which opened in 1913. Grab a seat on the "catwalk" and watch the show below.

Richmond Arms (D1), 5920 Richmond; 713-784-7722. This is as close to an authentic British pub as you will find in Houston. For a real party, visit during a telecast of a British football (soccer) match.

Slainte Irish Pub (I10), 519 Main; 713-237-0000. This $1.2 million theme pub is a little bit of Dublin dropped onto Main Street. Its comfy couches and balcony are popular gathering spots late into the night.

SIGHTS

Most newcomers and first-time visitors don't think of Houston in typical tourist terms. With an image of smoke-belching refineries, trade and high finance, many think of this as a severe business-only town with little time for frivolity. But you will find it does have a surprising number of manmade and natural tourist attractions, some yet to be discovered even by many Houstonians.

The biggest surprise is the variety of things to see and do that are either free or nominally priced. Some of these sights and happenings will be mentioned in other chapters on visual art, sports and special events. Here, we will discuss the points of general interest for the tourist.

Consider the wide range of choices: a celestial show or a visit to a medical museum; a day of family fun at an amusement park or an excursion down a ship channel; a serene stroll through a forest preserve or joining thousands of fans cheering their home team in a sports palace.

However brief your visit or whatever the season, there is always a changing slate of things to do.

Armand Bayou Nature Center (E6 & F6), 8600 Bay Area Blvd.; 281-474-2551; www.abnc.org. *NCH.* About 25 minutes from downtown. In early days, this was a dwelling site for the Karankawa Indians, a nomadic Gulf Coast tribe that survived by hunting and fishing. The center is on nearly 2,500 acres at a point where three ecological systems merge, and it affords the visitor an exceptional view of the upper Texas coast as it was before the French and Spanish explorers arrived. There is a mix of native plants and animals reflecting Houston's curious blend of sub-tropical and continental elements.

Start at the main building where there are displays of the plant and animal life, then follow some of the five miles of trails that lead into the heart of the preserve. Among the animals you might encounter are deer, armadillos, nutria and mink, cottontails, and with any luck, you might spot an alligator.

The center boasts rich educational programs for children and families, including wildlife walks, canoe outings and birding instruction. Guided tours of the trails are available weekends at 11 A.M. and 1 P.M. Open 9 A.M.-5 P.M. daily. Closed Mondays.

Art Car Museum (C3), 140 Heights Blvd.; 713-861-5526; www.art-carmuseum.com. *NCH*. Each year in April, Houston artists, eccentrics and spectators brake for a whimsical parade featuring rolling sculptures and cars decorated with objects such as Pez dispensers, doll heads and tennis balls. Some of these over-the-top automobiles make pit stops at the Art Car Museum, a combination gallery and garage. Exhibits change frequently. Open 11 am-6 pm Wed-Sun.

Astrodome—Harris County Domed Stadium (E2), Kirby at I-610 Loop; 713-799-9500. Once dubbed the "Eighth Wonder of the World," this is one star in the Houston galaxy of attractions that needs little introduction. Of all the developments in the city's tourist industry, none has had greater impact than the Astrodome. Since its opening in 1965, millions have come from around the world to see the tremendous variety of events here. Until recently, it has even been a magnet for visitors who paid admission just to take a look at an empty building. Unfortunately, tours of the stadium have been discontinued.

Battleship Texas (D6). See San Jacinto Battleground State Historical Park below.

Children's Museum of Houston (D3), 1500 Binz; 713-522-1138; www.cmhouston.org. *CH*. The city's funnest museum bursts with colorful, hands-on exhibits for children. Includes a KID-TV studio, computer technology, a mini-market, and other areas of interest for the young. Open 9 am-5 pm, Tue-Sat; noon-5 pm Sun. Closed Mondays. Free family nights Thursdays.

Forbidden Gardens, 23500 Franz Road in Katy; 281-347-8000; www.forbidden-gardens.com. *CH*. About 30 minutes from downtown. This unusual outdoor museum pays homage to the Forbidden City of Beijing. Intricately detailed models represent the many palaces and official buildings of the city, which was built between 1406 and 1420 and was reserved for the Imperial family and the emperor's guards. A highlight of your visit is a 1/3-scale re-creation of the 6,000-piece terra-cotta army of China's first emperor, Qin, who died in 210 BC. Open 10 am-5 pm Wed-Sun. Closed major holidays. Extended hours during the summer.

Glenwood Cemetery (C3), 2525 Washington; 713-864-7886. *NCH*. As Houston's oldest private cemetery, it is estimated that Glenwood goes back some 160 to 185 years. Unusual for pancake-flat Houston, this 65-acre park-like setting is on hilly terrain overlooking Buffalo Bayou with a view of the downtown skyline. At the center is a caretaker's office, which itself is an attraction, a petite German "gingerbread"-style house commonly found in older sections of the city such as The Heights. Many of Houston's rich and famous are buried here including billionaire Howard Hughes. Open 7 am-5 pm daily.

Gulf Greyhound Park, I-45 South, exit 15 at La Marque; 409-986-9500; www.gulfgreyhound.com. *CH*. About 25 minutes from downtown.

Billed as the world's largest pari-mutuel greyhound racing complex, the 315,000-square-foot facility operates seven days a week, with live racing Tue-Sun. The complex features more than 300 teller windows and 1,100 closed-circuit televisions; its full-service restaurant is the largest in the state, seating 1,900.

Hermann Park (D3), bounded by Fannin, Almeda, Hermann Dr., and N. MacGregor; 713-845-1000. CH for some attractions.

One can spend days and evenings in this beautiful municipal park enjoying a host of activities and participating in recreational diversions including jogging, fishing, and golf. Principal points of interest are a natural science museum, a zoo, a Japanese garden, an amphitheater and a garden center.

Attractions within the park:

Museum of Natural Science, One Hermann Circle, 713-639-4629; www.hmns.org. CH. The most visited museum in Texas, the Museum of Natural Science offers four attractions in one. The museum's permanent exhibits include cavernous halls dedicated to dinosaurs, petroleum and space science and the hall of the American Indians. A stunning gallery is devoted to gems and minerals. The museum also frequently stages traveling international exhibitions of art and artifacts from Egypt, Peru, and other fascinating parts of the globe.

In addition to the galleries, the complex includes the Cockrell Butterfly Center, with a 40-foot waterfall and more than 1,500 gaudy butterflies; an IMAX theater; and the Burke Baker Planetarium, which when not occupied by the public is used to train NASA astronauts in starfield identification.

Open 9 am-6 pm daily; noon-6 pm Sun. Admissions vary by attraction, but visitors may see the museum's permanent exhibits for free each Tuesday after 2 pm.

Houston Zoological Gardens, 1513 N. MacGregor, 713-523-5888, www.houstonzoo.org. CH. This 55-acre zoo features more than 5,000 animals, including koalas, sea lions and an outstanding collection of vampire bats. Feeding time for the bats is 2:30 pm, a bit gory but interesting. Other features include a terrific primate habitat, a children's zoo with petting area and an aquarium.

Open 10 am-6 pm daily with extended hours during the summer. Admission is free on City of Houston holidays.

Near the zoo is a *miniature train* that provides rides through the woods and around Hermann Park. CH

Japanese Garden, 713-284-1914. CH. In the center of Hermann Park is this peaceful garden, a gift from the Japanese people to Houston in 1992. Boasting ornamental grasses, inviting bridges, exotic flowering trees and a teahouse, this garden is a pleasant respite when the park becomes crowded. Open daily.

Bob Fowler's The Elephant   *Courtesy of Dale Young*
outside Houston Zoological Gardens

Miller Outdoor Theater, 100 Concert Dr., 713-284-8350. NCH. A manmade grassy knoll provides casual seating for more than 15,000 for this amphitheater, which April through November presents productions ranging from grand opera and Broadway musicals to Shakespearean dramas and zydeco music festivals.

The recently renovated theater has 1,582 covered, theater-style seats for which tickets are required. Tickets are free and are provided on a first-come, first-served basis at the theater box office between 11:30 am and 1 pm on performance days.

Houston Garden Center, 1500 Hermann Dr., 713-284-1986. NCH. The center's gardens showcase 5,000 species of roses as well as a colorful pavilion, a gift to Houston from its oldest "sister city," Taipei, China.

There are objects of art throughout the park plus a children's playground, picnic facilities and snack bars.

Holocaust Museum Houston (D3), 5401 Caroline; www.hmh.org. CH. Artifacts, film, documents and photographs tell the story of Jewish life in Europe before and after the Nazi reign of terror at this powerful museum, which is both memorial and educational center. Particularly moving are the oral histories recorded by Houston-area Holocaust survivors. Open 9 am-5 pm Mon-Fri.; noon-5 pm Sat-Sun.

Houston Fire Museum (C3), 2403 Milam; 713-524-2526; www.houstonfiremuseum.org. CH. Housed in the city's oldest firehouse, No. 7, this kid-friendly attraction displays old pumper and steam-powered trucks, firefighter badges and helmets and other equipment such as bells, extinguishers and lanterns. Open 10 am-4 pm Tue-Sat.

Houston Garden Center (D3). See Hermann Park above.

Houston Zoological Gardens (D3). See Hermann Park above.

Kemah Boardwalk (F6), 701 Fourth St. in Kemah; 281-334-5425; www.kemahboardwalk.com. CH for some attractions. About 35 minutes from downtown. This 30-acre complex fronting Clear Creek Channel and Galveston Bay features a collection of themed restaurants, high-end shops and boutiques, a luxury hotel and old-fashioned amusements such as a Ferris wheel, a carousel and a miniature train. Children love to splash in the dancing fountains and playground.

Museum of Health & Medical Science (D3), 1515 Hermann Dr.; 713-521-1515; www.mhms.org. CH. Take a walking tour through the human body at this museum dedicated to promoting good health. Among the interactive exhibits are a 22-foot-long backbone, a 10-foot tall walk-through brain, and a huge walk-in eyeball. A science lab, kid-friendly demonstrations and two theaters enhance the experience. Open 9 am-5 pm Tue-Sat; noon-5 pm Sunday. Free admission after 4 pm on Thursdays.

Museum of Natural Science (D3). See Hermann Park above.

Museum of Printing History and Graphic Arts (C3), 1324 West Clay; 713-522-4652; www.printingmuseum.org. CH. Printing has long been a major industry in Houston, and this museum spotlights this fascinating pursuit. It boasts some of the oldest known examples of printing pieces and rare documents. A feature is the world's oldest printed example of a temple scroll dating to 764 AD. Old printing equipment includes an Albion Press introduced in England in 1817. The gift shop offers new and old samples of wood types and other authentic pieces. Open 10 am-5 pm Tue-Sun.

NASA Lyndon B. Johnson Space Center (F6), 2101 NASA Rd. 1; 281-244-2100; www.jsc.nasa.gov. About 25 minutes from downtown. Known the world over, the space complex is frequently called the nerve center of the nation's space program. As headquarters for NASA's astronauts, it is here that they train, where humans and machines

Kemah Boardwalk   *Courtesy of Kemah Boardwalk*

An exhibit at Space Center, Houston

Courtesy of Greater Houston Convention & Visitors Bureau

undergo testing for endurance in outer space environments, and where all space flights are monitored. JSC also plays a pivotal role in the International Space Station program.

While all visitor services have been shifted to Space Center Houston (details to follow), JSC hosts an open house one day each August. About 120,000 visitors turn out each year to see more than 150 exhibits and 20 of the center's buildings. Many of JSC's more than 3,000 employees—including astronauts—are on hand to answer visitors' questions and to discuss space flight programs.

Among the featured attractions at the free open house are Mission Control center, life-size mock-ups of the space shuttle and the Neutral Buoyancy Lab, where astronauts train for space walks in a 6-million gallon pool.

National Museum of Funeral History, 415 Barren Springs; 281-876-3063; www.nmfh.org. *CH.* Because Houston is the home of Service Corp. International, the first funeral service company to have its stock traded on the New York Stock Exchange, what more logical locale for the giant firm's collection of historic funeral service memorabilia and artifacts? Learn about funerals of the famous and the history of embalming. See antique hearses and ornate coffins. Open daily.

Observation Deck (I10), Chase Tower. *NCH.* Facing the corner of Milam and Capitol is the 75-story Chase Tower, Houston's tallest skyscraper with an observation deck on the 60th floor, providing a panoramic view of Downtown, Uptown and the South Main Corridor. Open 8 am-5 pm weekdays.

The Orange Show (D4), 2402 Munger; 713-926-6368; www.orangeshow.org. *CH.* A unique attraction. Houston postal worker Jeff McKissack died in 1979, but his monument to citrus lives on. A one-of-a-kind folk art playground, the Orange Show features elaborate sculptures, displays, portals, gates and railing all created with found objects such as tiles, gears and tractor seats. Days, hours vary.

Port of Houston (C5), Gate 8 off Clinton Dr.; 713-670-2416. *NCH.* This port is the eighth-largest in the world. Ships making the 50-mile channel voyage upstream from Galveston to the Turning Basin must do a round-house turn at the dead end with the aid of tugs for the return trip to sea. A two-story observation deck is a good lookout point to observe this action.

A short distance away is the Sam Houston tour boat; its popular narrated expeditions last about 90 minutes and afford a close-up look at the mighty industries and ships lining the channel. The boat offers tours daily, except Mondays and holidays. Tours are free; reservations should be made well in advance.

Sam Houston Historical Park (J8), 1100 Bagby; 713-655-1912. *CH* for tours only. This is the oldest municipal park in Houston, a small green oasis and peaceful retreat from the frenetic pace of downtown Houston. A project of the Harris County Heritage Society, the park reflects the city's lifestyle during its early years. There are eight principal structures:

The *Kellum-Noble House*, built in 1847, is the city's oldest house on its original site;

The *Nichols-Rice-Cherry House* is a Greek Revival house built about 1845-50 and was once owned by William Marsh Rice, founder of Rice University;

The *Old Place* is a picturesque cedar cabin believed to have been built about 1823;

The *Pillot House*, built in 1868, features what is believed to have been the first indoor kitchen in Houston;

The *San Felipe Cottage* is a simple six-room house typical of the 1870s;

St. John Church, Houston's oldest church (1891), was moved to the park from its original spot in a former colony built by German settlers;

The 17-room *Staiti House* featured all the latest amenities, including electricity, when it was built in 1905.

The *Yates House* was built in 1870 by a freed slave who later became one of Houston's most prominent religious leaders;

Also on the grounds of the park is the Long Row, a reconstruction of Houston's first business building. It houses the Heritage Society offices as well as a museum.

Open 10 am-4 pm Mon-Sat and 1 pm-5 pm Sun.

Sam Houston Race Park, 7575 N. Sam Houston Parkway W.; 281-807-8700; www.shrp.com. CH. This pari-mutuel racetrack opened in the spring of 1994. The $84 million complex showcases thoroughbred and quarter horse racing with an annual purse running around $20 million. The park can accommodate up to 30,000 spectators and stable up to 1,000 horses. Call for race schedule. Closed Christmas Day.

San Jacinto Battleground State Historical Park (D6), 3523 Highway 134, in La Porte; 281-479-2431. CH for some attractions. This park marks the site where Texas won its independence from Mexico in 1836. It holds several major attractions, plus granite markers throughout relating the details of this famous battle. Picnic facilities are available, but no camping is permitted. You may fish along the riverbank.

Within the park:

The *San Jacinto Monument* is the world's tallest masonry column at 570 feet. At the base is a museum featuring regional history, NCH, from the time of the Indian civilization to Texas as a state of the Union. Near the top is an observation deck, CH, for a good view of the surrounding

San Jacinto Battleground and Monument   *Courtesy of Texas Highway Dept.*

marshlands. A 160-seat theater, *CH*, presents a film about the Texas revolution and the battle. The museum and observation deck are open 9 A.M.-6 P.M. daily.

Nearby in permanent berth is the *Battleship Texas, CH*, the only remaining dreadnought of its class. The battleship fought in two world wars and several other engagements. Visitors can tour the ship from the bilges to the wheelhouse, and aboard are several specially dedicated museums. Open 10 A.M.-5 P.M. daily. Closed Christmas Eve and Christmas Day. Information: 281-479-2431.

Six Flags AstroWorld and Waterworld Theme Parks and (E2), I-610 Loop at Kirby; 713-799-1234; www.sixflags.com. *CH*. AstroWorld brings the Six Flags family brand of amusement, fun and games to Houston's Astrodomain. Built on land that once was inhospitable to anything but mesquite, sage and jack rabbits, this 75-acre park has been converted to a veritable garden land complete with fountains, streams and a lagoon, plus many species of tropical flora.

AstroWorld leads the state in the number of rollercoasters with 11. The Texas Cyclone, a replica of Coney Island's famous wooden coaster, is the grande dame of the park's coasters, which includes thrillers such as Greezed Lightnin', Viper, and Texas Tornado. In all, the park offers more than 100 rides, shows and attractions for all ages.

Next door is **Waterworld,** which offers acres of raft rides and water slides. Among the attractions are a six-person family raft ride called the Big Kahuna; Hook's Lagoon, a five-story interactive tree house; and a water playground reserved for little kids.

Adjacent to the theme parks is the Southern Star Amphitheater, which presents musical acts ranging from gospel to rock.

The theme parks are open daily from late May to mid-August. Variable days and hours at other times of year. Call to check in advance. Also inquire about the discount admissions and passes that provide admission to both parks.

Space Center Houston (F6), 1601 NASA Road 1,800-972-0369; www.spacecenter.org. *CH*. About 25 minutes from downtown. This $79 million, 183,000-square-foot, state-of-the-art concentration of educational and entertainment facilities features a walk-in vault containing the earth's largest display of moon rocks (including one you can touch), escorted tram tours of the Johnson Space Center, and appearances by astronauts. High-tech interactive exhibits and demonstrations offer opportunities for visitors to simulate space flight experiences. Open 10 am-5 pm daily. Extended hours during the summer. Closed Christmas Day. Inquire about discounts and annual passes.

Splash Town, 21300 North Interstate 45, at Spring Cypress Road in Spring; 281-355-3300; www.splashtown.com. *CH*. About 25 minutes from downtown. This attractive water park features acres of rides, slides, and attractions. Favorites are a five-story raft racing speedway; a gentle river for tubing; and Space Rapids, where riders enjoy special fog and light effects as they shoot down a dark tunnel into an 81,000-gallon pool. Open daily June to mid-August. Variable days and hours at other times of year. Call to check in advance.

Texas Medical Center (D3), bounded by Fannin, Holcombe, N. MacGregor, and Braeswood; 713-797-0100. *NCH.* This vast center is made up of 32 institutions and hospitals and is still expanding. It is a magnet for students, patients, doctors, and scientists from around the world. Many know this center for care and treatment of childhood diseases, cancer, and open-heart surgery, as well as other areas of specialization.

An Assistance Center, on the ground floor of Parking #II at 1155 Holcombe (D3), offers free 75-minute bus tours through the complex. *NCH.* Call 713-797-0100 for reservations. The information center is open 10 am-4 pm weekdays.

HISTORIC CHURCHES
(Open daily)

Annunciation Catholic Church (I11), 1618 Texas Ave.; 713-222-2289. Built in the style of the great European churches, Annunciation was begun in 1867 by the Rev. Joseph Querot, a French missionary in Texas who was a canon of the Cathedral of Lyons. The most important feature of the church is the steeple. Its architectural style is Norman Romanesque. The Texas Historical Survey Committee has placed a historical medallion at the front of this church, which is open for services daily.

Christ Church Cathedral (I10), 1117 Texas Ave.; 713-222-2593. This was the second Episcopal parish in the Republic of Texas, established in 1839 by William Fairfax Gray. The initial structure was erected in 1845 and a second was added in 1859. The present structure was built in 1893 and is Gothic Revival in style. The interior is especially beautiful with handsome wood carving throughout and one Tiffany stained-glass window among others. The church is open daily for services at noon and there is a public chapel open for masses daily.

VISUAL ARTS

Perhaps it was the longing to shed its cowboy boots or the need to polish its oil field roughneck image. Or maybe it was just a desire to show off a little. Whatever the inspiration, Houston has established itself as a cultural center with grand theaters, well-endowed museums, and stimulating galleries.

Visitors will find a long list of museums, galleries, schools of art and art events. And while space does not permit a complete roster, we offer a varied selection. For information on the medley of arts organizations, schools, museums, and galleries in Houston contact the **Greater Houston Convention & Visitors Bureau** , 901 Congress, which produces a handy cultural guide. You will also find listings for museum and gallery events in the Thursday and Sunday editions of the Houston Chronicle and in the weekly Houston Press.

PRINCIPAL MUSEUMS

Bayou Bend (C2), #1 Westcott; 713-639-7750; www.mfah.org. CH. Bayou Bend is part of the Museum of Fine Arts Collection and houses one of the finest assortments of American art, artifacts, and furnishings in the nation. It provides a wonderful opportunity to view pure Americana in paintings, silver, ceramics, and other accessories rarely found anywhere else.

Bayou Bend was the home of Miss Ima Hogg, daughter of Texas' first native-born governor and one of Houston's most passionate philanthropists. Miss Hogg began collecting American decorate arts in 1920, seven years before construction began on the house that eventually would showcase treasures. Miss Hogg donated the house to the museum in 1957 and lived there until in 1965. The estate was opened to the public in 1966.

The museum is on 14 acres of beautiful gardens and woodlands overlooking Buffalo Bayou. Guided and self-guided tours of the home and gardens are offered Tuesday through Sunday. Hours vary and reservations are required for most tours. Allow one to 1 1/2 hours for tours.

One Sunday each month from September through May is designated a Family Day. These fun-filled free events include craft activities, performances and self-guided garden tours. A select number of rooms in the house also are open for viewing. Call for dates.

Contemporary Arts Museum (F2), 5216 Montrose Blvd.; 713-284-8250; www.camh.org. *NCH.* Housed in a striking stainless-steel structure, this museum enjoys national acclaim, making bold statements in new directions. A recent $3.5 million renovation has increased gallery space for the museum, which features post-1945 American art with changing exhibitions. Ambitious programming includes concerts, dance programs, lectures and films. Open Tue-Sun. Closed Mondays and holidays.

The Museum of Fine Arts (D3), 1001 Bissonnet; 713-639-7300; hearing impaired call TDD/ITY line 713-639-7390. *CH.* With the spring 2000 opening of the $85 million Audrey Jones Beck Building, this museum became the sixth-largest museum space in the United States. The Beck Building, connected by a cleverly lighted tunnel to the original exhibit space, showcases the museum's European art, the heart of which is an Impressionist and Post-Impressionist collection with works by Monet, Renoir and Seurat.

The permanent collections at this museum, founded in 1900, also include Spanish and Italian High Renaissance works, Indian art of the Southwest, a classical collection of pieces from Greece, Rome, and Egypt, and pre-Columbian art. The museum boasts one of the finest collections of Frederic Remington Westerns, the Glassell collection of African gold and a terrific photographic collection.

Across the street is the Glassell School of Art, an exciting glass-brick, art-deco building, which is perhaps the largest museum-affiliated school in the Southwest. The complexes are bridged by the Lillie and Hugh Roy Cullen Sculpture Garden designed by the architect-artist, Isamu Noguchi. Another sculpture garden on the south side of the museum features a number of fine pieces, including one by the Spanish artist Eduardo Chillida.

Throughout the year, the museum presents events of interest such as films, concerts, and lectures, and, with fair regularity, a major traveling exhibit of wide interest. Open 10 am-5 pm Tue-Sat; noon-6 pm Sun. Closed Mondays and holidays.

The Menil Collection (F2), 1515 Sul Ross; 713-525-9400; www.menil.org. *NCH.* One of the world's most outstanding private collections is found in a pretty residential area of Montrose. The collection consists of more than 15,000 pieces with emphasis on primitive art and sculpture, Byzantine and Medieval art, Cubism, Surrealism, Pop art, contemporary Minimalism, mid-century New York School, and contemporary work from Europe. The museum's light-filled galleries were designed by architect Renzo Piano, co-creator of the Pompidou Art Center of Paris. Open 11 am-7 pm Wed-Sun.

The Rothko Chapel (F2), 3900 Yupon at Sul Ross; 713-524-9839; www.menil.org/rothko.html. *NCH.* Like the Menil, this chapel was a gift to Houston from the late John and Dominique de Menil. The octagonal sanctuary houses the last works of Mark Rothko, an American abstract expressionist.

Rothko's 14 monumental paintings are complemented by sculptor Barnett Newman's *Broken Obelisk* in its own reflection pool at the front of the building. These huge canvases emphasize color and scale and are effectively illuminated by natural light from strategically placed skylights.

Apart from the Rothko experience, the chapel also is the scene of rare ethnic performances, such as the Bhutan Dancers and Whirling Dervishes. And it has served as a venue for such visiting speakers as the Dalai Lama and Nelson Mandela.

It is open 10 am-6 pm daily.

MUSEUMS AND GALLERIES

Blaffer Gallery (D4), University of Houston Central campus, Entrance #16 off Cullen Boulevard; 713-743-9530; www.hfac.uh.edu/blaffer/. *NCH.* This museum's exhibits range from the old masters to the leading contemporaries plus exhibitions of student works. Regular hours are 10 am-5 pm Tue-Fri; 1-5 pm Sat-Sun. Closed Mondays.

John T. Biggers Art Center at Texas Southern University Arts Center (D3), 713-313-7337. *NCH.* This center houses a large collection of student and faculty works. You also will find several interesting works scattered around the campus. Hours vary by season. Closed holidays and summer months.

COMMERCIAL GALLERIES

As might be expected in a city with several art museums and schools and a growing appreciative audience with the means to support them, galleries are spread throughout the city. They usually are located in the affluent areas or around professional centers of artistic endeavor.

There is sufficient variety to suit all interests as well as most budgets. While we would like to present a full list, we must limit the discussion to the following, many of which are members of the Houston Art Dealers Association and have long-established reputations in the city.

John Cleary Gallery (F2), 2635 Colquitt; 713-524-5070. Specializes in photography, from the famous of the nineteenth century to the contemporary. Open 10 am-5:30 pm Tue-Sat.

Barbara Davis Gallery (F2), 2627 Colquitt; 713-520-9200. Contemporary American, primarily abstract, is the focus here. Open 10 am-5:30 Tue-Sat; 11 am-5 pm Sun.

Gremillion & Co. (D2), 2501 Sunset; 713-522-2701. Contemporary mid-career American artists and fine art furniture. 10 am-5 pm Tue-Sat.

Inman Gallery (D3), 1114 Barkdull; 713-529-9676. Specializes in edgy contemporary work from Texas and elsewhere. Open 11 am-5 pm Tue-Sat.

Meredith Long & Co. (C2), 2323 San Felipe; 713-523-6671. The oldest commercial gallery in the city focuses on historic American artists from nineteenth-century impressionists to twentieth-century moderns and contemporary realists. Open 10 am-6 pm, Tue-Sat.

Moody Gallery (F2), 2815 Colquitt; 713-526-9911. Arguably the most important gallery in the state, it is dedicated to emerging or established Texas artists. Open 11 am-5 pm Tue-Sat.

Texas Gallery (C2), 2012 Peden; 713-524-1593. Avant-garde art from around the country is shown here. Open 10 am-5:30 pm Tue-Sat.

ART IN PUBLIC PLACES

There is growing momentum in Houston to bring quality art to public buildings, plazas, parks, and campuses. We have selected some of the distinguished examples of works by resident, national, and international artists. For the convenience of the viewer, we have grouped these works by location.

Downtown

Armillary Sphere, by Kenneth Lynch, in Sam Houston Historical Park (J8).

Ballet Dancer, bronze by Marcello Mascherini. Jones Hall for the Performing Arts (I10), 615 Louisiana.

Central Public Library, 500 McKinney (J9). NCH. The library features monthly exhibits ranging from art objects to antique dolls.

Eye Shutter, by Dean Ruck, in (H10) 800 block of Congress.

The Family of Man, by Barbara Hepworth, on South Plaza of First City Tower (J10), 1001 Fannin.

Frozen Laces-One, by Louise Nevelson, on Enron Plaza (K9), 1400 Smith.

Gemini Two, sculpture by Richard Lippold, in the Grand Lobby of

Jones Hall for the Performing Arts (I10), 615 Louisiana. Except during performances, you can only see this through the glass over the marquee; it is suspended from the ceiling.

Geometric Mouse X, sculpture by Claes Oldenburg, Central Public Library Plaza (J9), 500 McKinney.

High Plains Drifter, sculpture by Peter Reginato, Two Allen Center (J9), 1200 Smith.

The Market, mural by Suzanne Sellers, (H10) 315 Travis.

One Step for Mankind, engraved stainless steel panels by Naomi Savage. Located in Tranquillity Park, Smith at Rusk.

Reliant Energy HL&P (I9), 611 Walker. The lobby of this building features art exhibitions.

Julia Ideson Library and Archives (J9), corner of McKinney and Smith streets. A treasure-trove of permanent art plus temporary exhibitions. Included are bronze and marble busts, portrait paintings, stone sculpture, steel engravings, and a number of Spanish murals of special interest. Also interesting is the intricately carved and painted ceiling in the rotunda.

Large Spindle Piece, by the British sculptor Henry Moore, located in Buffalo Bayou Park between downtown and Montrose Boulevard. (C3).

Monument au Fantome, by Jean Dubuffet, on Louisiana Plaza, 1100 Louisiana (J9).

Neuhaus Fountain, bronze coyotes and fountains by Gwynn Murrill, in Sam Houston Historical Park (J8).

Pair of Horses, sculpture by Robert Fowler, in Lower Lobby at entrance to Jones Hall for the Performing Arts (I10), 615 Louisiana.

Palm Columns, mosaic and masonry by Ned Smyth, (K9) 1201 Milam.

Passage Inacheve, steel, concrete and photographic images by Linnea Glatt and Francis Merritt Thompson. Located within Buffalo Bayou Park (C3), between Montrose and Bagby.

Personage and Birds, a 55-foot sculpture by the world-renowned Spanish artist, Joan Miro, on the plaza of Chase Tower (I10), corner of Milam and Capitol.

Points of View, by James Surls in Market Square Park (H10), Travis at Preston.

The Quilting Party, mural by John Biggers. Located within the Wortham Theater Center (I9), 501 Texas.

Rolled Up Sidewalk, by SWA Group of Houston, (K8) 1600 Smith.

Sam Houston, a bronze by David Adickes. Located within the Houston Visitors Center (J9), 901 Bagby.

Seven Wonders, stainless steel columns by Mel Chen. Located at Sesquicentennial Park (I9), Bagby at Prairie.

Spirit of the Confederacy, sculpture by L. Amateis, in Sam Houston Historical Park (J8). Can be seen from Lamar Avenue.

Virtuoso, by David Adickes. Designed with its own system to play music throughout the day. On plaza of the Lyric Centre building (I10), 404 Louisiana.

Wortham Theater Center (I9), 501 Texas. The eight, 28-foot-tall Albert Paley sculptures may be seen from the plaza in front of the 90-foot glass archway of this grand structure. It is the largest such contemporary project in the United States and is a mix of steel monuments to the movement of life, setting the mood for patrons of the arts.

Ziggurat Playscape, Jesus Bautista Moroles. The Houston Police Officers Memorial, off Memorial Drive between Montrose and downtown.

Montrose Area

Broken Obelisk, sculpture in pool by Barnett Newman, in front of the Rothko Chapel (F2), 1409 Sul Ross, behind the University of St. Thomas campus.

Passages, sculpture by Hannah Smith, on the University of St. Thomas campus (F2), can be seen from Mt. Vernon Street.

Pueblo Bonito, sculpture by Charles Ginnever at Heights Boulevard; Waugh Drive, and Feagan Street (C3), across Buffalo Bayou from the Montrose district.

South Main Corridor

Abesti Gorgora V, sculpture by Spanish artist Eduardo Chillida, South Main Sculpture Garden, Museum of Fine Arts (D3), between Main and Montrose.

Adam 1889, bronze by Emile-Antoine Bourdelle, Cullen Sculpture Garden (D3), Bissonnet at Montrose.

Atropos Key, sculpture by Hannah Smith, on top of the hill overlooking Miller Outdoor Theater (D3), on Concert Drive in Hermann Park.

Backs I, II, III, IV, bronze by Henri Matisse, Cullen Sculpture Garden (D3), Bissonnet at Montrose.

The Crab, sculpture by Alexander Calder, Cullen Sculpture Garden, Museum of Fine Arts (D3), Main at Montrose.

The Elephant, sculpture by Robert Fowler, in front of the Houston Zoological Gardens in Hermann Park (D3).

The Gorilla, sculpture by Robert Fowler, in front of the Primate Habitat (D3), in the Zoological Gardens.

Hercules Upholding the Heavens, sculpture by Paul Manship, South Main Sculpture Garden, Museum of Fine Arts (D3), Main at Montrose.

Houston Triptych, bronze by Ellsworth Kelly, Cullen Sculpture Garden (D3), Bissonnet at Montrose.

Magari, steel sculpture by Mark diSuvero, Museum of Fine Arts (D3), Bissonnet at Montrose.

Manila Palm, sculpture by Mel Chin, Contemporary Arts Museum (D3), 5216 Montrose.

Pieta, sculpture by Charles Umlauf, Museum of Fine Arts (D3), Main at Montrose.

Portable Trojan Bear, sculpture by Jim Love, Hermann Park (D3).

Pranath Yama, Kinetic sculpture, by Mark diSuvero. McCollum Plaza (D3), Texas Medical Center.

Sam Houston Equestrian Statue, sculpture on arch by Enrico Cerracchio, main entrance to Hermann Park (D3), Fannin at Montrose.

The Walking Man, sculpture by Auguste Rodin, Cullen Sculpture Garden, Museum of Fine Arts (D3), Main at Montrose. Also other works in Cullen Garden.

Airport

Perhaps the last place you might expect to find a delightful sculpture is outside an airport terminal, but that is just where Jay Baker's *Light Spikes* brightens arrivals and departures. Aluminum trusses and fluorescent lighting, just outside the Mickey Leland International Airlines Building at Bush Intercontinental Airport, depict the flags of eight major industrialized nations.

Campuses

There are numerous works of art on college campuses, especially at the University of Houston Central (D4), and Texas Southern University (D3).

Some of the works of interest are *African Queen Mother,* and *Jonah & The Whale,* sculptures by Carroll H. Simms, Texas Southern University. *Round-A-Bout,* sculpture by Linda Howard, *Tower of the Cheyenne,* sculpture by Peter Forakis, and *Troika,* sculpture by Charles Ginnever are just a few of the many outdoor works at the University of Houston.

SHOPPING

With its myriad shops of every description, Houston resembles a Southwestern Hong Kong aglitter with everything the buyer could possibly need or imagine. The city has a reputation as a land of opulence, and the world's merchants seem to have gotten the message.

Many of the leading names in retail are here, plus thousands of lesser-known shopkeepers yet to be discovered by you. In Houston you can find that one-of-a-kind item with a price tag to match, but you may also delight in your own clandestine discoveries in flea markets, resale shops and discount stores.

It's scattered over miles of urban sprawl, so we will orient you first to the various key regional centers before we define what's available by category of merchandise.

MAJOR SHOPPING DISTRICTS

Downtown

As little as five years ago, downtown shopping was dismal. Apart from a flagship department store and small mall that catered to convention-goers, there was not much to lure shoppers to the city's original center of commerce. But downtown's recent revival as a desirable residential neighborhood offers promise that retailers, particularly galleries and specialty shops, will return.

Downtown is not devoid of shopping. **Foley's,** the last of the major downtown retailers (a group that once included Sakowitz, Neiman-Marcus and Battlesteins), maintains its 10-story flagship store at 1110 Main. When it opened in 1947, the windowless building was hailed as the department store of the future. Folks marveled at its $12 million price tag and its electric stairways (escalators).

The Park Shops is a two-block-long, three-story atrium mall that has more than 70 stores and eateries plus a number of other services. For dining, you'll find everything from fast food to upbeat pubs and sidewalk-style restaurants. Specialty shops abound and there's an assortment

111

of jewelry and apparel stores. The center attraction is a pipe sculpture with cascading fountains. The mall, at 1200 McKinney, is connected to Houston Center buildings via skywalks.

And don't forget downtown's pedestrian tunnel system, which harbors a variety of specialty shops and services.

Galleria/Post Oak (F1)

Shoppers from far and wide make the pilgrimage to **The Galleria,** 5015 Westheimer. Known as the "city under glass," this sprawling mall offers one of Texas' most colorful parade of stores, including Neiman-Marcus, Lord & Taylor, Saks Fifth Avenue and Macy's. Valet parking available.

Always the place for trendy goods, in recent years Post Oak Boulevard has attracted more affordable, but no-less-popular retailers such as FAO Schwarz, Marshall's, Barnes and Noble and Old Navy.

Westheimer at Post Oak.

Highland Village

Just inside The Loop from The Galleria is the up-and-comer among Houston shopping districts. Built in 1952, this shopping center got a much-needed face-lift several years ago. Today it is sophisticated yet friendly, and boasts some fine retailers, including Tootsies, Pottery Barn, Williams-Sonoma, James Avery and Restoration Hardware. Just as appealing are its restaurants, among them Anthony's, P.F. Chang's China Bistro and Grotto.

4001 Westheimer.

Katy Mills

Cross a discount shopping center with a high-tech entertainment complex and you have Katy Mills, an enormous mall that cost $200 million to build and greets about 18 million visitors each year. Don't miss Bass Pro Shops Outdoor World, with its indoor ranges for golf and archery, and an aquarium large enough for angling demonstrations. Outlet stores here include Benetton, Banana Republic, Gap, and Casual Corner.

A multiscreen theater and themed restaurants such as Rainforest Café and Johnny Rockets add to the diversions.

I-10 at Pin Oak Road in Katy.

Memorial City Mall (B1)

This nearly 40-year-old mall with a terrific location on the well-trafficked Katy Freeway is always re-inventing itself and with much success. Anchor stores include the top-producing outlet in Foley's 57-store chain, Sears Roebuck, Mervyn's and Sun & Ski Sports Expo.
I-10 at Gessner.

Sharpstown (D1)

Houston's first air-conditioned, covered mall is still one of the busiest in town. Famous names found here include Foley's, Montgomery Ward, and Victoria's Secret. This mall raises the question: Which came first, the hordes of teens or the shoe stores?
Southwest Freeway at Bellaire Boulevard.

Town and Country Mall & Village

The glory days of Town and Country Mall appear over. Recently, Saks Fifth Avenue abandoned the mall, leaving anchors Dillard's, J.C. Penney and Neiman-Marcus to fend for themselves. If the mall survives, credit might go to its new next-door neighbor. A sprawling, invitingly landscaped outdoor complex, **Town and Country Village** boasts upscale stores such Restoration Hardware, Williams-Sonoma, The Gap and the largest Hallmark store you've ever seen.
I-10 West (Katy Freeway) at Beltway 8.

MINI CENTERS

China Town

Just on the fringe of the George R. Brown Convention Center is a thriving concentration of Asian—mainly Chinese and Vietnamese—shops, jewelers, boutiques, food markets and cafés. Exotic offerings range from fungus to herbal medicines. Also fine jewels, tapestries, architectural pieces, furniture, clothing, plants, Asian wines, carvings, paintings, souvenirs and, of course, Oriental food.

Covering a large area downtown, but primarily bounded by St. Emanuel, Chartres, Rusk, and Lamar.

Other large concentrations of Asian shops and markets can be found in the Midtown district (bounded by Gray, Hamilton, Bagby and Wheeler) and upper Bellaire, between Fondren and Beltway 8.

Old Town Spring

This too-cute collection of more than 100 shops and cafés surrounds a long-abandoned railroad center. Antiques and handicrafts are the most popular goods here. Old Town also is known for its many special events, which include a wine festival in March; a crawfish cook-off in May; a heritage celebration in the fall; and a holiday festival in December.

Take the Spring/Cypress exit off I-45 North to Main St., 1 1/2 miles to the railroad tracks.

Rice Village (D2)

Once a sleepy shopping district, the "Village," as it is known, has taken off in recent years. Perhaps because of its proximity to Rice University, the Village is filled with youthful clothing outlets such as The Gap, Banana Republic and Urban Outfitters and thinking folks' pubs such as the Gingerman.

Because this is Houston, you will still find plenty of sophisticated shops. The Village is particularly strong in art and specialty stores.

Morningside, University, Kirby, and Bolsover.

River Oaks Center (C2)

Tall stately palms along West Gray mark the perimeter of one of the oldest shopping centers in the city. Another area that caters to the River Oaks neighborhood with a mix of shops, dining, and entertainment. Options range from high-end boutiques and a canine bakery to an avant-garde film house and an extremely good comedy club.

West Gray at Shepherd.

Uptown Park (C1)

One of the city's newest shopping centers, Uptown Park aims for a European experience but with ample parking. High-end boutiques share sidewalks with an eclectic assortment of restaurants.

Post Oak at Loop 610.

SPECIAL STREETS

Many streets could be singled out for interesting shopping, but we will point out several in close proximity, yet diametrically different from each other.

Montrose Boulevard (F2-3)

Montrose Boulevard was once the street early Houstonians toured on Sundays to see majestic palms and gardens gracing fashionable homes. The Link-Lee Mansion, now headquarters for the University of St. Thomas, is a reminder of those times. More recently the boulevard has been revitalized with plantings, restorations and conversions, creating a variety of things to see and do. Beginning at the crossroad of Westheimer, Montrose is punctuated with shopping centers, sidewalk cafes and points of interest all along the way to the junction of the Mecom Fountains on South Main.

Westheimer—The Strip (F3-2)

From Ferndale back toward downtown on Westheimer is The Strip, where good dining and entertainment spots intersperse with some of the city's more bizarre curiosities. Here you can find fantasy accessories next to a tattooed ladies shop; wine tasting just a stone's throw from tarot card reading; and gourmet dining to just plain spuds.

OTHER MAJOR MALLS

Almeda Mall (E5), 12200 Gulf Freeway.
Baybrook Mall (F5), I-45 South at Bay Area Boulevard.
Carillon Shopping Center, 10001 Westheimer.
Champions Village, 5505 W. FM 1960.
Deerbrook Mall, FM 1960 at U.S. 59 North.
First Colony, 16535 SW Freeway at Sugar Land.
Greenspoint Mall (A1), I-45 North at Greens Road.
Gulfgate (E5), I-45 South at I-610 Loop.
Mall of the Mainland, 10000 Emmett F. Lowry at Texas City.
Meyerland Plaza (E1), Beechnut at I-610 South.
Northline Mall (A3), I-45 North at Crosstimbers.
Northwest Mall (B1), Highway 290 at I-610.
Pasadena Town Square, Tatar at Harris in Pasadena

San Jacinto Mall, I-10 at Garth in Baytown.
Sugar Land Mall, Highway 59 at Sugar Land
Weslayan Plaza Shopping Center (D2), 5564 Weslayan.
Westchase Mall, 10863 Westheimer.
West Oaks Mall, Hwy. 6 at Westheimer.
Willowbrook Mall, FM 1960 at Hwy. 149.
Windsor Plaza Shopping Center (F1), 4901 Richmond Ave.
The Woodlands Mall, I-45 North at The Woodlands.

MAJOR DEPARTMENT STORES

Most malls boast one or more of the following as anchor stores among their numerous boutiques and specialty shops.

Foley's. Now owned by the May Company, this is the largest department store chain, with headquarters downtown at 1110 Main (J10) plus numerous branches in shopping centers throughout the greater Houston area.

Dillard's. Born in San Antonio and now a well-established large chain of Dillard's stores, the main store is at 4925 Westheimer (F1).

J.C. Penney Co. Locations in malls throughout Houston.

Macy's. Most famous for its Thanksgiving Day parade in New York, Macy's boasts one Houston outlet—at The Galleria (F1).

Mervyn's California. Several locations, including Memorial and Baybrook malls.

Montgomery Ward. Full-line stores at local malls include auto services, formal-wear rentals and even pest control.

Sears Roebuck & Co. (D3), 4201 S. Main and throughout Houston.

ANTIQUES AND AUCTION HOUSES

Antique shops abound all over Houston with offerings from fine American and European pieces to primitives and Texana. For guidance, contact **Houston Antiques Dealers Association** at 713-764-4232.

Adkins Architectural Antiques (F3), 3515 Fannin; 713-522-6547; www.adkinsantiques.com. Houston's largest assortment of architectural embellishments in a three-story 1912 mansion crammed with decorative doors, inlaid mantels, large light standards, old Mexican masks, chandeliers, stained glass, wrought iron gates, and brass fittings.

Antique Center of Texas (B2), 1001 W. Loop North, 713-688-4211. A major venue for antiques.

Antiqueland, 1/2 mile west of I-45 at FM 2920 in Spring; 281-350-4557; www.antiquelandusa.com. Features more than 300 shops.

Antique Pavilion, 2311 Westheimer; 713-520-9755. A major assemblage of antiques shops.

The Emporium (F2), 1800 Westheimer, 713-528-3808; and 2303 Voss, 713-782-2223; www.the-emporium.com. Specializes in architectural antiques such as moldings, mantels, doors, gargoyles, fountains, and stained glass.

James A. Gundry Inc. (F2), 2910 Ferndale; 713-524-6622. Specialties include English Georgian furniture and period accessories.

Hart Galleries Antiques (C2), 2301 S. Voss; 713-266-3500. A long-established and highly reputable outlet dealing in fine European antiques, objets d'art, new and old Oriental rugs. A major auction house in Houston.

Made in France (F2), 2912 Ferndale; 713-529-7949. Specialties include country French antiques, accessories, objets d'art.

River Oaks Antiques Center (F2), 2030 Westheimer; 713-520-8238. Another significant outlet.

ART SUPPLIES

Expressing artistic creativity requires supplies provided by numerous outlets.

Larry's Art & Craft Supplies, 1510 Richey; 713-477-8864.

Pearl Art Supplies (D1), 6100 Westheimer; 713-977-5600.

Texas Art Supply (C3), 2001 Montrose, 713-526-5221; also (C1), 2237 S. Voss, 713-780-0440; and Baybrook Mall, 281-486-9320.

BOOKS

Houston reads. In fact, Houston reads a lot. Furthermore, Houston's many colleges and universities, technological industries, art schools and the Medical Center significantly affect the city's number and range of quality bookstores. We have selected a cross section by location and specialization.

B. Dalton Bookseller (E5), Almeda Mall, 713-944-9310; 1320 Baybrook Mall (F5), 281-488-3327; The Galleria (F1), 713-960-8191; Memorial City Shopping Center (B1), 713-464-2951; Deerbrook Mall, 281-446-4970; Willowbrook Mall, 281-890-6097.

Borders Book Shop and Café (E1), 570 Meyerland Plaza; 713-661-2888. (D1) 9633 Westheimer; 713-782-6066. These cavernous, yet comfortable bookstores stock more than 200,000 titles.

Brazos Bookstore (D2), 2421 Bissonnet; 713-523-0701. Literary specialties (fiction, poetry, drama, biographies, art, and architecture). Convenient to Rice University, the Medical Center, art museums.

Brown Book Shop (K10), 1517 San Jacinto; 713-652-3937. Specializes in technical books catering to industries in our area. General-line store—among Houston's oldest.

Cokesbury Bookstore & Church Supplies (D1), 3502 W. Alabama; 713-621-1755. General store with emphasis on religious publications.

Detering Book Gallery (F2), 2311 Bissonnet, 713-526-6974. Take a cue from the name. Specializing in used and rare books, this tasteful shop is more like a private library or literary gallery than bookstore.

Half-Price Books (C3), 2410 Waugh, 713-520-1084; (D2) 2537 University, 713-524-6635; other locations. Incredible collection of more than a million books, paperbacks, records, tapes and magazines. Will buy anything printed or recorded, but don't expect to get rich.

Majors Scientific Books, Inc. (E3), 7205 Fannin; 713-799-9922. Spectacular selection of medical and technical books and featuring a large computer collection.

Milam Book Store (F2), 1613 Richmond; 713-528-0050. One of the largest dealers in town for used novels. Buying and trading here for 18 years. Lots of science fiction, war stories, mysteries and comics.

Murder by the Book (F2), 2342 Bissonnet; 713-524-8597. Far more than the usual roundup of suspects, this treasure-trove of mysteries, detective fiction and similar writings—in volumes new and pre-read— is (dare we say it?) to die for!

Museum of Fine Arts Bookstore (D3), 1001 Bissonnet; 713-639-7360; www.mfah.org. Fine art books and magazine offerings.

Rand McNally Map & Travel Store (F1), The Galleria; 713-960-9846. A whole, wide world of excellent, up-to-date travel guides, maps, atlases and travel-related tools and novelties.

U.S. Government Bookstore (J9), 801 Travis; 713-228-1187. This is Uncle Sam's library. Here is where you'll find books and pamphlets on engrossing topics such as tax codes, military history, energy policy and computers.

Waldenbooks, Baybrook Mall (F5), 281-488-2330; The Park Shops (J10), 713-951-0041; Greenspoint Mall (A1), 281-875-0381; Northwest Mall, 713-682-2237; Willowbrook Mall, 281-469-1901. You'll find a good selection of best sellers, reference, and children's books.

CLOTHING

Clothing, Children's

There are children's, juniors, and misses' sections in department stores, but many shops cater exclusively to the young with jeans and things, plus clothing for children and newborns.

Bebe de France (F1), 1800 Post Oak; 713-621-2224.

Children's Collection (F1), 1717 Post Oak; 713-622-4415.

Chocolate Soup, 12850 Memorial; 713-467-5957.

Doodles (D2), 2518 Rice; 713-528-2900.

Gap Kids (D2), 2560 University, 713-942-9225; and other locations.

Gymboree (C3), 2010 W. Gray, 713-529-9095; and other locations.

Little Lords & Ladies (D1), 6100 Westheimer; 713-782-6554.

Second Childhood (F1), 6211 Edloe, 713-666-3443; and also (C1) 1438 S. Voss, 713-789-6456. Sells lightly worn clothes.

Clothing, Men's

Al's Formal Wear (J10), 7807 S. Main, 713-791-1885; plus many other Houston locations. Instant tuxedo rentals.

Brooks Brothers (F1), The Galleria; 713-627-2057. Selling fine traditional clothing and accessories since 1818. Also a women's section.

Custom Shop Shirtmakers (I10), 1331 Lamar, 713-655-8858; (F1) The Galleria, 713-621-7631. Since 1937, the best in custom-and ready-made shirts.

Harold's Menswear (B3), 350 W. Nineteenth St.; 713-864-2647. The clothier of the rich and famous—sportswear, suits 36 short to 60 extra long.

Norton Ditto Company (F1), 2019 Post Oak Rd., 713-688-9800. Since 1908, one of Houston's most reputable quality clothiers.

Taghi (F1), 5116 Westheimer, 713-963-0884. European labels dominate this store, which is a favorite with Houston's many sports stars.

Bill Walker Clothier (F1), 1801 Post Oak; 713-871-9811. A favorite with the well-dressed businessman who wants traditional attire.

Zindler's (F1), 3111 S. Post Oak; 713-629-0663. Since 1892, one of Houston's oldest traditional clothiers and the South's largest specialty store for big and tall men.

Clothing, Women's

In addition to a wide assortment of clothes in department stores, we suggest the following outlets.

Craig's. Branches in most Houston malls. National labels in prestige sportswear, ladies' suits, lingerie, high-fashion millinery. Featuring career women's clothing.

Esther Wolf (F1), 1702 Post Oak Blvd.; 713-622-1331. A leading women's fashion store featuring ready-to-wear dresses, suits, sportswear and gowns.

Lerner Shops of Texas (D1), Sharpstown Mall; 713-766-3134. Also outlets in malls and centers throughout the greater Houston area. Known for latest fashions at moderate prices.

Lord & Taylor (F1), The Galleria; 713-627-8100. Top-line accessories, as well as designer sportswear and dresses. Clothing for entire family.

Neiman-Marcus Co. (F1), The Galleria; 713-621-7100. 10615 Town & Country Mall; 713-984-2100. This world-renowned store has full-line, high fashion clothing. Also fine jewelry, a salon and furs.

Palais Royal (J10), 917 Main; 713-658-1182; plus branch stores at numerous other locations throughout Houston. Moderately priced fashions and accessories.

Pixie & Ivy (B3), 621 1/2 W. Nineteenth. The hottest names and hippest fashions are found in a cozy, inviting boutique located above a Heights antiques store.

Saks Fifth Avenue (F1), The Galleria; 713-627-0500. Saks is shopping for junior fashions or designer originals.

Tootsie's (D2), 4045 Westheimer; 713-629-9990. Exclusive designer clothes boutique. An outlet also is in The Galleria.

Wink (F2), 2429 Bissonnet; 713-533-0303. Hip, young designers are showcased at this newcomer to the shopping scene.

COINS AND STAMPS

For your convenience, we have selected three dealers: two are in close proximity downtown and the other is in Rice Village. All are reputable firms doing business here for many years. It is advisable to check out the numismatic credentials of companies with which you plan to trade.

Astro City Coins (F1), 6464 Westheimer; 713-626-8432.

Houston Numismatic Exchange (D2), 2486 Times Blvd; 713-528-2135.

Royal Coins, 4658 Beechnut; 713-664-0881.

CRAFTS

Blue Hand (D2), 2323 University Blvd; 713-666-2583. An extraordinary collection of arts and crafts from around the world. Pueblo Indian pottery, Texas Terlingua Indian crafts, unusual baskets, a large collection of jewelry, and an African crafts collection that is outstanding as are the Kilim rugs and Rafia pile samples from the Congo. Several Houston/Galveston artists are represented here.

Casa Ramirez (B3), 239 W. Nineteenth; 713-880-2420. This folk art gallery is an explosion of color and creativity with works representing all regions of Mexico. The gallery also presents Hispanic cultural programs such as its *Dia de los Muertos,* or Day of the Dead, exhibit.

Surroundings (D3), 1710 Sunset Blvd; 713-527-9838. Walls covered with Panamanian "molas," and masks from Mexico, Haiti, and New Guinea. This place brims with brilliant colors in unique handmade clothing, feathered headdresses, natural fiber rugs, large demon figures, and thousands of other items from around the world. Most interesting are the handmade cabinets, tables, benches and rockers by local craftsmen.

DISCOUNT, RESALE, AND OUTLET STORES

As in other major cities, Houston has many thrift outlets, some selling at greatly reduced prices. Merchandise includes appliances, furniture, variety goods, clothing, shoes, accessories, jewelry and gifts, housewares and sporting goods.

Al Goldman's Office Store (D3), 4120 Fannin; 713-526-4401. Unbelievable array of merchandise, office supplies from seals to paper shredders.

Blue Bird Circle Shop (F3), 615 W. Alabama; 713-528-0470. Charity center with a wide range of merchandise.

Encore (C2), 2308 Morse; 713-523-8936. Here you'll find Klein, Nippon, and Scaasi, gently worn and greatly reduced. Also sportswear, imported Indian cottons, some fancy beaded formal wear, pool and party wear, and some costume jewelry.

Goodwill Industries (B4), 5200 Jensen; 713-692-6221. As expected, bargains galore with emphasis on clothes. Stores located throughout Houston.

The Guild Shop (C2), 2009 Dunlavy; 713-528-5095. Everything here on consignment or a donation—clothes, kitchenware, furniture and books.

Salvation Army Thrift Store (C3), 2208 Washington; 713-869-3551. Everything from furniture to bicycles, jewelry, clothes, and appliances.

FABRICS AND LINENS

Leggett's Fabrics (C4), 2600 Capitol; 713-222-2471.
High Fashion (D3), 3101 Louisiana; 713-528-7299.
Houston Fabric Center (C4), 2712 Capitol; 713-205-2218.

FLEA MARKETS

Spreads of merchandise from around the world sell side-by-side with American goods—the old and the new, fine crafts and junk, and an occasional real find at a bargain price all make flea market-hopping a fun venture.

Coles Antique Village Flea Market, 1014 N. Main in Pearland; 281-485-2277. On Highway 35 near Houston city limits. A Texas-size complex with more than 500 dealers spread over this 70,000-square-foot, air-conditioned village. Dealers from many states show antiques and collectibles weekends starting Fridays at 8:30 am.

Houston Flea Market (Southwest Common Market) (D1), 6616 Southwest Freeway at Westpark exit; 713-782-0391. One of the largest and most popular markets in Houston with nearly 14 acres of stalls, indoor shops, and covered tables plus 5 1/2 acres of parking. Open Saturdays and Sundays.

The Market Place, 10910 Old Katy Rd.; 713-464-8023. Combines well-maintained, glass-partitioned booths with a maxi-mall open-area with some 160 dealers selling primitives, antiques, brassware, plants, and collectibles. Open weekends.

Trade Mart, 2121 W. Sam Houston Tollway N.; 713-467-2506. Gigantic air-conditioned building with more than 167 dealers. Lots of parking space. A clean, bright quality mart with antiques, specialties, and collectibles. Open Friday, Saturday, and Sunday.

Traders Village, 7979 N. Eldridge; 281-890-5500. Acres of collectibles, antiques and specialty items. Promotes a family atmosphere with frequent festivals ands special promotions. Open Fri, Sat, Sun.

Trading Fair II (E3), 5515 South Loop East; 713-731-1111. A unique indoor flea market featuring 400 dealers. Located near the Astrodome. Open Friday, Saturday, and Sunday.

FLOWERS AND GIFT BASKETS

The right arrangement for any occasion in Houston or anywhere in the world may be found in the following locations.

Blanton-Niday Florists, 10651 Harwin; 713-999-7673. A complete range of floral services, fruit baskets. Deliveries; 24-hour hotline.

Cookie Bouquet (D2), 2524 Rice Blvd.; 713-524-7900. Whatever your special occasion or event, these talented cookie cooks can create a fun and tasty tribute.

Empty Vase (F2), 2439 Westheimer; 713-529-7900. You will pay a little more here, but the arrangements are all top quality and stunning.

Food for Thought (E1), 4534 Beechnut; 713-668-7877. Cookies, chocolate, wine and cheese baskets; balloon bouquets.

Teas, (D2), 4400 Bellaire; 713-664-4400. Full-service nursery also offers fresh floral arrangements and attractive gift plants.

FOOD

Shopping for foods can be almost as much fun as the pleasure in dining. The wonderful aroma of freshly baked bread, freshly ground coffee and eye-tempting chocolates and cheeses all excite the senses.

Bakeries

The Acadian Bakery (F3), 604 W. Alabama; 713-520-1484. Breads and cakes from Cajun recipes. Boule, batard and mini-baguette are the basic breads; also Acadian cheesecake with sour cream and other flavors.

Andre's Swiss Candies and Pastry Shop (F2), 2515 River Oaks Blvd.; 713-524-3863. At the front of Andre's Tea Room are display samples of Swiss breads and sweets to cause even the staunchest dieter to succumb. The shop carries the best in chocolates, truffles (of which there are a dozen varieties), tortes, quiches, cakes, cheesecakes and hand-dipped tea cookies.

Dacapo's (B3), 1141 E. Eleventh St.; 713-869-9141. Homemade breads, Key Lime pie and coffeecakes covered in sugar glaze, pecans and caramel are just the beginning of the edible magic conjured at this Heights bakery.

Descours Desserts and Patisserie (B1), 1330 Wirt Road; 713-681-8894. Lemon tarts, enormous cinnamon rolls and cakes almost too pretty to eat fill the pastry case in this small but much acclaimed shop.

Droubi's Bakery & Delicatessen (D1), 7333 Hillcroft; 713-988-5897. The smell of pita and other Middle Eastern breads, still hot from the oven, combines with the aromas of herbs and spices of many other delicacies to welcome you to Droubi's delicious world of Mediterranean cuisines.

French Gourmet (C1), 12504 Memorial; 713-973-6900. (F2), 2250 Westheimer; 713-524-3744. Try this French bakery's heavenly *La Bombe,* a decadent concoction of chocolate mousse, strawberry, lemon and vanilla all wrapped and tied in a chocolate bow. Also breads, quiche, fruit tarts, and Belgian candies.

La Sultana (B3), 809 Quitman; 713-229-9460. A great Mexican bakery with a colorful array of cakes, sweet rolls, and breads baked fresh daily. While shopping you might try a cool glass of Tepache—homemade, fermented pineapple juice with piloncillo (Mexican sugar).

Three Brothers 2040 W. Gray; 713-522-2253. (E2) 4036 S. Braeswood; 713-666-2551. Houston's largest authentic kosher bakery offering the finest in products since 1949. No fats, sugars, or preservatives used in rye, pumpernickel, and sourdough breads. Superb onion rolls and sourdough rye bread (with or without caraway seeds). Staff artist can reproduce anything on cakes for special occasions—simply bring in the picture you want portrayed.

Health Food Stores

Moveable Feast (F2), 2202 W. Alabama; 713-528-3585; www.amoveablefeast.com. Named for the Ernest Hemingway's classic memoir, this combination health food store/deli stocks organic produce, vitamins, cosmetics, soaps, teas, coffees, and books. Enjoy a protein drink while you shop.

Whole Foods (F2), 2955 Kirby, 713-520-1937; 11145 Westheimer, 713-784-7776; and (C1) 6401 Woodway, 713-789-4477. The largest health and natural food stores in Houston with an unbelievable assortment of herbs and spices, vitamins, plus produce, meats, cheeses, sweets, and a deli for takeout orders. Massages available.

International and Gourmet Food

Shoppers have multiple choices among Houston's many foreign food stores, and we have selected some typical markets, plus several general-line gourmet food outlets.

Antone's (C3), 807 Taft; 713-526-1046. The original is now joined by nine other locations. One's sense of smell is titillated just by walking into Antone's, where cheeses, spices, and deli meats combine for a powerfully appetizing aroma.

British Isles (D2), 2366 Rice Blvd.; 713-522-6868. This is the largest British products store in Houston, if not all of Texas. Here are the widest selections of famous English teas, biscuits, cakes, and sauces. Also great candies and syrups.

Cost Plus World Market (D1), 5125 Richmond, 713-963-8833; 10519 Katy Freeway, 713-827-8611; and other locations. Large selection of imported foods, including more than 60 specialty coffees, 40 teas, mixes for scones and other breads, Thai spices, specialty noodles, beers from around the world and wine. Also ethnic-inspired housewares and decorative objects. Think Pier 1 with snacks.

Diho Market, 9280 Bellaire; 713-988-1881. Chinese ingredients, fresh seafood, and culinary specialties from all over East and Southeast Asia dominate this supermarket. Also a good stock of Pacific Rim wines and beers, including some from the People's Republic of China, plus woks and other Oriental kitchenware.

House of Coffee Beans (D2), 2520 Rice Blvd. in the Village; 713-524-0057. Create your own special blends and flavors in the House of Coffee, prepared fresh every time you come in. There are blends, extra specials, flavored and decaffeinated coffees, plus chocolate, green cardamom seeds, and cinnamon.

Korea Supermarket (E1), 7501 Harwin; 713-789-4959. Like so many of the Oriental markets in Houston, this one carries a full line of imported foods from throughout Asia, but it also has the best assortment of dried fish, seaweed and chiles in town. And what Korean store would be caught without an entire section stocked with kimchi (hot and spicy pickled cabbage)?

La Casita (D4), 7120 Canal; 713-926-1735. This little house in the huge, mainly Mexican-American neighborhood by the Ship Channel sells super-fresh homemade (mild) tamales, carnitas, menudo and chicharrones.

Latina (F2), 1972 Fairview; 713-521-2611. Here you will see Cuban expatriates and others shopping for dried cod, kippers, smoked herring, special cheeses, herbs, and spices popular among people of the Caribbean. In addition, the store sells Cuban records and tapes, Spanish-language novels, newspapers and toilet articles.

Markets

Grocery wars are one of Houston's favorite spectator sports. Powerhouses such as Randalls, HEB and Kroger duke it out at busy intersections in well-populated neighborhoods. Their weapons are special promotions such as Triple Coupon Days and club cards that offer everything from discounts to frequent flier miles.

Markets such as Whole Foods (see Health Food Stores) and Rice Epicurean (upscale, gourmet selections) have carved their niche, setting up shop in neighborhoods where people are willing to pay for service and exclusivity.

Here are some of the city's unique markets:

Auchan Hypermarket, 8800 W. Sam Houston; 281-530-9855. You could spend all day wandering this massive market (230,000 square feet), where you can buy a wheel of Brie and the refrigerator in which to keep it. Perhaps because its owners are French, it boasts an outstanding deli and a huge selection of imported beers and wine.

Eatzi's (D1), 1702 Post Oak Blvd.; 713-629-6003. This delightful outpost of the Dallas original is tough to classify. More than 30 chefs are on hand to cook for you, but this is a takeout establishment. Terrific bakery, grill and salad bar, where a chef tosses on demand. Also stocks gourmet condiments, specialty pastas and astounding variety of cheeses, olives and wine.

On busy evenings, crowds can be confounding. Just know as you are elbow-to-elbow that he or she who is the most aggressive gets the last chicken quesadilla.

Farmers Market (A3), 2520 Airline; 713-862-8866. Here it truly is cheaper by the bushel; that is if you co-op with your neighbors. There are acres of fresh fruit and produce plus many products from the Rio Grande Valley of South Texas and neighboring Mexico. Look around and compare prices.

Fiesta Marts(D1), 1005 Blalock, 713-461-9664. And dozens of others in various sizes, including several incredibly giant markets.

These Fiestas could be listed in the international and gourmet food section, but they also offer all manner of daily needs, including clothes and accessories, music, radios, jewelry, photographs, keys, bakery, et al.

There is such an abundance of everything one wonders how it's kept fresh, but when you see the crowds picking over beans, chiles, mangos, and tiny Manzano bananas, you have the answer. Here you can buy insurance, pick up a straw hat, and highstep right on into this unbelievable market. You'll see a lot of fruit and vegetables you might not recognize, and where, after walking from one end to another, you'll need to stop at the refreshment stand for fresh, cold watermelon, cucumber, cantaloupe, or jicama juice.

Seafood and Fresh Fish ——————————————

Airline Seafood (D2), 2333 W. Alabama; 713-526-2351.
J&R Seafood (D2), 7277 Brompton; 713-664-6630.
Lawndale Fish Market, (C4) 7060 Lawndale; 713-921-3409.

FRAMERS

Allart Framing & Gallery (F2), 2635 Revere; 713-526-3631.
Village Frame Gallery (D2), 2528 Rice Blvd.; 713-528-2288.

GIFT SHOPS
AND GREETING CARDS

Of so many fascinating shops that qualify, here are a few to underline for unusual and fine quality merchandise.

Ann's Clock Shop, 14090 Memorial; 281-589-0424. The clocks here are nice, but what makes this store special is its phenomenal assortment of music boxes.

Bering's (C1), 6102 Westheimer; 713-785-6400. This hardware store/gift shop has earned a loyal following thanks to commitment to service. A fine selection of crystal, kitchen gadgets and gourmet cookware makes this a favorite registry spot with brides. Stationery and gardening supplies.

Carlton House (F2), 2509 River Oaks Blvd.; 713-529-6148. This is the debutante registry headquarters in the small but elite Lamar River Oaks Shopping Center. It handles the finest gifts in imported china, silver, crystal, clocks, brass, Oriental urns, lingerie, soaps and perfumes, unusual dolls, bath sets and linen place sets.

Events (C2), 1966 W. Gray; 713-520-5700. Specialty and baby gifts, one-of-kind jewelry and a large selection of picture frames.

JEWELRY

Jerome Berger Jewelry (D1), 4950 Bissonnet; 713-665-2431. Continuing a family tradition of several generations as a jeweler's jeweler, Jerome Berger himself does custom design work, repair and even antique restorations. Setting or resetting of diamonds and other precious stones.

Cartier (F1), The Galleria; 713-871-0177. Jewelry, watches and gifts bearing the Cartier signature.

Fly High Little Bunny (F2), 3120 S. Shepherd; 713-520-9995. Original, often quirky, silver creations that have a youthful appeal.

Fred Joaillier Inc., (F1), The Galleria; 713-960-9441. This exclusive design house, based in Paris, is known for its contemporary classics with the finest in precious gems.

I.W. Marks (D2), 3841 Bellaire; 713-668-5000. Good, well-priced store with diamond settings, pearls, fine watches and jewelry repair.

Tiffany & Company (F1), The Galleria; 713-626-0220. The classic, simple pigeonhole window displays understate the finest quality merchandise.

LEATHER

Bag 'n Baggage (I10), 1200 McKinney; 713-650-8236; and Outlet and Repair (D4), 3900 Polk; 713-223-2181. Also outlets at other locations in major malls and shopping centers. Serving Houston for nearly 100 years, stores stock superior brands of luggage, trunks, briefcases, and travel accessories.

Luggage & Leather Outlet (D1), 9880 Harwin; 713-266-0237. Good to heavily discounted prices on brand-name luggage and accessories. Look for first-quality, discontinued items, and some factory seconds.

North Beach Leather (F1), The Galleria; 713-629-5880. A San Francisco tradition with all drum-tanned leather goods. Featuring high-fashion articles in leather and suede with feathers, coyote-collar jackets, lined leather pants, women's bikinis and many other designs.

Tandy Leather Co. (E1), 8028 S. Gessner, 713-777-6998; (B1), 8211 Long Point, 713-461-2109. This well-known national firm sells every kind of leather craft and supplies, plus finished goods, which include hats, belts, vests and a large collection of buckles.

Thunderbird Leather (D3), 1635 Richmond; 713-521-2473. Custom-made leather clothing, including jackets, chaps, boots for ladies and men and motorcycle jackets.

OFFICE SUPPLIES

For the business traveler and conventioneer, there are numerous outlets for emergency supplies and items you might have forgotten in your haste to get here.

Bellaire Office Supply (D1), 5805 Chimney Rock; 713-664-9829. Good selection of office and printing supplies.

Office Depot (D2), 3401 Kirby, 713-522-9981; about a dozen other locations. Enormous office supply source at reasonable to amazingly discounted prices.

Office Max (E1), 8100 S. Gessner, 713-772-1110; about 10 other locations. Another enormous office supply source with reasonable to amazingly discounted prices.

PHOTOGRAPHIC SUPPLIES

Check the following for camera sales and service. Please see NEW RESIDENTS chapter for processing and developing outlets.

Camera Co-op (D2), 3514 S. Shepherd; 713-522-7837. This shop buys, sells and trades new and used cameras, lights and darkroom supplies.

Houston Camera Exchange (D1), 5900 Richmond; 713-789-6901. A wide range of cameras, lenses, projectors, lighting equipment, darkroom equipment, plus underwater still and movie equipment. Also buys, sells, and trades used equipment. Good prices.

Southwest Camera (C2) 500 N. Shepherd, 713-880-2505; (D1) 5371 Westheimer, 713-960-9904; 133 W. Bay Area Blvd.,

281-332-5990. Excellent photography stores with brand-name equipment including digital cameras, printers, and scanners.

RECORDS, TAPES AND VIDEO

Allrecord (C3), 1960 W. Gray; 713-524-4900. Wide selection in a small, friendly store. Will locate hard-to-find titles.

Cactus Music & Video (F2), 2930 S. Shepherd; 713-526-9272. A large store featuring the pops plus.

Discomundo (D2), 7655 Clarewood; 713-777-5722. Specializes in Latin titles.

Saturday Matinee (F1), The Galleria; 713-626-8326. Enormous selection of mainstream music and movies.

Soundwaves (F2), 3509 Montrose, 713-520-9283; and seven other locations. New, used and imports, as well as music-related videos, T-shirts and gift items.

Suncoast (B1) Memorial City Mall, 713-467-5339; and Baybrook Mall, 281-286-1548. Good selection of current and classic movie videos, as well as movie- and television-related memorabilia.

Vinal Edge, 13171 Veterans Memorial; 281-537-2575. Here is the spot for imports, rare titles, and industrial rock. Buy or trade.

SHOES

If you follow our suggested trails around Houston, you'll wear your soles thin before long. For replacements, consider:

Bally of Switzerland (F1), The Galleria; 713-629-4180. One of the world's finest men's shoe stores with other items as well, including passport and briefcases, suede jackets, suede-trimmed sweaters and ties.

Brucal's Shoes (F1), 2027 Post Oak Blvd.; 713-621-2991. Name-brand merchandise at attractively reduced prices.

Gucci (F1), The Galleria; 713-961-0778. Strictly high-end, high fashion footwear.

Joseph Shoes (D2), 3920 Westheimer; 713-623-8034. The latest fashions as well as classic footwear—all top quality.

SPORTS EQUIPMENT

A temperate climate enables Houstonians to enjoy outdoor sports year 'round, and thus creates a big demand for sporting goods. Here are some of the best-known stores in town.

Academy (F2), 2404 SW Freeway, 713-520-1795; and many other locations. Specializes in sportswear and sporting goods at affordable prices.

Bass Pro Shops & Outdoor World, Katy Mills; 281-644-2200. This huge complex boasts everything you would need for an outdoor adventure: tents, boats, clothing, cookware and condiments. Try the indoor archery range or take part in a fishing clinic. Good selection of golf gear and more camouflage clothing than you've ever imagined.

Burnett Bowling Supply (C2), 1515 W. Gray; 713-526-3081. This nondescript building is a wonderland of bowling equipment. Balls, shoes and more. Good customer service.

Nevada Bob's Discount Golf (D1), 6516 Westheimer; 713-783-6224. The place to go for well-priced golf equipment.

Oshman's Sporting Goods (F1), 2131 S. Post Oak, 713-622-4940; (J10) The Park Shops, 713-650-8240. Also stores at other locations and in major malls. Started by a Houston family, this international chain offers everything you could possibly need from indoor ski ramp practice to complete freeze-dried dinners for backpackers. Also a wide selection in sportswear and accessories for men and women. You may purchase fishing and hunting licenses here.

REI (B1), 7951 Katy Freeway; 713-688-3500. An outdoors-loving and well-informed staff makes this store a hit with novice and veteran adventurers. Camping gear, ski wear, cycling and whitewater equipment are among its offerings. Try the indoor climbing wall or drop in on one of the many free workshops or slide shows. Rental gear available.

Whole Earth Provision Co. (F2), 2934 S. Shepherd, 713-526-5226; (C1) 6560 Woodway, 713-467-0234. Terrific lines of outdoor clothing, equipment, travel goods and books. Not inexpensive.

Wilderness Equipment (C2), 1977 W. Gray, 713-522-4453; 7538 FM 1960, 281-469-7721. High-end outdoors equipment, tents, hiking boots and clothing.

TOYS

FAO Schwarz (F1), 5000 Westheimer; 713-623-8292. It is hard to tell who is having more fun at this colorful store—the kids, the parents, or the employees. Good selection of educational toys and plush animals. Note: this is Barbie headquarters.

The Toy Maker (F1), The Galleria, 713-840-1099; (D2) 2368 Rice Blvd., 713-521-2251; and other locations. Expensive dolls and other collectibles.

Toys R Us (B1), 9655 Katy Freeway, 713-465-0087; (D1) 6145 Westheimer, 713-785-8697; (D1) 7887 SW Freeway, 713-270-9630; and 10 other locations. These supermarkets of the toy world offer acres of everything you could imagine from doll cribs to real baby beds. Aisle after aisle stacked high with party goods, sporting equipment, games, stuffed toys, bikes, gas-powered toys, radio-controlled vehicles, camping equipment and computer games.

WESTERN WEAR

For garb synonymous with Texas, there are dozens of Western stores in Houston, some of which are not simply keeping up with fads—they started them, as far back as 1870.

Boot Town (D1) 2335 Post Oak, 713-627-2668; and seven other locations. Reasonably priced boots, hats, belts and jeans.

Palace Boot Shop (I11), 1212 Prairie; 713-224-1411. A landmark in Western wear in Houston since 1919. The Palace people are personable and anxious to custom design and handmake a pair of boots just for you. They also have a large selection of ready-made name brands such as Tony Lama and Frye. There is a great variety of accessories.

Stelzig's of Texas (D1), 3123 Post Oak, 713-629-7779. This has been Houston's most complete Western store since 1870. Not only will you find a wide selection in clothing, boots, hats, and accessories but all of your needs in Western and English saddles, stockman's supplies and many authentically Texas gift items.

SPORTS

SPORTS TO SEE

We would love to say Houston is a great sports town. Unfortunately, that is just not the case. Houston fans are loyal if the weather is good, the team is winning, and if they have nothing else to do. But that is not to say sell-outs are unusual. Houstonians are as prone to playoff/pennant fever as the next fan. They also tend to pack the arenas/stadiums when marquee teams such as the Lakers and Cardinals come to town.

All this is good news for visitors, who most likely will find good seats available for almost every professional game.

Professional Teams

Houston Aeros, International Hockey League. Games from September through May at Compaq Center (D2). Information: 713-974-7825; www.aeros.com.

Houston Astros, National Baseball League. Games from April to October, at *Enron Field* (I12). Information: 713-259-8000; www.astros.com.

Houston Comets, Women's National Basketball Association. Games from May through August, at Compaq Center (D2). The Comets are the first dynasty of women's professional basketball, winning four consecutive titles starting in 1997. Information: 713-627-9622; www.wnba.com/comets.

Houston Hotshots, Continental Indoor Soccer League. Games from July through November at the Astroarena (E2). Information: 713-408-5100; www.houstonhotshots.com.

Houston Rockets, National Basketball Association. The team brought Houston its first national championship, winning back-to-back NBA titles in 1994 and 1995. Games from October through spring at Compaq Center (D2), but a new downtown arena will break ground soon. Information: 713-627-3865; www.nba.com/rockets.

Houston Texans, National Football League. After losing its National Football League franchise, the Oilers, to Tennessee in 1997, Houston was awarded an expansion team, which is scheduled to begin playing in 2002. The Texans will play in a spanking new Reliant Stadium that is being built adjacent to the Astrodome (E2). Information: 713-336-7700; www.nfl2002.com.

Houston ThunderBears, Arena Football League. Games April through July at Compaq Center (D2). Information: 713-627-7277; www.thunderbears.com.

Canoe Racing

The state's largest canoe and kayak race is held here each spring. With a 15-mile course, the **Buffalo Bayou Regatta** draws hundreds of participants and thousands of spectators.

College Football

With three major university teams, Houston fans have a full schedule of college football. The **University of Houston Cougars** and the **Texas Southern University Tigers** play their home games at Robertson Stadium (D4) on the UH campus. The Cougars play in Conference USA; the Tigers compete in the Southwestern Athletic Conference.

Members of the Western Athletic Conference, the **Rice Owls** play in their own 70,000-seat stadium (D2). A much-anticipated game each year is when the former Southwest Conference rivals, Rice and U of H, face off at home for a trophy called the Bayou Bucket.

Ticket information for the Tigers 713-313-7271; the Cougars 713-743-9444; and the Owls 713-348-4068.

Dog Racing

Gulf Greyhound Park, I-45 South, exit 15 at La Marque; 409-986-9500; www.gulfgreyhound.com. Sleek greyhounds—and the occasional dachshund—compete at the world's largest dog racing complex. Seminars offer wagering tips for novices. Matinees, evening races and Texas' largest full-service restaurant.

The Houston Astrodome

Golf

A crowd-pleasing event is the **Shell Houston Open,** which draws 50 of golf's best professionals to the Tournament Players Course in The Woodlands each spring. The course is north of Houston in Montgomery County off I-45 North. Information: 281-367-7999; www.shellhoustonopen.com.

Horse Racing

Sam Houston Race Park, 7575 N. Sam Houston Parkway W.; 281-807-8700; www.shrp.com. *CH* This pari-mutuel racetrack features two racing meets. Thoroughbreds race October through April; quarter horses run July through September. Check out the track's Las Vegas-style race book and sports bar, where simulcast racing is presented every day except Christmas.

Motor Sports

Houston Raceway Park, located off I-10 East, exiting at Texas 146 in Baytown. This sprawling complex features races weekly and is home to several major events each year, including the National Hot Rod Association O'Reilly Nationals, an NHRA Winston Drag Racing Series and the Pro Stock Superbowl. Information: 281-383-7223; www.houstonraceway.com.

Texaco Grand Prix, downtown (J11). Each fall, the streets of downtown Houston are turned into a speedway for a Championship Auto Racing Team (CART) event. An international field of drivers push their cars in excess of 200 mph over the 1.53-mile course. Ten tricky turns and a downtown backdrop make this race a favorite with spectators. Information: 713-739-7272; www.texacogp.com.

Tennis

The intimate setting of a country club's courts makes the **River Oaks International Tennis Tournament** (C2) a favorite with tennis fans. The April tournament draws the future (and past) stars of professional tennis. Information: 874-713-6333.

One of the world's largest tennis tournaments with more than 2,000 entrants, the **Coca-Cola Open** is spread over dozens of courts each April. The Houston Tennis Association can provide details on the tournament, as well as a calendar of tennis events. Information: 713-973-7636; www.houstontennis.org.

SPORTS TO DO

Houstonians lead active lives and the emphasis is on keeping fit with participatory and recreational activities. Just look at the figures: more than 500 city and county parks, more than 150 public tennis courts and 174 public basketball courts. This vast range provides opportunities for everyone, no matter how brief your visit or how busy your schedule.

Archery

Rebel Arms Archery, 1513 Genoa-Red Bluff Road; 281-487-5985. Indoor and outdoor ranges. Open daily. CH

Basketball

The Parks & Recreation Department (713-845-1000) can provide information on league play. The city-run Fonde Recreation Center (C3), 110 Sabine, is home to some of the best pickup basketball games in the country. Many stars of the NBA, including Nick Van Exel, Sam Cassell and members of the Rockets, are occasional visitors, and the area's top college and high school players congregate here for pickup games.

Bicycling

For easy riding along scenic trails, Houston's flat terrain is ideal for this excellent form of exercise. The city and county have developed more than a hundred miles of bike and hike trails.

For information on bike shops, road racing and cycling clubs, contact the Houston Area Bicycle Alliance at 713-729-9333; www.bikehouston.org.

The Houston Bikeway Program was initiated in the early 1990s to construct more than 360 miles of bike trails citywide. Many of these routes incorporate abandoned rail trails or follow traditional paths along the city's many bayous. The project is ongoing.

For additional information and bike-path maps call the City Parks & Recreation Department, 713-845-1000.

The Alkek Velodrome, 19008 Saums Rd. Out I-10 West to Katy to Barker-Cypress exit, turn right and proceed to first light, then to the left on Saums Road; 281-578-0693. This facility is open for riding Tue-Sun. Riders need a 10- or 12-speed or track bike and helmet. *CH*.

Bowling

This is a great way to beat the heat and still get your exercise in a friendly social atmosphere. Houston has some of the largest bowling alleys in the Southwest. For general information try the **Houston Bowling Association** (C3), 2805 Bagby; 713-524-3185.

AMF Bunker Hill Lanes (B2), 925 Bunker Hill; 713-461-1207.

Delmar Lanes (A1), 3020 Mangum; 713-682-2506.

Max-Bowl West (B1), 1710 Hillendahl; 713-932-8594.

Palace Lanes (D2), 4191 Bellaire; 713-667-6554.

Golf

With more than 130 courses in the greater Houston area, golf is extremely popular. Visitors will find reasonable fees at public courses, but they might have a difficult time snaring a desirable tee time.

The most conveniently located public courses are, not unexpectedly, two of the city's most popular. The **Hermann Park Course** opened recently after a two-year renovation project. A compact course on just 109 acres, Hermann has been a favorite of senior golfers since it opened in the 1920s and hosts an average of 75,000 rounds of golf each year. The **Memorial Park Course,** founded in 1936, is considered one of the best municipal courses in the state.

One of the more spectacular courses is **Tour 18** in Humble, which reproduces famous holes from some of the most celebrated courses in the United States.

For a calendar of local golf events, call the Houston Golf Association at 281-367-7999; access www.hga.org. Here is a selection of public courses:

Bay Forest, (E6), 201 Bay Forest, La Porte; 281-471-4653.

Bear Creek, 16001 Clay Road; 281-859-8188.

Brock Park (B5), 8201 John Ralston Rd.; 281-458-1350.

Cinco Ranch, 2303 Cinco Ranch Blvd.; 281-395-4653.

Clear Creek, 3902 Fellows; 713-738-8000.

Clear Lake (F6), 1202 Roseda; 281-488-0252.
Cypresswood, 21602 Cypresswood, Spring; 281-821-6300.
Eagle Pointe, Mont Belvieu; 281-385-6666.
Evergreen Point (C6), Baytown; 281-837-9000.
Glenbrook (E5), 8205 North Bayou; 713-649-8089.
Greatwood, 6767 Greatwood Parkway, Sugar Land; 281-343-9999.
Gus Wortham Park (D4), 311 S. Wayside; 713-921-3227.
Hermann Park (D3), 6201 Golf Course Dr.; 713-526-0077.
Houston Hills, 9720 Ruffino; 713-933-2300.
Jersey Meadow, 8502 Rio Grande; 713-896-6931.
Kingwood Cove, 805 Hamblen, Kingwood; 281-358-1155.
Lake Houston, 27350 Afton Way, Huffman; 281-324-1841.
Longwood, 13300 Longwood Trace, Cypress; 281-373-4100.
Meadowbrook Farms, 9595 So. Fry Road, Katy; 281-693-4653.
Melrose, 401 E. Canino; 281-847-1214.
Memorial Park (C2), 6001 Memorial Park Dr.; 713-862-4033.
Old Orchard, 13134 FM 1464, Richmond; 281-277-3300.
Pasadena, 1000 Duffer Lane; 281-481-0834.
Sharpstown Park (D1), 660 Harbortown; 713-988-2099.
Southwyck, 2901 Club House Dr., Pearland; 713-436-9999.
Tour 18, 3102 East FM 1960, Humble; 281-540-1818.
TreeLine, 17505 N. Eldridge Parkway, Tomball; 281-376-1542.
The Woodlands-TPC, 2301 N. Millbend, The Woodlands; 281-367-1100.
World Houston, 4000 Greens Road; 281-449-8384.

Miniature Golf

Malibu Grand Prix Family Entertainment Center (C1), 1105 West Loop North; 713-688-5271.
Mountasia Family Fun Center, 17190 Hwy. 249, 281-894-9791; and also 26000 US 59, Kingwood, 281-359-4653.
Putt-Putt Golf (E1), 7914 Fondren; 713-995-5161.

Hiking ———————————————————————

The abundance of trees and park trails make hiking a pleasant form of exercise here. We recommend four possible routes convenient to the three major commercial centers. Walking alone after dark is not recommended on any of these trails.

Buffalo Bayou Park (J7), is on the edge of downtown, and its trails follow the sloping banks of the bayou several miles west, then back east on the other side into town. Start at Sam Houston Park (J9), corner of Bagby at Lamar, and follow the hike and bike trail along Allen

Parkway. At the Shepherd Street bridge (C2), cross over and come back in on the path along Memorial.

Hermann Park (D3), is convenient both to downtown and to the South Main Corridor. It, too, is wooded but with more open spaces dotted with things to see along the way such as a fragrance garden, outdoor art, Chinese pavilion, museums, and refreshment stands. It is bounded by Fannin (the main entrance), N. MacGregor, Hermann Dr., and Almeda Rd.

Houston Arboretum and Nature Center (C2), is farther out west off Memorial on Woodway, at the I-610 Loop. This is convenient to those staying in hotels in The Galleria-Post Oak area. The expansive Arboretum features gardens as well as an abundance of native trees and flora. Keep your eyes peeled for small animals foraging along the rustic trails. It is located at 4501 Woodway. Information: 713-681-8433.

Memorial Park (C2), Houston's largest, is between downtown and the Post Oak area. Besides more than 1,500 heavily wooded acres, there is a three-mile exercise trail with workout stations, water fountains and night lighting along Memorial Drive, which divides the park. This park is bounded by I-610 Loop, I-10, Crestwood, and Buffalo Bayou.

Horseback Riding

While you are here, you might as well "Go Texan" and saddle up.

If you have your own horse, try the Hermann Park equestrian trails for a slow and easy ride.

Blue Fox Farms, 14801 Old Chocolate Bayou; 713-731-1193.
Cypress Wood Stables, 21415 Cypresswood; 281-446-7232.
Hermann Park Stables (D3), 5716 Almeda, 713-529-2081.
Sunrise Stables, 14807 Jarvis Road; 281-373-4651.

Hunting

The variety of game in Texas is good and includes deer and antelope. Of course, bird hunting is popular seasonally as well, and includes such game fowl as geese, ducks, doves, quail, and turkey. Most hunting is done on private property, and owners require lease fees. There is often a waiting period just to secure a lease for the better ranches and lodges. Limited public hunting is available.

You must have a license for hunting, which is obtainable at major sporting goods stores such as Oshman's with several locations in town. Also, the Texas Parks & Wildlife offices here sell licenses for fishing and hunting.

For details on hunting in Texas you may call the **Texas Parks & Wildlife Department** toll-free number in Austin, 800-792-1112, or the Houston office, 281-931-6471. They can tell you where to get a copy of their "Regulations Handbook" on hunting. Information is available online at www.tpwd.state.tx.us.

Ice Skating

Curiously, for a town that almost never sees ice except in drinks, Houston's many skating facilities and hockey leagues have proven popular.

Aerodrome Ice Skating Complex, 16225 Lexington, Sugar Land, 281-265-7465; and also 8220 Willow Place North, 281-847-5283. The Sugar Land complex is the training home of the Houston Aeros professional hockey team. Both complexes offer public skating, lessons and hockey leagues.

Galleria Ice Rink in The Galleria (F1), 5015 Westheimer, 713-621-1500. The most fashionable spot also is the most convenient one for visitors. Skating lessons are alternated with public sessions.

Sharpstown Ice Center (D1), 7300 Bellerive; 713-981-6667. Public sessions and lessons daily. Pro shop.

Texas Ice Stadium (F5), 18150 Gulf Freeway; 281-488-7979. Figure skating lessons, hockey and party rentals.

Racket Sports

The fast-paced action of racquetball and paddle, which melds tennis and racquetball, are popular with fitness-conscious Houstonians.

Chancellors Racquet Club (E1), 6535 Dumfries; 713-772-9955.
Memorial Athletic Club, 14690 Memorial; 281-497-7570.
Paddle Recreation Center (D1), 5010 West Park; 713-665-7576.

Rifle and Pistol Ranges

There are a number of good rifle and pistol ranges with day and night practice, indoor and outdoor ranges, skeet trap, turkey shoots, gunsmiths, boresighting, and gun and ammunition sales. One-day practice fees available. Here are some major public shooting ranges:

American Shooting Centers, 16500 Westheimer, 281-556-8086.
Bailey's Rifle and Pistol Range, 3626 Blue Bonnet, 713-433-2475.

Carter's Country, 6231 Treaschwig, 281-443-8393.
Clear Creek Gun Range, FM 1266, League City; 281-337-1722.
Hot Wells Shooting Range, 24815 Hempstead Highway, 281-373-0232.

Rock Climbing

Can't get to the mountains? Several local companies offer indoor, air-conditioned areas where climbers can hone their skills or just enjoy a blast of adrenaline. Recommended:

Exposure Indoor Rock Climbing, 6970 W. FM 1960, 281-397-9446.
REI (B1), 7951 Katy Freeway, 713-688-3500.
Sun & Ski Sports, Katy Mills Mall, 281-644-6040.
Texas Rock Gym (B1), 9716 Old Katy Road, 713-973-7625; and also 201 Hobbs Road, League City, 281-338-7625.

Roller Skating

Most roller rinks rent inline and traditional roller skates. Lessons available.

Airline Roller Skate Center, 10715 Airline, 281-448-7845.
Almeda Skate Center, 10750 Almeda-Genoa, 713-941-7000.
Bear Creek Roller Rink, 5210 N. Highway 6; 281-463-6020.
Dairy Ashford Roller Rink, 1820 S. Dairy Ashford; 281-493-5651.

Running

You'll find Houstonians running not only for exercise but for the social scene. The city boasts dozens of running and racing clubs, and nearly every weekend you can find a competitive running event. For a list of clubs, running events and suggested running routes, contact the Houston Area Road Runners Association at 713-797-8602; www.harra.org.

The major running event of the year is the Houston Marathon, which is in January. The marathon attracts more than 6,000 runners and thousands more spectators. The route begins and ends downtown, passing through Hermann Park, Rice University, The Galleria, Tanglewood and Memorial Park. Information: 713-957-3453; www.houstonmarathon.com.

Motor Boating

With your own equipment you would enjoy boating on **Lake Houston** (A6), **Lake Conroe,** and **Clear Lake** (F6), the latter being the closest to Houston. We suggest you call the **Texas Parks & Wildlife Department** for details on safety rules required by the state: 713-779-8977 or 281-931-6471.

Sailing

If you don't have your own boat, you may rent one at **Clear Lake Park** (F6), NASA Road 1 just past the LBJ Space Center. This is Harris County's oldest park with a lake seven miles long. There are many facilities for children and adults, and you may rent sailboats, catamarans, wind surfboards, and canoes here. There are free public boat ramps and there is a free fishing pier as well.

If you own a boat, you will find assorted marinas in this area all the way down NASA Rd. 1 to Galveston Bay at Seabrook and Kemah, on major area lakes, and, of course, at Galveston.

Other resources for boat and sailboard rentals and sailing lessons:
Clear Lake Charter in Clear Lake, 281-334-4858.
Gateway Charters in Kemah, 281-334-4606.
Sacketts Sailing Center in Clear Lake Shores, 281-334-4179.

Before you hit the water, review Texas boating laws. You can obtain a copy from the Texas Parks and Wildlife Department by calling 512-389-4800; access www.tpwd.state.tx.us.

Soccer

On playgrounds around the city, soccer is the game of choice of Houston's school-age athletes. Men's, women's and coed soccer leagues are popular with adults. For information, contact the Houston Soccer Association (281-531-0320; www.hfasoccer.com) or the Houston Women's Soccer Association (713-267-1517; www.hwsa.org). The City Parks and Recreation Department (713-845-1000) also can recommend neighborhood soccer programs.

Water Sports————————————————

With your own equipment, there are numerous spots on rivers, lakes, and some bayous for water skiing. Check with the **Clear Lake/NASA Area Chamber of Commerce** as one source of information, 281-488-7676. This area has many waterways such as **Clear Lake, Clear Creek, Dickinson Bayou,** and **Taylor Lake** where skiing is permitted.

For water-ski equipment, turn to Liquid Excursions, 19211 No. I-45, 281-355-9253; and Sun & Ski Sports Expo, 1355 West Bay Area Blvd., 281-316-1365. Sun & Ski has several other stores in the greater Houston area.

Water sports involving windsurfing, parasailing and personal water-crafts such as jet skis are extremely popular on Clear Lake. Resources for rentals and instruction:

Clear Lake Parasail in Nassau Bay, 281-333-2816.

North Shore Water Sports in Seabrook, 281-326-2724.

Parkside Marina Rentals in Seabrook, 281-326-4949.

Windsurfing Sports in Seabrook, 281-291-9199.

Diving

Houston's proximity to the Gulf of Mexico makes diving a popular activity. The following firms offer instruction, certification, and equipment:

Houston Scuba Academy, 12505 Hillcroft, 713-721-7788; and also 14609 Kimberly, 281-497-7651.

Sea Sports Scuba (D1), 7543 Westheimer, 713-977-0028; and several other locations.

Fishing and Crabbing

Houston hubs a fishing paradise of lakes, rivers, bays, and the Gulf of Mexico nearby. Texas law requires that you have a current fishing license, which may be purchased at major sporting goods stores such as Oshman's and at most bait camps.

A fishing license and saltwater fishing stamp are required of any person 17 or older who fishes or crabs in coastal waters. For information, contact the Texas Parks & Wildlife Department, at 800-792-1112, or access www.tpwd.state.tx.us.

There is good fishing on several lakes, such as **Lake Houston** (A6), **Lake Conroe,** and **Lake Livingston. Galveston Bay** is lined with piers at fishing camps, from La Porte (E6), all the way south to Texas City, where there is a great facility for day and night fishing called the Texas City Dike Pier. Pier information: 409-948-8172.

Just a few miles south of Kemah is the village of **San Leon** (F6), which has a beautiful public pier with a bait camp called **Spillway Fishing Pier** at Bayshore Park. Also in this area are several good private piers with equipment and boat ramps, which charge a nominal fee to put in. Pier information: 281-339-1917.

Deep-sea fishing at its best is with **Galveston Party Boats,** 713-222-7025, or **Williams Party Boats,** 713-223-4853, on Galveston Island. To get there continue on Broadway over the causeway until you get to

Nineteenth Street. Turn left and go to the end of the wharf. This company has full-day trips daily starting in early morning. Everything is included. Seasonally you might catch the big snappers and groupers from about mid-December until mid-May. After May the good catches include ling, amberjack, dolphin, king mackerel, jack fish, and sharks.

Crabbing is a fun and easy family activity. You will find crabs during summer months along the bays, off the jetties in Galveston, on canals and river deltas.

Surf fishing is also extremely popular on Galveston Island toward West Beach and farther toward the end of the island just before the San Luis Pass toll bridge.

Surfing

We don't promise to deliver the Oahu Pipeline, but there are areas along Seawall Boulevard on Galveston Island where surfing is permitted. During certain periods, especially in the winter, the surf gets lively enough to catch the occasional wave. Call the **Galveston Island Convention & Visitors Bureau,** 2106 Seawall Blvd., for the best locations, 409-763-4311.

Swimming

There are a few places you are not allowed to swim, but they are the exception to the rule. Houstonians flock to Galveston during the spring and summer and even into early fall. There are 30 miles of public beaches.

The most popular is **Stewart Beach Park**, Seawall at Broadway. It has cafes, a bathhouse, parking, a children's playground, a water coaster, restrooms, lifeguard stations and clean, wide, sandy beaches with lounge chair and umbrella rentals, all within close proximity. It also is alcohol-free, which means no beer, booze, or other intoxicating beverages may be carried or consumed on that beach.

The City of Houston maintains 44 swimming pools open to the public during the summer. For the nearest public pool, call 713-854-1000.

SPECIAL EVENTS

You'd be hard pressed to find a dull weekend in Houston. With more than 500 special events, festivals and celebrations on the calendar, visitors and residents can take their pick of diversions: a sporting event, a cultural affair or a fun-filled fete of foods.

In October alone, you'll find events celebrating the heritages of African-Americans, Asian-Americans, Cajuns, Chicanos, Germans, Greeks, Italians and Turkish-Americans.

We have selected events that occur on or about the same dates each year. Visitors and newcomers alike are encouraged to join in the Houston style of fun.

A good source for current event and festival information is Preview, which appears each Thursday in the Houston Chronicle.

January

Houston Auto Show (E2)—Reliant Hall, Kirby at I-610 Loop; 713-799-9500. Come kick the tires and conquer sticker shock as you admire hundreds of new vehicles, concept cars and classic automobiles. *CH*.

Houston Marathon (J11)—Begins and ends at Brown Convention Center, 1001 Avenida de las Americas; 713-957-3453; www.houston-marathon.com. This 26.2-mile challenge attracts more than 6,000 runners and thousands more spectators. *NC*.

International Boat, Sport & Travel Show (E2) —Reliant Hall and Reliant Arena, Kirby at I-610 Loop; 713-526-6361. More than 40 years old, this boat show overwhelms with 19 acres of boats ranging from skiffs to yachts. Other attractions include recreational vehicles, outdoors equipment, and related seminars. *CH*.

Martin Luther King Day —Parades and celebrations marking the birthday of the civil rights leader are held at various locations throughout the city. Information: Black Heritage Society, 713-645-9598.

Motor Spectacular (E2)—Reliant Astrodome, Kirby at I-610 Loop; 713-629-3700. Testosterone levels are high at this popular event, which features monster trucks, a destruction derby and other car-crunching thrills. *CH*.

Weiner Dog Nationals —Gulf Greyhound Park, 1000 FM 2004, La Marque; 800-275-2946. Speedy dachshunds compete for the title of top dog in this event that draws more than 80,000 bemused spectators each year. CH.

February

Chinese New Year—Several locales. The city's Chinese, Filipino, Indian, Japanese, Korean, Vietnamese and Thai communities gather for traditional celebrations featuring dragon dancers, fireworks, entertainment and food concessions. *NCH.*

Houston Antiques Dealers Association Annual Spring Show (J11)—Brown Convention Center, 1001 Avenida de las Americas; 713-764-4232. Dealers arrive from all across the country, Canada and England to be in this highly lucrative marketplace, where buyers can shop for days, pondering everything from primitives to antique jewelry. HADA hosts a similar show each fall. *CH.*

Houston Livestock Show & Rodeo and Parade (E2)—Reliant Park, Kirby at I-610 Loop; 713-791-9000. Parade downtown. This is arguably Houston's favorite annual tradition. From late February and into early March champion rodeo riders gather to compete for big money. Really big money, as this is the richest regular-season rodeo in the world. And it is also the world's largest livestock show. Superb specimens of the finest breeds of livestock are on view for judging and auctions. But what really pulls in the crowds—more than 100,000 visitors a day—is the galaxy of music stars that entertain during each rodeo performance. In recent years, rodeo schedulers have offered an outstanding variety of musical guests and appear no longer interested in just country-western acts. Among recent headliners: Perry Como, Enrique Iglesias, and Rod Stewart.

It all begins with a huge one-of-a-kind parade that brings back the nostalgia of the old West. Proceeds go to scholarships for young people. *CH.*

Houston Supercross (E2)—Reliant Astrodome, Kirby at I-610 Loop; 713-629-3700. This off-road motorcycle event features some 80 contestants in head-to-head competition of speed and skill. *CH.*

Mardi Gras—Galveston, various locations. The island celebrates what has grown into one of the nation's top week-long, pre-Lenten festivals, culminating in a night parade. The Momus Parade features magnificent floats, giant walking heads, bands, and colorful performers from the United States and abroad. Also street bands, dances, live entertainment and concessions line the route. Parties everywhere. For details and dates, contact the Galveston Island Convention & Visitors Bureau, 409-763-4311; www.galvestontourism.com. *CH.*

Texas Home and Garden Show (J11)—Brown Convention Center, 1001 Avenida de las Americas; 713-529-1616. This huge lifestyle exhibition features information and seminars on home remodeling, furnishings, gardening and more. A similar event is held each fall. *CH.*

March

Azalea Trail (F2)—River Oaks Garden Club, 2503 Westheimer; 713-523-2483. Houston is a horticulturist's dream with bouquets of club programs and flower shows almost year-round.

This one is the granddaddy of them all and ranks as another must-see event. It is largely contained within the confines of Houston's most exclusive residential district, River Oaks. Visitors get a chance to see Houston's "silk-stocking" crowd in their formidable mansions.

Visitors may tour any or all of the seven sites selected each year, but if time is limited stop by Bayou Bend, the highpoint on the trail. *CH.*

Bayou City Art Festival (C2)—Memorial Park; 713-521-0133. Boasting a lovely wooded backdrop, this juried art show features more than 300 artists and works ranging from ceramics to leather goods. Live music and a wine café. *CH.*

Bob Marley Festival (J7-8)—Buffalo Bayou Park; 713-688-3773. Reggae and world-beat bands provide the accompaniment for this popular event. *CH.*

Foto Fest—Various venues; 713-223-5522, www.fotofest.org. Held every other year, this excellent celebration of photography features simultaneous exhibits at museums, galleries, and corporate spaces all over town. *NCH.*

Houston Children's Festival (J9)—Downtown; 713-437-5200. This sprawling family-focused event fills Sam Houston Park, Tranquillity Park, and Hermann Square, which is the plaza surrounding City Hall. Kids enjoy games, play areas, interactive exhibits, art projects, storytelling, musical entertainment and a hands-on farm. *CH.*

St. Patrick's Day Parade —Downtown. This is one of the largest such parade in the Southwest. It features floats, drill teams, bands and everything Irish. *NCH.*

April

Art Car Weekend—Downtown; 713-926-6368; www.orangeshow.org. The highlight of this celebration of the eccentric and Houston's arts scene is the Art Car Parade. The parade, which rolls through the Houston

International Festival (see below), features more than 250 vehicles embellished with everything from handcrafted buffalo heads to Barbie doll shoes. Trophies and cash prizes award art car builders for craftsmanship, design and originality. Don't miss these amazing motorized works of art.

Just as fun and accessible is the Art Car Ball, held the evening of the parade on the roof of a downtown parking garage. Costumes not required, but never more appropriate. *CH.*

Earth Day (J7-8)—Buffalo Bayou Park; 713-266-1000. Sponsored by Enron and radio station KRBE, this family event offers environmental education, games, and an excellent music lineup. *CH.*

Heights Home Tour (B3)—713-861-4002; www.houstonheights.org. Creative construction and historic homes are spotlighted on self-guided tours of one of Houston's most charming neighborhoods. *CH.*

Houston Astros Baseball (I12)—Enron Field, Crawford at Texas streets; 716-627-8767; www.astros.com. Houston's National League baseball team opens its season this month. *CH.*

Houston International Festival (J9)—Downtown; 713-654-8808; www.hif.org. This expansive street festival draws hundreds of thousands for its impressive array of events. Artists and performers featured in such realms as acting, dancing, puppetry, singing, music and mime entertain on 10 stages, while Houston restaurateurs offer foods ranging from the exotic to the familiar.

A juried arts fair and festive African, Latin, and gypsy marketplaces draw serious shoppers, while children's activities abound. Definitely a family affair. Free weekday concerts at City Hall, 900 Bagby, link the two weekend blowouts. *CH.*

Japan Fest (D3)—Hermann Park; 713-963-0121. Tea ceremonies, origami demonstrations and martial-arts presentations are highlights of the culturally rich event adjacent to the park's Japanese Garden. *NCH.*

River Oaks International Tennis Tournament (C2)—River Oaks Country Club, 1600 River Oaks Blvd.; 874-713-6333. *CH.* Get a look at tennis' future stars at this exhibition tournament in the rarefied air of River Oaks. The players like the event's casual atmosphere; tennis fans love it. Get your tickets early. *CH.*

Westheimer Street Festival—713-522-6548. This longtime favorite bash for artists and spectators is experiencing growing pains. Traditionally concentrated in Montrose between the 100 and 1000 blocks of Westheimer (F2-3), the festival was recently exiled to the banks of Buffalo Bayou, where its 300,000-plus fans could be more easily accommodated. Organizers hope to win over Montrose neighbors and move the festival back to its roots. Stay tuned. Wherever it is, this is a super event for good art buys, people-watching, entertainment, and extremely casual fun. A similar event is held each fall. *NCH.*

Worldfest—Various locations, 713-965-9955; www.worldfest.org.

Feature-length movies, 35mm shorts, experimental and student films, commercials and music videos makeup the lineup for this 10-day celebration of independent film. *CH.*

May

Cinco de Mayo (D3)—Hermann Park; 713-225-8522. This colorful event featuring a parade, mariachi bands and folklorico dancing marks an important battle won by a small band of Mexicans over French troops in 1862. *NCH.*

Crawfish Festival—Preservation Park in Old Town Spring; 800-653-8696. Mudbug madness overwhelms this historic shopping district. Live music and children's games. *CH.*

Houston Comets basketball (D2)—Compaq Center, 10 Greenway Plaza; 713-627-9622; www.wnba.com/comets. The four-time Women's National Basketball Association champs open their season this month. *CH.*

Shell Houston Open—The Tournament Players Course in The Woodlands, in Montgomery County off I-45 North; 281-367-7999; www.shellhoustonopen.com. Golf's elite turn out to play this nationally recognized course for big ($1 million-plus) money. Pro-Am events Monday through Wednesday lead up to the four-day tournament. This benefit event provides millions of dollars to local charities each year. *CH.*

Strawberry Festival—Pasadena Fairgrounds, Pasadena; 281-991-9500. Texas' largest strawberry shortcake is a highlight of this family-oriented berry bash. *CH.*

June

Accordion Kings Music Festival (D3)—Hermann Park; 713-284-8350. Cajun, Czech, conjunto and zydeco music are the focus of this jubilant celebration of the squeezebox. *NCH*

Bay Day (E6)—Sylvan Beach Park in La Porte; 713-863-9993. Marine conservation and ecology are the focus of this bayside event. Children's games and good bands enliven the learning environment. *CH.*

Gay and Lesbian Pride Parade (F3)—713-529-6979; www.pride-houston.org. With more than 50,000 participants and another 100,000 spectators, Houston's Pride Parade is the third-largest of its kind. The colorful night parade rolls through Montrose, a neighborhood with strong ties to the gay community. *NCH.*

Juneteenth —Downtown parade and various events around town; 713-529-4195. This celebration marks June 19, 1865, the day the

Emancipation Proclamation was first read in Galveston, two years after the order was signed. *NCH*.

Sand Castle Competition —East Beach in Galveston; 713-520-0155. Architects, engineers, interior designers, and college students in those fields compete in a day-long sculpting contest sponsored by the Houston chapter of the American Institute of Architects. Elaborate and whimsical, the "castles" constructed here are just as likely to be cars, film characters or American icons such as the Statue of Liberty. *NCH*.

July

Astro World Series of Dog Shows (E2)—Reliant Park, Kirby at I-610 Loop; 800-884-2443. More than 4,000 canine competitors try to paw their way to the top in conformation judging. Demonstrations in handling, training, and agility courses. *CH*.

Freedom Festival (J8-9)—Sam Houston Historical Park (J8-9), 1100 Bagby, An old-fashioned July Fourth celebration complete with music, flags, and a major fireworks display. A real family-oriented day and evening of fun with entertainment sprawling from this charming gas-lit park at the edge of downtown Houston to the banks of Buffalo Bayou. *NCH*.

Houston Shakespeare Festival (D3)—Miller Outdoor Theater in Hermann Park; 713-284-8350. Two of the Bard's best plays are performed on alternating nights. Bring a blanket, a picnic basket, and plenty of bug spray. *NCH*.

Joy Fest (E2)—Six Flags Astroworld, I-610 Loop at Kirby, 713-799-1234. Youth-oriented festival of Christian music with concerts in the theme park's Southern Star Amphitheater. *CH*.

August

Ballunar Liftoff (F6)—Johnson Space Center in Clear Lake; 281-488-7676. More than 100 hot-air balloons fill the skies at this festival that features a carnival, arts and crafts, and live music. Meanwhile, JSC hosts a once-a-year open house, allowing visitors to chat with astronauts and other space experts. *CH*.

Houston International Jazz Festival (J9)—Hermann Square at City Hall; 713-839-7000. Houston copes with August's heat with some cool jazz. *CH*.

September

Texaco Grand Prix (J11)—Downtown; 713-739-7272; www.texacogp.com. Each fall, the streets on the eastern edge of downtown Houston are turned into a speedway for cars racing in excess of 200 mph. *CH*.

Theta Charity Antiques Show (E2)—Reliant Arena, Kirby at I-610 Loop; 713-942-8699. This huge antiques show features elaborate displays and more than 55 dealers from the United States and Great Britain. Fine antiques but few bargains. *CH*.

October

Fright Fest (E2)—Six Flags Astroworld, I-610 Loop at Kirby; 713-799-1234. Rollercoaster thrills and Halloween chills await visitors to Houston's theme park, which takes on a temporarily eerie tone with cobwebs, coffins and monsters. *CH*.

Houston Rockets Basketball (D2)—Compaq Center, 10 Greenway Plaza; 713-627-0600; www.nba.com/rockets. The two-time champs (1994 & 1995) of the National Basketball Association open their season this month. *CH*.

Texas Renaissance Festival —Located near Plantersville, 50 miles northwest of Houston; 800-458-3435; www.texrenfest.com. This re-creation of fifteenth-century England draws hundreds of thousands of Houstonians and out-of-towners to a giant festival held every weekend in October. There are music, drama, games, contests, jugglers, mimes, jousting, horse races, and other events under the trees in a medieval country-village setting. *CH*.

Quilt Festival (J11)—Brown Convention Center; 713-781-6864; www.quilts.com. Elaborate, one-of-a-kind pieces are among the more than 1,000 quilts and textile artworks on display at this three-day event that draws more than 50,000 visitors annually. *CH*.

Zoo Boo (D3)—Houston Zoological Gardens in Hermann Park; 713-523-5888; www.houstonzoo.org. Costumed kiddies trick or treat throughout the zoo. Don't miss dinnertime at the vampire bat exhibit. A similar event with a holiday theme is staged each December. *CH*.

November

Nutcracker Market (E2)—Reliant Hall, Kirby at I-610 Loop;

713-535-3271. This is serious shopping (nearly 300 vendors from around the country) for a good cause (proceeds go to scholarships for the Houston Ballet Academy). Wear comfortable shoes and bring a big wallet. *CH.*

Thanksgiving Day Parade —Downtown. For many Houstonians, this is the official kickoff of the holiday season. Huge floats, balloon characters, bands, and drill teams plus celebrities highlight the parade, which culminates with the arrival of Santa Claus. *NCH.*

Uptown Holiday Lighting (C-D1)—Westheimer at Post Oak; 713-621-2011. Fireworks, an electric-light parade, and musical entertainment signal the start of the holiday season in this imaginatively decorated shopping district. *NCH.*

Warehouse Art Crawl (H11-12)—Downtown; 713-225-0993. Nearly 100 artists open their studio doors and exhibit their wares at this casual event that draws an eclectic crowd. Metro Trolleys deliver patrons to the doors of warehouse studios throughout the downtown area. Live music and munchies are offered at many of the sites. *NCH.*

December

Dickens on the Strand —Galveston; 409-765-7834. A popular re-creation of Dickens' London of the 1800s with costumes, live performances, parades and fun for the entire family. Festivities are on The Strand, one of the island's most historic streets. *CH.*

Galleryfurniture.com Bowl (E2)—Reliant Astrodome, Kirby at I-610 Loop; 713-799-9500. This new college bowl game pits Big 12 Conference and Conference USA teams. Game expected to move to new NFL stadium when it is completed in 2002. *CH.*

Christmas Candlelight Tours (J8-9)—Sam Houston Historical Park, 1100 Bagby; 713-655-1912. Houston's oldest municipal park takes on a special charm during the holidays when its historical homes and church are decorated in the fashion of yesteryule. Refreshments add cheer. *CH.*

Jingle Bell Run (K9)—Downtown YMCA, 1600 Louisiana; 713-775-5700; www.jinglebellrun.org. This annual charity event attracts more than 6,000 runners and walkers, many of whom wear holiday-themed costumes. Good fun and good cheer. *NCH* for spectators.

Lights in the Heights (B3)—Norhill Esplanade, 200 Norhill; 713-683-5188. This festival of lights features more than 20 blocks of twinkling decorations and 8,000 luminaries. Bands and choirs performing on porches add to the old-fashioned holiday atmosphere. Sponsored by the Woodland Heights Civic Association. *NCH.*

SELF-GUIDED
CITY TOURS

The Greater Houston area offers numerous points of varied interest. To touch on some of the highlights we recommend one downtown walking tour—with a trolley ride and detour underground—and one easy metro driving tour.

Dress comfortably, wear good walking shoes and take along a compact umbrella in case of rain. It is fun to compare notes and exchange comments on such jaunts, so consider going with a companion. Certainly on the driving tour it will help to have someone along to follow map directions and read the legend. Many of the sights are covered in detail in the SIGHTS and VISUAL ARTS chapters.

DOWNTOWN WALKING TOUR

It is possible to simply cross the street to pass from the shadows of pioneer days to space age underground walks, to see Houston as it was and how it is. Along this path you begin with Houston's past and quickly move into Houston today where glass, chrome and polished steel reflect ultra-modern skyscrapers that give Houston the name, the "Future City."

This tour should last about two and a half hours, depending on your pace. Your best starting times are about 9 a.m. when it should be cooler or around 2 pm after the noon pedestrian rush.

We encourage you to pause, look in on several buildings and perhaps enjoy a meal, snack or beverage along the way. As walking tours go, this one is a little long, but there is a trolley ride and a trip underground, both of which offer a chance to escape the heat.

Begin at Market Square

If you have driven into downtown you will find convenient parking in the commercial lots scattered around the square. Or consider the

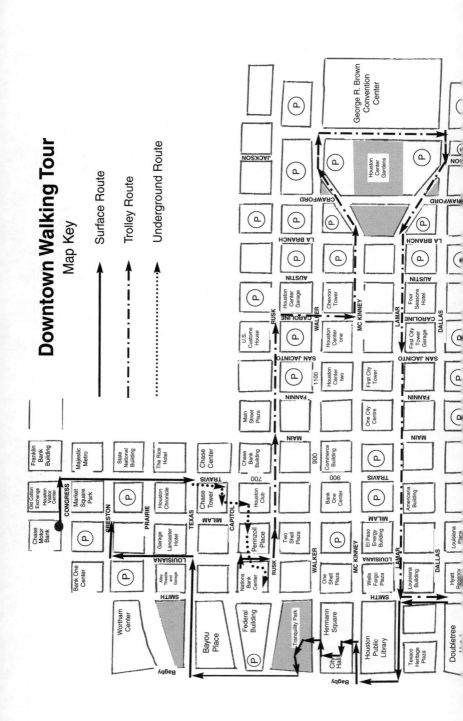

Downtown Walking Tour

Map Key

→ Surface Route

–··– Trolley Route

······ Underground Route

Market Square Garage just across the street from where you **begin at the northwest edge of the park on the corner of Congress and Milam streets.** Market Square is the city's original business district and it was the location of the first five city halls. Looking to your right across the square, you can see three downtown landmarks. From the left, there is the historic Rice Hotel; the world's tallest bank building, the 75-story Chase Tower; and the gothic-inspired triple spires of Bank of America. In the middle of the square is a pine sculpture (*Points of View*, 1991) by James Surls.

Walk east toward Travis Street and the Friedman Clock Tower. To your left is the Henry Henke Building. Constructed in the 1800s, it once housed the Henke & Pillot grocery. On the same block is the leaning La Carafe (c. 1845), the best of what is left of old downtown. Hardly the Ritz—only wine, beer and champagne are served—but it's heavy on nostalgia and character. Among its early uses were as a stage-coach inn where Sam Houston is believed to have slept, and an Indian trading post. An eclectic clientele appreciates its history and its juke-box, which features a curious collection of opera and old Broadway tunes, among other selections.

Proceed to the corner of Congress and Travis. To your left at the end of Travis, you can see the red and sand-colored brick of the down-town branch of the University of Houston. Near the university is Allen's Landing, a park near the spot where the Allen brothers found-ed Houston in 1836.

Stay on the square, and **walk right on Travis.** When you reach the end of the block, look to your left. A mural by Houston artist Suzanne Sellers pays tribute to the area's history as a farmer's market. The Majestic Metro opened in 1926 as the 800-seat Cine Ritz. It was restored in 1991 and today is a special-events venue. **Proceed another block.** After crossing Prairie, on your right will be large glass windows exposing the printing presses of the Houston Chronicle Publishing Company, which produces Texas' largest-circulation newspaper.

To your left is The Rice. Listed on the National Register, the old Rice Hotel oozes history. Although temporary, it was the first capitol of the Republic of Texas in the late 1830s. Later it became the favorite hotel among visiting dignitaries, including queens, kings and congress-men. One of its more tragic stories: President John F. Kennedy dined here the night before he was assassinated in Dallas on Nov. 22, 1963. Today it is a loft-apartment complex.

Explore Underground Houston————

Cross Texas Avenue and enter the Chase Tower through its revolving door to your immediate right. Directly ahead is an escalator offering access to the world's largest pedestrian tunnel, already more than six miles long and still expanding.

This tunnel is unique in that each of its 60 blocks is privately designed, being built by the overhead buildings' owners; therefore, no two segments are identical. Some are old; others are glimmering, mirrored corridors that have been used in sci-fi films such as *Futureworld*.

As you come off the escalator, walk straight ahead to the tunnel marked "Houston Club Building;" enter and follow it the right. You'll pass several eateries catering to downtown's lunch crowds, including pint-size versions of Ninfa's and La Madeleine French Bakery and Café. Watch for signs labeled "North Travis Tunnel" as you **proceed under the Houston Club Building.**

As you walk through the tunnel, keep to the right. You'll want to enter the next tunnel through glass doors marked "Pennzoil Place." Follow the tunnel's curving trail into a popular arcade that includes several cafés, florist and gift shops and a Pennzoil logo store.

On the far right past the Pennzoil store is another tunnel entrance. **Head into the "Bank of America" tunnel.** Its curving route will take you to another set of escalators. The escalators will be on your left, opposite a small bakery.

Proceed up the escalator and into the soaring lobby of the 56-story Bank of America building with its Dutch Renaissance architecture. **Take an immediate right off the escalator and then another right; use the revolving door to exit** to Louisiana Street. Directly across the street is the famous Pennzoil Towers, which prompted a leading architectural critic to claim "Houston is the American future." These trapezoid-shaped towers linked by an eight-story glass arcade are the creation of world-renowned architects Philip Johnson and John Burgee, who, like many of their counterparts, have made Houston an architect's playground.

Take a right and proceed to the corner. Looking east (to your left), you will have a terrific view of a buff-colored building with a classic cupola. The Niels Esperson building was Houston's first skyscraper, constructed during the city's first big building boom in 1927. Listen on the hour and you may hear carillon chimes emanating from that dome.

Cross the street twice, so that you end up on the eastern corner of Louisiana and Rusk. Proceed to the left down Rusk. At the corner of Rusk and Milam is a Metro bus stop. Take the B route Metro Trolley. The trolleys, which service five downtown routes, are free and pass approximately every seven minutes.

While waiting for the trolley, look to your left down Milam. The colorful sculpture you see is *Personage and Birds*. The 55-foot piece by Spanish artist Joan Miro enlivens the gray exterior of the Chase Tower, the tallest building in the United States outside of New York and Chicago. A free observation deck is on the sixtieth floor.

A Ride on the Trolley

For the purposes of our tour, try to get a seat on the left side of the trolley. Eight blocks into your trolley ride, Annunciation Catholic Church with its graceful steeple will come into view. But the church is dwarfed by Enron Field, which made its debut in March 2000. The 40,950-seat ballpark with its retractable roof is home to the Houston Astros.

The trolley will make a right turn in front of the George R. Brown Convention Center. With its air funnels, pipes and porthole accents, the 900-foot-long Brown Center, designed by Mario Bolullo, resembles a land-locked ship. After another right, the trolley will proceed down Lamar. (Note: From 11 am-2 pm, the trolley will detour past the Brown Center and make stops in Chinatown for lunchtime diners before looping back to Lamar.) If you are ready for a break, get off the trolley just past the Houston Center gardens at Lamar and Austin streets. For an elegant lunch, consider the Four Seasons' well-regarded DeVille. For more casual fare, visit the food court at The Park, where you also will find a nice selection of specialty stores in the three-story mall.

If you do not need a break, stay on the trolley. Another four blocks into your ride, on the left, will be Foley's, the last of downtown's great department stores. **Exit the coach after it makes a left turn on Smith. Then walk right on Smith to the corner of Smith and Lamar. Cross Lamar.**

To your right is the historic Julia Ideson Library and Archives. This Spanish Renaissance-style building is one we encourage you to enter, for on the first, second and third floors are Spanish murals, changing exhibits and an ornately carved and painted oak rotunda.

The Library and City Hall

Walk down the left side of the Ideson Building. Straight overhead is an outstanding view of the Texaco building's Mayan-inspired architecture. Soon you will be on the plaza facing Houston's Central Public Library, an octagonal structure with sweeping glass front and Dakota mahogany granite facing. **Keep to the left of the library and walk another block to Bagby.**

Across Bagby is Sam Houston Historical Park. The city's oldest park features several historic structures, including Houston's earliest home on its original site, plus the city's oldest church and oldest home, which have been moved to this location.

Niels Esperson Building in front of Pennzoil Place　　　　　　*Courtesy of Dale Young*

You may opt to pay a nominal charge for a tour of Sam Houston Historical Park, but that will add time to the estimate of our tour. If you decide to tour the park, stop by the Long Row, which is across Bagby to your left. It is a replica of Houston's first commercial structure. It houses a gift shop and the offices of the Harris County Heritage Society. There you can watch a brief presentation that provides good historical background on the park and Houston. If you have a camera, the park offers one of the best angles for shooting the downtown skyline, contrasting old against the new.

To continue our walking tour, **make the block around the library, turning right on McKinney and proceeding to the library plaza.** The large orange sculpture is Claes Oldenburg's *Geometric Mouse* X. From the position of the sculpture, **cross over the middle of McKinney Street** to the stepped-up walk in front of City Hall.

Above the building's cast-aluminum doors are medallions of great lawgivers, from ancient Egypt's Akhenaten to early America's Thomas Jefferson. In front of the building is Hermann Square, a popular noonday oasis for downtown workers.

Enter this art-deco building, which was remarkably controversial for downtown when it opened in 1939. Today, it houses not only the mayor and city council offices, but also the Greater Houston Convention and Visitors Bureau. In addition to finding brochures and information on area attractions, visitors also will find exhibits, public restrooms, an imaginatively stocked gift shop and a refreshment kiosk.

Tranquillity Park and the Bayou ——————

Exit the visitors center via the Walker Street doors. Use a crosswalk on your right to cross Walker Street. You have entered Tranquillity Park, which commemorates man's moon landing on the Sea of Tranquillity in July 1969. In front of you there is a landscaped mound. **Walk up to the left of the mound to the edge of the fountain then down the brick ramp on your left. Just ahead is a smaller grass-covered mound. Go around** that to the cut-away rest area on the other side to see an authentic footprint made from the same boot astronaut Neil Armstrong wore when he took that historic step onto the moon and said, "One small step for man, one giant leap for mankind."

This end of the park provides another great angle for shooting the skyline, especially if the fountains are turned on and if flowering lilac and crepe myrtle are in bloom.

If you walk to the other side of the park, there is a wall depicting the path of the Apollo 11 flight and the history of Tranquillity. Bronze disks embedded at the entrances to the park tell the Tranquillity story in brief in the major languages of the world.

Go back to the footprint and **exit up the steps leading to the corner of Walker and Bagby. Cross Bagby and proceed right,** past the Hobby Center for the Performing Arts. Scheduled to open in 2002, the center will include two performance venues and will be home to Houston's Theatre Under the Stars and the Houston Broadway Series. On the corner between Rusk and Capitol is a small traffic island, home of the Sweeney Clock. The clock was purchased in 1908 and adorned the Sweeney Jewelry store before finding its way to this spot in 1971. Look to your right, and you will see a building with small square windows. That is the Federal Building.

Move along across the streets to the shade of the live oak tree just ahead to the left.

The long rectangular building you see is the old Albert Thomas Convention and Exhibit Center and on this site, where the building curves, stood the old County Jail. The building was designed this way to preserve Houston's "Old Hanging Oak." About 400 years old, this tree has been the scene of several hangings.

Continue past the tree through the overhead pass on Bagby one block to the corner of Memorial/Texas.

Immediately to your left is the Houston Fire Department central station, and just beyond that to the right is Houston's central U.S. Post Office. Look over the bridge railing at this corner to see Buffalo Bayou down below. This is the largest and most historic bayou in the city, for it was this waterway that sparked the city founders' idea to establish Houston as a port city.

Now **cross Bagby, and walk past Bayou Place to the corner of Smith.** Bayou Place, the entertainment complex widely credited with sparking a downtown revival, rose from the ruins of the Albert Thomas Convention Center, which was dormant for 10 years after the opening of the Brown Center in 1987 rendered it obsolete. The center offers several notable restaurants including the Hard Rock Café; a comedy club; an upscale pool hall; the Angelika, an eight-screen theater specializing in art films; and Aerial Theater, a popular venue for national touring acts.

To your left is the $74 million Wortham Theater Center, home to the Houston Ballet and the Houston Grand Opera.

A Theater and Arts Center

On the adjacent corner to your left is the world-famous Alley Theatre, the second-oldest permanent resident theater in the country. In this fortress-looking building are two stages, bringing the finest in professional productions to the Houston boards. The Alley has earned many awards, including a Tony for best regional theater.

Cross Smith and, continuing past the Alley, you come to the corner of Texas and Louisiana.

To your right is a giant travertine marble colonnaded structure. The Jesse H. Jones Hall for the Performing Arts, an American Institute of Architects honorary-award winner, is the home of the Houston Symphony and a venue for major touring road shows. If interested, proceed right to the main entrance of the building and notice that it is curved; if you go inside you will see the curve continues in the pattern of a seashell, thus the style is called "Caracol," from the Spanish for shell. At the head of stairs leading to city tunnels, parking, and offices of performing arts groups, is the bronze *Dancing Girl* by David Parsons.

If you look through the glass over the marquee, you can make out the sweeping jet stream-like sculpture called *Gemini II*. It is by artist Richard Lippold who, with the help of only one assistant, spent weeks hanging thousands of aluminum rods suspended from the ceiling on golden wires. In the lobby below is another sculpture titled *Pair of Horses* by Robert Fowler.

Across Texas Street from Jones Hall is the Lancaster Hotel, one of Houston's smallest, but most luxurious inns. It was previously the Auditorium Hotel, housing delegates to the 1928 Democratic National Convention at which Franklin D. Roosevelt nominated Al Smith for president.

Cross Texas and proceed down Louisiana to the left of the Lancaster. On your right is a three-story, red-brick building that used to be the Texas Boxing Association Gymnasium, where some of our nation's greatest fighters worked out. It now houses the Longhorn Café.

At the corner of Louisiana and Prairie, you will see a taller red building with white trim, a tile rooftop and a gazebo. This is the Hogg Building, which is named after brothers Mike and Will Hogg. The latter, together with Hugh Potter, developed the exclusive residential district, River Oaks. Miss Ima Hogg, Mike and Will's sister, had the rooftop gazebo built for entertaining friends. Miss Ima, as she was known, was one of the great ladies of Houston and a leading philanthropist. She was instrumental in forming the Houston Symphony Society, and she ultimately donated Bayou Bend, her famous River Oaks mansion, to the city as a museum of American furnishings and artifacts.

Walk past the Hogg Building, now residential lofts, to Preston. Take a right and walk one block before arriving back at Market Square.

METRO DRIVING TOUR

In a couple of hours driving, you should be able to capture a very good overview of this dynamic city. There are several points along the way that are good stops for lunch or dinner. Consider any restaurant mentioned by name a recommendation. If you do pause for refreshments, add another hour to the driving time for a total excursion of approximately three to four hours, depending on traffic.

Leaving Downtown

As in the walking tour, you may begin at Market Square. **Simply proceed south on Milam.** As you cross Prairie, to your left is the Houston Chronicle building. Across the street is downtown's tallest building, the 75-story Chase Tower. The colorful sculpture in front of Chase Tower is Joan Miro's *Personage and Birds.* To your right, is Jones Hall.

Farther down Milam, on your left at Pease, are the Houston Press offices, home of the city's popular alternative weekly. Three blocks later, you will pass under I-45 at Pierce. This section of the interstate often is referred to as the Pierce Elevated.

Watch for blue street signs in the coming blocks. These Vietnamese street signs were added in 1998 and reflect the importance of the immigrant business people who set up shop in midtown. In other Asian neighborhoods in Houston, you will find Chinese and Korean street signs. The Asian street name often has nothing in common with its American counterpart.

At the corner of McIlhenney and Milam is the Houston Fire Museum, located in old Fire Station #7.

Once dominated by strip centers packed with Asian restaurants and services, this neighborhood is changing rapidly. New housing developments are popping up as empty-nesters and young professionals move back to Houston's urban center.

Van Loc Restaurant, on your right at the corner of Anita, is a standout among the many Vietnamese restaurants in this neighborhood.

Watch for Elgin, where you will turn right. Proceed west on Elgin. As you cross Louisiana, on your left is the Houston branch of Brennan's specializing in New Orleans cuisine.

As you cross Bagby, Elgin becomes Westheimer. Westheimer is one of the longest streets in Houston and is named after the family of novelist David Westheimer. With miles of restaurants, nightclubs, stores, and galleries, this is the shopping, dining and entertainment mecca of Houston and is one of the busiest streets in town.

Lively Neighborhood

As you proceed west on Westheimer, you enter one of the city's most funky and fun neighborhoods. With strong links to the arts and gay communities, Montrose is a lively patchwork of tattoo parlors, art galleries, chic restaurants, leather bars and psychic readers. Montrose at Westheimer is the epicenter of this cultural storm.

Among the landmarks: On your right at Grant, the white stucco Felix Mexican Restaurant, where tasty Tex-Mex specialties have been served since 1948; on your left at Yoakum is Hollywood Video, which is housed in the former Tower Theater, an art deco showplace built in 1936.

Soon you will be making the Westheimer Bend, where vintage clothing stores dominate. You also will start to pass some antique stores. Generally, the farther west you travel on Westheimer, the more upscale the antique store.

As you cross Shepherd, to your right is the Spanish-style St. Anne's Catholic Church, which was constructed in the 1930s. It is home to one of the largest parishes in the Greater Houston area.

Farther down the street, on your left, is Avalon Diner, an old-timey soda fountain that serves open-face roast beef sandwiches and chocolate shakes.

After crossing Kirby, you'll want to be in the right lane. Approaching River Oaks Boulevard, Lamar High School is to your left. Among its alumni are showman Tommy Tune and actor Robert Foxworth.

Turn right on River Oaks. You are entering Houston's most exclusive district. Planned by Will Hogg and Hugh Potter, this residential area features magnificent homes shrouded by huge oaks, magnolias, and pines. It is an idyllic neighborhood, a well-insulated escape from the bustle of Houston.

Proceed north on River Oaks to where it dead-ends at the gated River Oaks Country Club. **Make a U-turn in front of the ROCC, admiring the mansions as you return to Westheimer.**

Turn right onto Westheimer. To your right is St. John the Divine Episcopal Church. At Claremont, on your left, is St. Luke's Methodist Church.

As you cross Weslayan, the palm-lined Highland Village shopping district will come into view. Both sides of Westheimer are crammed with upscale stores such as Restoration Hardware, Pottery Barn, and Williams-Sonoma. The district also boasts several good restaurants, including the distinguished Anthony's and the more casual P.F. Chang's.

Don't Stop to Shop

You'll want to be in the inside left lane as you approach the Loop 610 overpass. This area can be heavily congested and changing lanes can be difficult. As you cross under the Loop, you are entering Houston's premier shopping area, the Galleria/Post Oak district.

Turn left on Post Oak, where futuristic street signs float like space ships above the intersections. (If we were to turn right on Post Oak, we would find more upscale shopping and fashionable restaurants such as Americas and Tony's.)

As you turn left on Post Oak, Neiman-Marcus is on the right. It is one of several anchor stores of the Galleria, an expansive and expensive shopping mall that sucks in tourists and shoppers with the power and efficiency of a vacuum cleaner. Among the fine stores are Macy's, Emporio Armani, Tiffany & Co., Saks Fifth Avenue and Lord & Taylor. Bargain hunters and budget shoppers need not bother.

Just past the Galleria is the Williams Tower, 65 glass-clad stories topped by a revolving beacon. Adjacent to the skyscraper, the nation's tallest building outside a central business district, is the Williams Fountain, a cascade often referred to as the Water Wall. It is a favorite backdrop of Houston photographers, both professional and amateur.

Proceeding on Post Oak, move into the far left lane in preparation to turn left onto Richmond. (If you were to turn right, you soon would be on the Richmond Strip, an area known for nightclubs and eating and drinking establishments that cater to a college-age crowd.)

Turn left and proceed east on Richmond. As you approach the railroad tracks, to your left is one of Houston's colorful and casual restaurants. Ragin' Cajun specializes in crawfish and tasty Louisiana cuisine such as gumbo and jambalaya.

The next major intersection is Weslayan. To the left is a fortress-looking building that is headquarters for the Houston Independent School District.

Farther east is a cluster of silver reflective glass buildings known as Greenway Plaza. Within this development, but not visible from Richmond, is Compaq Center, which is home to many of the city's professional sports teams including the Rockets, Comets, Aeros and Thunderbears.

Continue along Richmond, crossing Buffalo Speedway. Keep to the right lane. At Kirby, turn right. Keep to the inside or far left lane. This area can become congested. As you approach Westpark, you are in Goode Company. Houston grilling guru Jim Goode's tasty dynasty includes the Goode Company Taqueria to your right. Another block down Westpark is Goode Company Seafood. A block ahead on Kirby, to your left, is Goode Company Barbecue, which is next door to Goode's Hall of Flame, a barbecue shrine-cum-store, which sells barbecue grills, supplies and Texas-inspired goods.

Turn left on Bissonnet. You will drive about 1 1/2 miles before arriving at the intersection with Montrose. There, to your left, is the Contemporary Arts Museum; ahead to the right is the Museum of Fine Arts.

Rice and the Village

Turn right on Montrose. Straight ahead is the Mecom Fountains, a gift to the city from the late John Mecom Sr., who opened the luxurious hotel on your left.

Keep right as you circle the fountains and proceed down South Main. At the next light, at the corner of Sunset Boulevard, look to the right and note the long tree-lined drive that leads to the administration building of Rice University. The land for this school was given to the city by William Marsh Rice, who also built the old Rice Hotel. Founded in 1891, Rice is the city's oldest university. The private institution is known for its science and engineering programs.

At the end of the Rice campus, you come to the area of business supporting the mammoth Texas Medical Center. (We will return to the Medical Center.)

Take a right on University. Soon Rice Stadium will be in view. Built in 1950, the 70,000-seat stadium was home to Super Bowl VIII in 1974. The Rice football team might never win a national championship, but the games still draw good crowds, who come as much for the halftime entertainment as the athletic competition. Rice's Marching Owl Band, known affectionately as the MOB, is famous for its irreverent halftime shows.

As you cross Greenbriar, you are entering another one of Houston's popular shopping/dining districts. Rice Village features more than 325 shops, including Eddie Bauer, Banana Republic and Urban Outfitters. If you would like a quick bite here, stop by Jason's Deli or Berryhill's Hot Tamales, both offer dependable fare in a casual setting.

Turn left on Kirby. Notice as we proceed down Kirby that on your left are green street signs and on the right are blue street signs. And none of the names match. On your left is Houston. To your right is West University Place, one of several cities within the big city.

Continue south on Kirby. As you cross Braeswood, you also will cross Brays Bayou. It along with other urban waterways such as Buffalo, Sims, Greens and White Oak bayous have earned Houston the nickname, The Bayou City.

As you cross Main, to your left, is Droubi's, an excellent Lebanese fast-food spot.

Home Sweet 'Dome

Continue south on Kirby. On your left as you cross Old Spanish Trail, you will get your first glimpse of what once was called the "Eighth Wonder of the World." When it opened in 1965, Harris County Domed Stadium, better known as the Astrodome, was the world's first covered air-conditioned arena. But like many older sports stadiums, the Astrodome has outlived its usefulness. Going up next door to the Astrodome is a 69,500-seat football stadium with a retractable roof.

Here you can also see the rest of the Astrodomain, or Reliant Park as it is now known. The complex includes the Reliant Hall, actually larger in area than the Dome, and the Reliant Arena. The new construction is Reliant Stadium and Reliant Center, which will open in fall of 2002.

At the I-610 Loop up ahead on your right is the Radisson Astrodome hotel. Note the dark windows along the full length of the tower's top floor. That penthouse once was the "Celestial Suite" of the Astro Village Hotel. In the 1960s, it was listed in the *Guinness Book of World Records* as the world's most expensive hotel accommodation ($3,000 per night).

Go under the Loop and turn left onto the feeder road.

Now you will pass directly in front of Six Flags AstroWorld amusement park with more than 100 rides and shows. The overhead bridge leading into the park is the only privately owned bridge over an interstate highway. Next to AstroWorld is Six Flags WaterWorld, still another theme park full of rides, thrills and water-oriented activities.

Watch now for the Fannin Street sign as you proceed down this feeder road along the freeway. Turn left at the light onto Fannin and get over into the right lane. At a fork in the road, bear right to stay on Fannin.

What's up, Doc?

Just as you cross Braeswood, to your left is the University of Texas-Houston Health Science Center. You have entered the world-famous Texas Medical Center, the largest of its kind in the United States. Covering more than 675 acres, the center comprises 41 institutions, including 13 hospitals, 2 medical schools and four nursing schools.

Follow Fannin through the underpass. You will want to be in the right lane.

Two of the world's most recognized and respected heart specialists are closely associated with the Texas Medical Center: Dr. Michael DeBakey with Methodist Hospital and Dr. Denton Cooley of St. Luke's Episcopal Hospital.

Turn right on MacGregor, keeping to the left lane. To your right is the old entrance to Hermann Hospital. Turn left on Golf Course Drive. Hermann Park Golf Course, one of seven city-owned courses, is to your right.

On your left is the Houston Zoo, home to more than 5,000 critters including Indonesian tigers, Australian koalas and endangered Mexican wolves.

Follow Golf Course Drive as it snakes through park. As the road narrows to one lane, you can see through the trees to your left, Miller Outdoor Theater. To your right is the Houston Garden Center.

Pull up and park at the theater if you would like to stretch a bit and take a closer look at this innovative auditorium. There are restrooms and a snack stand if you care to pause before the remainder of the tour.

Miller Theater has permanent seating for 1,500 but many thousands show up regularly for free summer performances that include Shakespearean dramas, Broadway musicals and a wide range of other entertainment.

Past the garden center, to your right is the Museum of Natural Science, which is home to Cockrell Butterfly Center. You can see the center's glass atrium as you approach Fannin.

To your left is a statue of Gen. Sam Houston, the hero of Texas independence from Mexico.

Cross Fannin and head toward the Mecom Fountains, where you will follow the curve and access Montrose Boulevard. As you approach the fountains, to your right is the Cancer Survivors Plaza and beyond that the grande dame of Houston hotels, The Warwick.

As you make the right turn onto Montrose, to your right is the MFA. Crossing Bissonnet, to your left is the Contemporary Arts Museum; to your right are mounds that make up a wall of the MFA's Cullen Sculpture Garden.

Proceed north on Montrose. To your left is the Glassell School of Art, the teaching wing of the MFA.

Soon you will back in Montrose, a culturally rich and ethnically diverse neighborhood. Both sides of Montrose offer diversions such as galleries, boutiques and cafés.

Just past Colquitt, on your left, is the Freed Library, housed in the Italian Romanesque sanctuary of the former Central Church of Christ.

More of Montrose

As you approach Alabama, the University of St. Thomas is to your left. Founded in 1947, this Catholic institution is known for its liberal arts programs. St. Thomas' administration offices are housed in the stately 1912 Link-Lee Mansion, which fronts Montrose.

Nearby on your left is La' Colombe d'Or, a tiny luxury hotel with a well-regarded restaurant and clubby bar.

Continue traveling north. Off Montrose, just a block down Clay Street, is the Museum of Printing, which features a gallery of historic headlines.

Overpasses will take you past Allen Parkway, Buffalo Bayou and Memorial Drive. Buffalo Bayou Park runs along both sides of the bayou and is worth exploring. The park features several interesting works of art such as *The Spindle Piece* by Britain's Henry Moore and the Police Officers Memorial, a pink granite pyramid designed by Texas-born sculptor Jesus Moroles.

Stay in the right lane, making a right onto Washington. After several blocks, Glenwood Cemetery will be on your right. This pretty plot of plots has spectacular views of downtown, though it is doubtful any body here notices. Glenwood is the final resting place of recluse millionaire Howard Hughes.

On your left is the Pig Stand, which opened in 1924. It is one of just a handful of Pig Stands that remain since the chain's heyday in the 1940s and '50s, when more than 60 of the restaurants operated in the South. A little trivia: Texas toast, fried onion rings and car-hops were all inventions of a Pig Stand.

This area is the Old Sixth Ward Historic District, Houston's oldest neighborhood. A working-class neighborhood with turn-of-the-century cottages, the district was embraced by immigrant communities, including the German, French, Italian, Polish, Irish and Mexican. Great efforts are under way to revitalize the district while retaining its character and historic structures.

Crossing Houston Street, keep to the right as the road forks. You now are on Preston.

Return to Downtown

Across the Preston Street Bridge is the Wortham Center, home to the Houston Ballet and the Houston Grand Opera, and Sesquicentennial Park on Buffalo Bayou. Inspired by the artwork of elementary schoolchildren and designed by Houston artist Mel Chin, the seven towering metal columns are known as the *Pillars of the Community*.

Across Louisiana, to your right, is the Hogg Building, which was constructed in 1921. Listed on the National Register, the building has been developed into loft apartments.

Your tour ends back at Market Square at the corner of Preston and Milam.

ONE-DAY EXCURSIONS

As much as we love the big city, taking a break from the bustle is worthwhile. And you don't have to travel far to see a dramatic change in scenery.

Two suggested excursions offer a different mix of things to see and do. Both have historical stops, recreational possibilities and interesting dining and shopping options.

Taking these trips during early spring adds the pleasure of seeing the highways in bloom with Texas wild flowers. The northern route's rolling hills become a fantasyland with Texas bluebonnets, and the southeastern route weaves a patchwork of Indian paintbrush winecups, and dandelions.

We hope you enjoy these excursions as much as do the locals who head for the hills or the coastline on weekends.

NORTH TO COLLEGE STATION
(9 to 10 hours or overnight)

A Taste of Texas History ————————

On any highway north of Houston it doesn't take long before the coastal flatlands meet gentle rolling hills.

There should be no need to stop until arriving at Chappell Hill, unless you have the urge to check out some of the roadside produce stands and antiques stores. It's fun to poke around even if you don't buy.

Take I-10 West out of downtown Houston and travel west. About nine miles outside of downtown, take Loop 610 North, watching for US 290 signs. This section of the freeway can get congested. Once turning onto the Loop, you'll want to make your way to the one of the three inside left lanes, which will exit to US 290 West toward Austin. This area of northwest Houston has experienced tremendous growth in recent years.

While the speed limit on much of this tour will be a generous 70 mph, be aware of areas of reduced speeds where limits are strictly enforced.

169

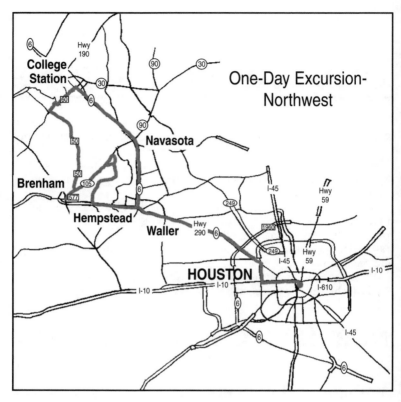

One-Day Excursion-
Northwest

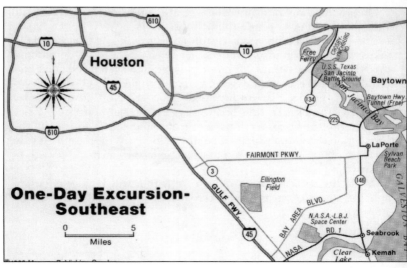

One-Day Excursion-
Southeast

0   5
Miles

Continue north on US 290 until you reach Chappell Hill. As you approach the Brazos River, you'll begin noticing subtle scenic changes as the coastal plain becomes a more rolling landscape.

At the Chappell Hill stoplight, take a right onto FM 1155. This also is known as Main Street in Chappell Hill's historic district.

A Polish farming community founded in 1847, Chappell Hill was once home to five churches and two universities. The town survived the Civil War and Reconstruction, but was not able to recover after a yellow fever epidemic in 1867, which decimated its population.

Today the community is known for its many historic homes and its Bluebonnet and Scarecrow festivals, which attract thousands of Houstonians annually.

Just past the 1873 Providence Baptist Church, take a right on Poplar Street. At the end of Poplar at Church Street is the Museum of the Chappell Hill Historical Society and the 1901 Chappell Hill United Methodist Church. The museum is open Wednesday through Sunday, and presents historic and art exhibits. You also can pick up a free guide to the town's historic buildings.

To leave, go one block north on Church and take a left on Cedar Street. Follow Cedar to Main Street and take a right. Follow FM 1155 North out of Chappell Hill.

Washington-on-the-Brazos State Historical Park is about 19 miles outside of Chappell Hill. FM 1155 is dotted with farms and ranches, simple and spectacular. The park entrance is well-marked.

Take a right into the park and follow the signs to the Visitors Center parking lot. The park is on the site of the once-bustling town of Washington-on-the-Brazos, which was twice the capital of the Republic of Texas.

For our purposes, you have about an hour to explore the park, which includes two museums and a living history farm. You may opt to take a guided tour of Independence Hall, where the Republic of Texas was born, or Barrington Farm, which re-creates 1850s rural life. Admission to the park is free; nominal fees for tours, which can be arranged at the Visitors Center.

This Must Be Heaven

To leave, follow park exit signs and take a right on FM 1155 North. After about two miles, you will come to the intersection of Texas 105. Take a left on Texas 105 West. About nine miles into your drive, you'll see a sign for the Monastery of St. Clare Miniature Horse Farm. The farm is home to the Franciscan Poor Clare Nuns and is open to visitors 2 pm- 4 pm daily except during Holy Week and on Christmas Day. Call 979-836-9652.

Brenham is another nine miles down Texas 105. Take a left on FM 577, which also is known as Horton Street. Approximately two miles down Horton, Blue Bell Creameries is on the left. Park in the lot just past the red-brick building. Tours of the plant are offered several times each weekday and last about 40 minutes. Established in 1907, Blue Bell entices customers with frozen treat flavors such as Chocolate Covered Cherry, Banana Pudding and Buttered Pecan. A Blue Bell logo store with an ice cream parlor is open Monday through Saturday March to December. Call 800-327-8135.

Lunch and Free Time

To leave the creamery, take a left from the parking lot on Horton Street, then take a right at the intersection onto Tom Green Street. At the first stoplight is Market Street, where you should turn right. Market Street will take you to Brenham's historic downtown district. You can park free anywhere around town square for two hours.

The downtown district features several eateries. We suggest the home-cooked buffet at Fluff Top Roll Restaurant, 979-836-9441; soup and salad at Must Be Heaven, 979-830-8536; or a burger at the friendly Legend Billiards & Grill, 979-251-7665.

After lunch, you can explore the many gift and antiques shops located downtown or check out the Brenham Heritage Museum, which is housed in an attractive 1915 Classical Revival building and is open Wednesday through Saturday.

George Bush Library

When you are ready to leave Brenham, take Alamo Street east out of downtown. Turn left on Chappell Hill Street, which will become Texas 105 East as it leaves the city. About two miles outside of Brenham, take a left on FM 50 North.

A few miles outside of Brenham on your right will be the Antique Rose Emporium. The retail center is an explosion of color and fragrance with eight acres of rose gardens, herb gardens, a wildflower meadow and several historic structures. Visitors are welcome to stroll about the gardens. Call 979-836-5548.

Not too far down the road from the Emporium is Independence. As you pass through town, you will see Independence Baptist Church & Museum on your left. Founded in 1839, the church was the site of Gen. Sam Houston's baptism in 1854, as well as the original site of Baylor University, which was established in 1845.

College Station is located about 40 miles from Brenham. As you cruise FM 50 toward College Station, you will soon see farms and orchards belonging to Texas A&M University, an institution famous for its agriculture and animal husbandry research and its military Cadet Corps.

Take a right on the first major intersection, which is FM 60 North. Take another right at FM 2818. From here you can see Kyle Field, where the spirit of the Twelfth Man is celebrated. Aggies, as A&M students and alum are known, never sit during football games. They stand, always ready to go into the game should the coach ever need a twelfth player.

At the first light, take a left on George Bush Drive. Look for signs for Barbara Bush Drive, take a left and follow the road into the visitors parking lot of the George Bush Presidential Library.

The library traces the life of President Bush from his boyhood in Connecticut, to his years as ambassador to the United Nations, director of the CIA and later his election as forty-first president of the United States. Highlights of a self-guided tour include a re-creation of the Oval Office, Barbara Bush's ballgowns and a fine collection of gifts given to Bush as head of state. The library is open to 5 pm daily.

Return to Houston

To return to Houston, take Barbara Bush Drive to George Bush Drive. Turn right. Take a left onto FM 2818. Watch for Texas 6 South, also known as Texas Avenue, where you will turn right.

Follow Texas 6 South to US 290. Follow 290 East to Houston. Once in Houston, take Loop 610 South. Exit the Loop at I-10 East and follow the signs into downtown.

SOUTHEAST TO
GALVESTON BAY
(8 to 9 Hours)

If you could leave downtown Houston at about 9 am, preferably on a weekend when traffic is not so congested, and take all of the tours offered on this excursion, you could be back downtown by approximately 6 pm.

NASA/Space Center

Take Jefferson or Pierce, both are crosstown one-way streets that from downtown will take you directly **onto I-45 South (Gulf Freeway)**. **After Bay Area Boulevard, get into the right lane, for the next exit will be marked "NASA—Alvin—1 mile." Exit and stay in the middle lane on the feeder road until you go under the overpass, then cloverleaf to the right** onto NASA Rd. 1 headed east. Continue for about three miles.

On your right across from the Space Center is a tall building—brick, with white trim and with mortared arches painted white. This penthouse used to be all glass and was the network pool for all television stations for shooting the exterior of NASA during the Mercury, Gemini, and Apollo space flights.

Watch for signs directing you to the entrance of the spectacular Space Center Houston, which serves as visitor and interpretive center for the Johnson Space Center. (Please see SIGHTS chapter for details.)

Allow at least 3-4 hours for visiting the center and its various activities and attractions.

A Boardwalk Lunch

To leave the Space Center, **turn left onto NASA Rd. 1 and head east toward Galveston Bay.**

This road curves frequently, passing Clear Lake on the right and the Lunar Planetary Institute across the street on the left. The Institute was formerly the summer home of the late Houston millionaire Jim West. West had a ranch at the site where the Space Center is located. He sold it to Humble Oil, which later gave 1,000 acres to Rice University; Rice in turn donated the land to the U.S. government, which then purchased more acreage to bring its land commitment up to the 1,642 acres required to build what was originally called the Manned Spacecraft Center.

As you get closer to the bay, you will begin to see marinas and other water-oriented businesses. **Continue until you cross some railroad tracks, then turn right at the traffic light onto Texas 146 South.** As soon as you make the turn you'll see a tall bridge that crosses Clear Creek.

Stay in the left lane, cross over the bridge, and you will be in Kemah, an Indian word meaning "Facing the Wind." **Just across the bridge is a stoplight, turn left there and go to the end, then take another left and follow the signs to the Kemah Boardwalk. Go to the end** and on the right you will see a cluster of restaurants.

Not that long ago, this area was a tangle of privately owned restaurants and shops. Nothing fancy. Just fresh seafood and terrific views of pleasure boats entering and leaving Clear Creek and Galveston Bay. In the mid 1990s, the entire neighborhood was bought by one company and renovated into what you see today. A dining and entertainment complex that features high-energy restaurants, a hotel, amusements such as a passenger train and Ferris wheel, and a collection of high-end gift shops.

Most of the restaurants still concentrate on seafood, although the Cadillac Bar offers Tex-Mex specialties. Particularly popular is the Aquarium, a fine-dining room that wraps around four 50,000-gallon tropical fish tanks. While all the restaurants afford good views, we recommend Landry's for its sweeping views of the bay.

Before exploring the boardwalk, check in with the restaurant of your choice. On busy weekends, waits for tables can be long and you can use the wait time to browse nearby shops or let the children splash in the boardwalk's water playground. If lines are prohibitively long, go for the restaurant with the shortest wait. Because a single company owns all the restaurants, menus, quality and presentation are similar.

Galveston Bay is rich in lore from the days of pirate Jean Lafitte, who headquartered nearby at Galveston Island. Tales of buried treasure are still told today. Some hoards of gold are believed buried on land; others lie at the bottom of the sea in galleons wrecked during hurricanes. The last treasure discovered in the Kemah area was a cache of gold and silver Spanish coins found in 1965. (Please see GALVESTON chapter for more on pirate days.)

Sylvan Beach Park and Sterling Home ——

Leaving here, return to Texas 146 and go back north over the bridge; continue for about five miles. Turn right at sign indicating "146 Business—1/4 mile to the right"; **follow to dead-end junction with Broadway; turn left; then turn right at Sylvan Beach sign onto Fairmont Parkway leading to Sylvan Beach Park. Drive through the park, around the circle to the left, out the other end, and turn right onto Bayshore Drive. Past the church on the left, turn left onto Kansas for one block, right onto Park Avenue.** This road makes two "s" curves and crosses two small canals before you come to the Sterling mansion on the right with the historical marker in front of a hurricane fence.

This famous home was constructed in 1927 by Houston architect Alfred Finn for former Gov. Ross S. Sterling. The portico faces the bay, and in its day it was the largest home in Texas. Its 34 rooms included a dining room that seated 300 for dinner. Built at a cost of $1.4 million, the mansion had silver and gold sconces and Tiffany chandeliers. It is an exact, one-fifth scale replica of the White House.

In the '20s and '30s this stretch between Sylvan Beach and Morgan's Point was known as the Texas "Gold coast," and at Sylvan Beach many of the great names in big bands played to high society.

San Jacinto via a Tunnel and Oil Derricks

From the Sterling home **turn around and go back south on Park Avenue, across San Jacinto Street to Fairmont and turn right. Continue on Fairmont to TX 146 and turn right again. Take TX 146, watching for signs for TX 225 West. This will be your exit.**

As you exit to TX 225, you will see to your right the Fred Hartman Bridge, which links Baytown and La Porte. With its 40-story cable towers, the $95 million, two-mile bridge is stunning. Shortly you will begin to spot plastics and chemical plants.

In about five miles turn right onto Texas 134 north toward the San Jacinto Battleground. Proceed north on Texas 134, which is part of the State of Texas Independence Trail. Just past a polymer plant on the right, you will see the towering San Jacinto Monument. Shortly this highway veers off to the right onto Battleground Road, leading straight to the base of the monument.

San Jacinto Battleground, Monument and USS *Texas*

For a tour around the battleground, turn right at the sign with directions to Battleship Road, just after the park gates. Drive into the **game preserve,** cross over a spillway, and go to the end at the water's edge, where there is a cul-de-sac to turn around. You will see people out in the water fishing; this San Jacinto River is popular with sportsmen. Turn back and go to the **monument.** You can ride to the top of the 570-foot tower for a great view of the marshes stretching for miles around. On a clear day you can see downtown Houston. *CH.* The **Regional Museum of History** is at its base, *NCH.* (Please see SIGHTS chapter for details on the battleground, monument, museum and battleship).

Leaving the monument, **go to Battleship Road and turn right.** Follow the signs to **USS** *Texas.* Tickets are available at the foot of the gangplank.

Return to Houston

Leaving here, you will see a historical cemetery and picnic grounds along the banks of the Houston Ship Channel. At the gate **turn left onto TX 134** and shortly you will be nearly surrounded by the back bay waters and the San Jacinto River.

To cross the channel, board a ferry, one of the few remaining small, free, vintage ferries in the United States.

On the other side you will be on the Crosby-Lynchburg Road, which also is elevated above water on both sides. **When you come to I-10 East (East Freeway), cross over and turn left onto the freeway to head west back into Houston.**

Watch the overhead signs for the lane into downtown. You may take the Capitol Street exit off the freeway, which puts you in the heart of downtown Houston and over to Main Street. As you exit you will spot the massive George R. Brown Convention Center and further east, Enron Field.

THE INTERNATIONAL VISITOR

Houston is a humming global marketplace where the world beats a steady path to place its stake in the city's business and industrial circles.

Recognizing this emergence as an international gateway, Houston's civic and business leaders have taken steps to assure the international traveler a convenient, rewarding, and enjoyable stay. The U.S. Customs facilities at Bush Intercontinental Airport accommodate 1,000 foreign passenger arrivals an hour. In addition, there are directional signs in several languages and foreign currency exchange facilities.

The **Greater Houston Convention & Visitors Bureau** maintains a multilingual staff and distributes brochures in several languages at its visitors center at 901 Bagby.

Business travel constitutes the bulk of international arrivals. In 1999, more than 500 foreign companies did business in Houston and

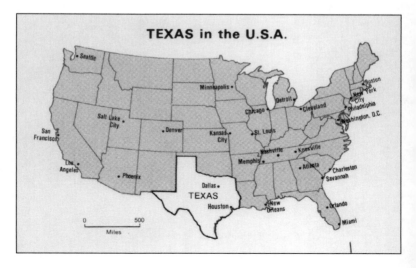

TEXAS in the U.S.A.

more than 3,000 Houston companies reported international business activities.

But all foreign travel here is not just commercially oriented. Many visitors come to Houston for their health. The Texas Medical Center wields a sizable impact on the city's international visitor industry. Thousands of foreign patients visit Houston annually for medical reasons. The vast network of colleges and universities contributes as well, with perhaps 10,000-plus students registered from abroad. And apart from international business people, patients, and students, more than 200,000 foreign seamen call on the city every year via the Port of Houston.

As the city's international image grows, Houston is realizing significant increases in foreign tourism.

Of all the organizations involved in programming international visits to Houston, the forerunner is the **Institute of International Education**, 515 Post Oak Blvd.; 713-621-6300. The IIE works closely with the medical centers, the Greater Houston Partnership, the Port of Houston, and others in planning such visits. Under a program sponsored by the U.S. Information Agency, the IIE follows up on requests from consulates, bi-national chambers, major business firms and others requesting assistance in planning visits for guests and specialists in such areas as medicine and education. Working parallel to the IIE is the **Houston International Protocol Alliance**, 901 Bagby, Suite 100; 713-227-3395.

The alliance is the city's protocol office and serves as liaison with the consular corps, as well as with Houston's 13 Sister Cities and visiting dignitaries. The alliance also advises city officials, as well as the corporate and public sector, on matters of protocol and cultural sensitivities.

Consulates and Trade Offices

Houston has the fifth-largest consular corps in the United States and the largest in the South. There are 70 consulates and trade offices here. The following is the latest Houston International Protocol Alliance list of consulates, consulates-general, and honorary consulates arranged alphabetically by country. Most function as, or can direct callers to, trade offices for their respective countries.

Albania, 20682 Sweetglen, Porter; 281-354-0789.

Argentina, 3050 Post Oak Blvd.; 713-871-8935.

Austria, 7887 Katy Fwy.; 713-723-9979.

Bangladesh, 35 N. Wynden; 713-621-8700.

Belgium, 2929 Allen Parkway; 713-529-0775.

Belize, 7101 Breen; 713-999-4484.

Bolivia, 800 W. Sam Houston Parkway; 713-977-2344.

Botswana, 10000 Memorial; 713-680-1155.

Brazil, 1700 W. Loop S.; 713-961-3063.

Cameroon, 2711 Weslayan; 713-774-7319.

Chile, 1360 Post Oak Blvd.; 713-621-5853.

China, People's Republic of, 3417 Montrose; 713-524-0780.

Colombia, 2990 Richmond; 713-527-9093.

Costa Rica, 3000 Wilcrest; 713-266-0484.

Cyprus, 1128 River Glyn; 713-928-2264.

Czech Republic, 4544 Post Oak Place; 713-629-6963.

Denmark, 45455 Post Oak Place; 713-622-9018.

Dominican Republic, 3300 Gessner; 713-266-0165.

Ecuador, 4200 Westheimer; 713-572-8731.

Egypt, Arab Republic of, 1990 Post Oak Blvd.; 713-961-4915.

El Salvador, 6420 Hillcroft; 713-270-6239.

Finland, 31 Pinewold Circle; 713-552-1722.

France, 277 Post Oak Blvd.; 713-572-2799.

Georgia, 3040 Post Oak Blvd.; 713-585-3500.

Germany, 1330 Post Oak Blvd.; 713-627-7770.

Ghana, 3434 Locke Lane; 713-960-8806.

Greece, 1360 Post Oak Blvd.; 713-840-7522.

Guatemala, 3600 South Gessner; 713-953-9531.

Haiti, 6310 Auden; 713-661-8275.

Honduras, 4151 Southwest Freeway; 713-622-4572.

Hungary, P.O.Box 27253, Houston 77227; 713-529-2727.

Iceland, 2348 W. Settlers Way; 281-367-2440.

India, 1990 Post Oak Blvd.; 713-626-2148.

Indonesia, 10900 Richmond Ave.; 713-785-1691.

Ireland, 2711 Weslayan; 713-297-8841.

Israel, 24 Greenway; 713-627-3780.

Italy, 1300 Post Oak Blvd.; 713-850-7520.

Jamaica, 7737 Southwest Freeway; 713-541-3333.

Japan, 1000 Louisiana; 713-652-2977.

Jordan, P.O. Box 3727, Houston 77253; 713-224-2911.

Korea, 1990 Post Oak Blvd.; 713-961-0186.

Kyrgyzstan, 2302 Greens Court, Richmond; 281-341-5309.

Latvia, 5847 San Felipe; 713-785-0807.

Madagascar, 1400 El Camino Village; 281-222-3599.

Malta, 910 Travis; 713-428-7800.

Mexico, 10103 Fondren; 713-271-6800.

Mongolia, 1221 Lamar; 713-759-1922.

Morocco, 2121 Kirby; 713-521-7607.

Netherlands, 2200 Post Oak Blvd.; 713-622-8000.

New Zealand, 246 Warrenton; 713-973-8680.

Nicaragua, 2825 Wilcrest; 713-953-0237.

Norway, 2777 Allen Parkway; 713-521-2900.

Panama, 24 Greenway Plaza; 713-622-4451.

Peru, 5177 Richmond; 713-355-9517.

Philippines, 8 Greenway Plaza; 713-877-6700.

Poland, 2718 St. Anne, Sugar Land; 281-565-8900.

Portugal, 700 Louisiana; 713-759-1188.

Qatar, 1990 Post Oak Blvd.; 713-355-8221.

Saudi Arabia, 5718 Westheimer; 713-785-5577.

Senegal, 3602 South MacGregor; 713-747-4711.

Slovenia, 2925 Briarpark; 713-430-7350.

Spain, 1800 Bering Dr.; 713-783-6200.

Sweden, 2401 Fountainview; 713-953-1417.

Switzerland, 1000 Louisiana; 713-650-0000.

Syria, 5433 Westheimer; 713-622-8860.

Thailand, 600 Travis; 713-229-8241.

Turkey, 1990 Post Oak Blvd.; 713-622-5849.

United Kingdom, 1000 Louisiana; 713-659-6270.

Venezuela, 2925 Briarpark; 713-974-0028.

Auto Rentals

There are dozens of auto rental firms in Houston that follow standard procedure for rentals to international travelers. They require a valid driver's license, and, if you have no major credit card, passport, proof of a return ticket to your country of origin and a cash deposit. It is advisable to ask for insurance when you take a car. For a list of auto rental companies, please see the MATTERS OF FACT chapter.

Bank Hours

Houston's banking hours are generally from 9 am to 5 pm. Some branches of some banks remain open on weekends as well.

Currency Exchange and International Banking

It is possible to exchange foreign currency at Bush Intercontinental Airport or in a bank, but to obtain the best rate, try an exchange specialist such as Thomas Cook. Some major hotels might post signs indicating the currencies they accept with current information on the daily rate of exchange, but such willingness is subject to wide and unpredictable fluctuation.

At Bush Intercontinental Airport, there are foreign exchange facilities at the International Airlines Building dealing in currencies of nations linked by air with Houston, plus selected others.

Several private firms that handle foreign currency and/or buy and sell travelers checks, drafts, or gold coins include: **International Money Exchange,** 1130 Travis, 713-654-1900; **Thomas Cook Currency Services,** 11077 Westheimer, 713-782-8092; and **American Express,** 1200 McKinney, 713-658-1114.

Some Houston banks have international banking departments that include services such as buying and selling foreign currencies, foreign travelers checks, transfers, Eurodollar service, foreign drafts on overseas banks, foreign collections, import/export financing, acceptance financing and issue of commercial letters of credit.

In addition, 28 foreign banks operating in Houston can provide service to international guests. Contact the Greater Houston Partnership (713-844-3600; www.houston.org) for a current list of foreign-owned banks.

Customs Allowances

Foreign nationals are allowed to bring certain items into the United States duty-free for personal use only:

One liter of alcoholic beverages per adult non-resident; 200 cigarettes, 50 cigars, or 2 kg smoking tobacco or proportionate amounts of each. An additional 200 cigars may be brought in under the gift exemption. But remember that Cuban cigars are prohibited for even personal use. Also, items or products made from endangered species are strictly prohibited and are subject to confiscation.

It is highly recommended that international visitors learn all of the details on customs allowances before departing for the United States A handy guide is titled "Know Before You Go." You may secure a free copy by writing the **U.S. Customs District Office,** 2350 N. Sam Houston Parkway East, Suite 1000, Houston, TX, 77032, by calling 281-985-6700, or from your nearest U.S. Embassy or consulate. Internet: www.customs.gov.

Driving

Driving in the United States is done in the right-hand lane. You will need a valid international driver's license, which should be secured before you leave home. Most gasoline stations are self-service operations and stay open 24 hours. Full-service stations are difficult to find and you will pay extra for the service.

The urban 70-mph maximum speed limit is enforced on Houston freeways and expressways. The speed limits decrease as you get into the city. The speed limit on most residential streets is 30 mph. Watch for posted signs to be sure you are driving at the correct speed.

In Houston you may turn right on a red light after stopping and looking in both directions; you may turn left on a red light only when turning onto a one-way street from another one-way.

Electricity

110 volts 60 cycles alternating current (AC). You will need a plug adapter and a voltage converter for foreign electrical appliances.

Hospitals—Emergency

In case of medical emergency, call 911. Or seek out a medical facility offering comprehensive services. Please see the NEW RESIDENTS chapter for a list of hospitals providing 24-hour emergency care.

International Publications and Newspapers

Some bookstores, newsstands, universities, hotels, libraries, and consulates have international publications that can be purchased or that may be read on location.

The **Central Public Library** (J9), 500 McKinney, has foreign language newspapers, magazines and journals. Information: 713-236-1313; www.hpl.lib.tx.us/hpl/.

Another downtown source for foreign publications is Globe News Stand, 809 Pierce; 713-650-6397. Superstand, 5348 Westheimer, also carries foreign newspapers and magazines. Information: 713-626-4888. Superstand has a half-dozen locations in the greater Houston area.

For a list of newspapers, including foreign language publications, please see MATTERS OF FACT.

Medical Insurance

Medical insurance should be secured prior to arrival. There is no national health service. Health care is costly and payment often is required immediately.

Money

The U.S. dollar ($) is divided into 100 cents (¢). The coins are the penny worth 1¢ (copper-colored), nickel 5¢, dime 10¢, quarter 25%¢, half-dollar 50¢ (all silver-colored), and the dollar coin, which is gold-colored. The bills or notes are predominantly printed in green and black ink on special white paper in denominations of $1, $5, $10, $20, $50 and $100.

Pharmacies

With the large number of international patients visiting Houston, it is good to know of a 24-hour pharmacy for emergency needs, and medical supply rentals such as crutches and wheelchairs. Please see MATTERS OF FACT for a list of 24-hour pharmacies.

Postage

Mail service is generally good, and letters can cross the country in one to three days. ZIP codes must be used for guaranteed delivery. Express mail (guaranteed overnight delivery) is available. Two-day Priority Mail transports up to 2 pounds in two days for about $3 with surprising dependability.

Call 800-275-8777 or access www.new.usps.com for information on mailing rates, ZIP codes and for the location of the nearest post office.

Post offices generally are open 8 am-5 pm weekdays. Hours may vary during holiday periods. The **Central Post Office** (H10) is at 401 Franklin; 713-226-3066.

Public Holidays

The following holidays are considered legal holidays in most businesses, including government offices. Some holidays are celebrated on the closest Monday to the holiday in order to give working people a long weekend. This is indicated in the listing.

Jan. 1, New Year's Day.
Jan. 18, Martin Luther King Day.
Feb. 22, George Washington's Birthday, celebrated as Presidents Day on closest Monday.

May 30, Memorial Day, celebrated on closest Monday.
July 4, Independence Day.
September, Labor Day, first Monday after first Tuesday.
Nov. 11, Veteran's Day.
November, last Thursday, Thanksgiving Day.
Dec. 25, Christmas.

Taxes

In Texas there is an 8.25 percent state sales tax on purchases except non-restaurant food and prescription medicines. There is an additional 17 percent tax on hotel and motel rooms in Houston.

Telephone and Telegrams

Pay phones require a 30¢ deposit. When calling long distance, first dial 1, then the area code number, then the telephone number. Telephone numbers preceded by an 800, 877 or 888 are toll-free. You dial 1, 800 and the number.

If a telephone number is preceded by 900 or 976, it is a toll call and you will be charged an additional amount for each minute of the call.

You can get operator assistance by dialing 0 or directory assistance by dialing 1-411.

Prepaid phone cards that can be used for local and long-distance service are gradually gaining acceptance in the United States. Most convenience stores, pharmacies and post offices sell phone cards.

To send a mailgram (guaranteed next-day delivery by mail and less expensive than a telegram), telegram, international message, or charge-card money order, call **Western Union,** 800-325-6000.

Tipping

Some businesses such as restaurants and bars automatically add a gratuity to a check, so be mindful of this and look at your bill before you pay the normal 15 percent tip for services rendered. Tipping may exceed the standard 15 percent when and if you observe that service has been exceptional. Bellhops and porters generally receive $1 per bag and, while it is not required here, taxi drivers appreciate a nominal tip.

Tours

Several sightseeing firms offer special tours of the city with narration in foreign languages. Please see TRANSPORTATION chapter.

Translators

AE Inc. Translations, 14780 Memorial Dr.; 281-870-0677. Specializes in business and technical translations in most major languages.

SpanTran Educational Services, 7211 Regency Square Blvd., Suite 205; 713-266-8805. Unusual firm evaluates foreign educational credentials for purposes of further study, immigration, employment, and professional licensure in the United States. Also certified translations of educational and non-educational documents. Deals with all languages.

The Language Co.; 713-952-6704. Translations and interpreters for most languages.

Transportation

Please see TRANSPORTATION chapter.

TV Channel and Radio Stations Broadcasting in Foreign Language

Radio and television stations vary news, entertainment, and talk shows in Spanish, Mandarin Chinese, Cantonese, Vietnamese, and other languages. See the Houston Chronicle listings for current programming.

KXLN-TV Channel 45 and KTMD-TV Channel 48 broadcast almost entirely in Spanish.

METRIC CONVERSIONS

Length

1 millimeter = .039 inch (in.)	1 inch = 2.54 cm.
1 centimeter = .39 in.	1 foot = 0.30 m.
1 meter = 3.28 feet (ft.)	1 yard = .91 m.
1 kilometer = .62 mile (mi.)	1 mile = 1.61 km.

To convert miles to kilometers, multiply the number of miles by 8 and divide by 5.

Weight   1 oz. = 28.35 g.
1 gram = .04 ounce (oz.)   1 lb. = .45 kg.
1 kilogram = 2.2 pounds (lbs.)   1 ton = .91 metric ton

Liquid
                  2.11 pints (pt.)   1 pt. = .47 liter
1 liter =   1.06 quarts (qt.)   1 qt. = .95 liter
                  .26 gallon (gal.)   1 gal. = 3.79 liters

Temperature
To convert Fahrenheit temperatures to Centigrade (Celsius): Take the Fahrenheit temperature, minus 32 and divide by 1.8 equals the Centigrade temperature.

CONVERSION CHARTS
FOR CLOTHING

Dresses, coats, suits and blouses (Women)

British	10	12	14	16	18	20
American	8	10	12	14	16	18
Continental	40	42	44	46	48	50

Suits and overcoats (Men)

American/British	34	36	38	40	42	44
Continental	44	46	48	50	52	54

Shirts (Men)

American/British	14	14½	15	15½	16	16½	17	17½
Continental	36	37	38	39	40	41	42	43

Shoes (Men) for ½ sizes add ½ to preceding number

British	6	7	8	9	10	11
American	7	8	9	10	11	12
Continental	39½	40½	41½	42½	43½	44½

Shoes (Women) for ½ sizes add ½ to preceding number

British	3	4	5	6	7	8	9
American	4½	5½	6½	7½	8½	9½	10½
Continental	35	36	37	38	39	40	41

THE SPECIAL TRAVELER

SENIOR CITIZENS

Senior citizens are a vital segment of the tourist industry according to the nation's travel-market experts, who are developing programs and bus tours aimed at this sizable and growing group of travelers.

A good source of information on travel resources and discounts available to seniors is the American Association of Retired Persons. You don't have to be retired to join this nonprofit organization and annual membership is just $8 a year for people age 50 and older. Members save on airlines, auto rentals, cruise vacations, motels and vacation packages. Call 800-424-3410. Internet: www.aarp.org.

Texas boasts more than 1.8 million AARP members. The state office is at 98 San Jacinto Blvd. #750 in Austin. Call 512-480-9797.

Houston has a host of exciting things to see and do, and amenities and special considerations will make your stay more comfortable and rewarding. As in other parts of the country, senior citizens find various establishments here offering discounts on tickets, ranging from airlines to attractions.

Few phenomena have proved flightier than airline fares. All the major airlines offer coupon booklets for people age 62 and older that provide considerable savings on air travel. But investigate prices before using coupons; you might find cheaper fares through advertised sales or via online travel providers. You can find airline contact information in the TRANSPORTATION chapter.

You also should inquire about savings when making lodging arrangements; virtually every major hotel chain offers senior discounts.

AMTRAK provides discounted fares for its senior rail passengers. Call 800-872-7245 for details. Internet: www.amtrak.com.

Greyhound, which has a terminal here, offers senior discounts on its bus fares. Call 800-229-9424. Internet: www.greyhound.com.

Metropolitan Transit Authority public bus system has two discount programs for seniors. Persons age 62 and older can ride any route for at least 50 percent off the regular cash fare by showing a Metro ID card. The card costs $2 and can be purchased at any Metro RideStore. (RideStore locations can be found in TRANSPORTATION chapter.)

The other program is available for people age 70 and older. The 70+ Lifetime Pass allows seniors to ride all Metro fixed routes free of charge. Visit a Metro Ridestore to apply for the pass, which can be renewed annually by mail.

Call Metro at 713-635-4000. Internet: www.ridemetro.org.

Many **movie theaters** and performing arts groups offer discounts with proof of senior citizenship. Check with them for individual policies. You will find their numbers in the PERFORMING ARTS chapter.

Newcomer residents with special needs will find an abundance of agencies offering varied assistance programs, ranging from nutrition to recreation.

One such agency is **Sheltering Arms,** which provides telephone assurance, foster home programs, hot meals and transportation for more than 200,000 area senior citizens. Call 713-956-1888.

Texas Department of Human Resources offers home- and community-based services to help the aged remain in their own homes, as an alternative to nursing homes and hospitals. Another important aspect of its program is protective services for the physically and mentally disadvantaged. Call 713-692-3236. A hotline offers assistance for elderly victims of abuse or neglect. Call 800-252-5400.

Another source is the **Houston-Harris County Council** on Aging, 713-794-9001.

For those unable to get around there is a **"Meals-on-Wheels"** service by Interfaith Ministries of Greater Houston, 713-522-3955.

If you need job assistance, call **Goodwill Industries,** 713-692-6221.

The **American Red Cross** provides transportation to and from clinics and hospitals for those with no other means. Call 713-526-8300.

Of course, **United Way** is the clearinghouse for numerous agencies and information on various types of assistance. Call 713-957-4357.

HANDICAPPED PERSONS

With today's advances in medical technology, innovative space-age aids, the multiplicity of self-help programs, the will to see the world and new laws on their side, the handicapped are finding a special welcome mat in most major cities in the country.

In Houston, not only the traveler, but also the newcomer will find an open-door attitude and a desire among the citizenry to accommodate the disabled in every way possible.

Handicapped persons arriving at **Bush Intercontinental Airport** will experience little difficulty getting around. This facility has international signage clearly marking wheelchair accessibility.

Many of the **Metropolitan Transit Authority's** fixed routes are designed to accommodate disabled riders. In addition to lift-equipped buses, the routes feature well-marked stops with flat concrete surfaces to facilitate boarding. These stops are designed not only for people in wheelchairs, but also to help those with sight and hearing impairments, the mentally ill and those who require crutches, canes or walkers. Bus operators on these routes are trained to provide assistance. Call 713-739-4018 for assistance in learning to use these buses.

In addition, Metrolift is available to persons unable to board, ride or disembark from a regular lift-equipped bus or for those who require transportation on a route that is not serviced by accessible buses. This curb-to-curb service is by reservation only. A Metrolift ID card is required. Call 713-225-0119 for details.

Houston has many attractions that, from the outset, were designed with the handicapped in mind.

The **Space Center Houston,** and **Six Flags AstroWorld** earn excellent marks for their efforts in planning and allowing for the disabled to fully enjoy their visit. Most new hotels, restaurants and shopping malls provide wheelchair accessibility and are increasingly barrier-free.

The City of Houston continues restructuring curbs at downtown intersections and other projects to assure that parks, streets and public buildings are wheelchair accessible and reasonably barrier-free.

Those who enjoy cultural performances will discover excellent conditions in venues such as **Jones Hall, Compaq Center, Wortham Theater Center** and others.

One could spend a day or more at **Hermann Park** with its museums, zoo, planetarium, garden center and other attractions and encounter few difficulties getting around.

Handicapped newcomers to Houston will find bountiful social, recreational and educational programs available. A good central source for information and referrals is **United Way,** 713-957-4357. The following are just a few other agencies offering a broad range of assistance:

Houston Center for Independent Living, 713-974-4621. Among its many key services is a TTY communications system enabling the deaf to call in on their teletype machine for a voice exchange. Job referrals, information on accessibility to buildings and care counseling are just a few of their programs.

Lighthouse of Houston, 713-527-9561. This agency offers the blind vocational evaluation and training, instruction in the use of canes and how to travel independently.

Texas Rehabilitation Commission, 713-334-1613. With offices all over town, this group works with the physically and mentally disabled who want to enter the Houston workforce.

Texas Department of Human Resources, Call 713-692-3236. This agency provides home- and community-based services, helping the disabled to remain in their own homes as an alternative to institutional care. Alternative living plans include clusters of apartments modified for the handicapped.

Center for the Retarded, 713-525-8400. Apart from providing high-rise living for qualified clients, this agency assists with job counseling and training. It also runs an organic farm and residential center near the town of San Felipe.

CHILDREN

Houston holds special promise of fascinating times for the young. The city's many playgrounds, pools, water parks, putt-putt golf courses, skating rinks and nearby beaches all hold real appeal for children of all ages.

Among attractions that have the most kid appeal:

At **Hermann Park,** the **Houston Zoo** and the **Museum of Natural Science** are educational and fun. Just a few blocks away is the **Children's Museum,** a playful paradise for younger kids.

A day or two could be spent exploring **Six Flags AstroWorld and Waterworld.** And **Space Center Houston,** with its interactive exhibits, certainly is entertaining.

Get away to Galveston for some fun in the sun. The beaches are dandy; **Moody Gardens** offers enough attractions and recreational options to fill a weekend. (See GALVESTON chapter for details.) Or get back to nature at the **Houston Arboretum** or **Armand Bayou Nature Preserve.**

For ideas on kid-friendly events and outings, check Thursday's Preview section of the Houston Chronicle.

STUDENTS

With more than 30 colleges and universities in the area, it follows that there are numerous youth-oriented outlets for students from teens to those in their 20s.

Many of the discounts and deals offered to senior citizens are available to students as well, so bear this in mind and inquire wherever you go. Invariably, valid student identification is required and must be presented in order to get a student discount.

Lodging

Houston has just one hostel. The **Houston International Hostel** is at 5302 Crawford (D3) in the Museum District, not far from Hermann Park and Rice University. It is a member of **American Youth Hostels.** Call 713-523-1009.

YMCA (K9), 1600 Louisiana; 713-758-9250. A limited number of rooms reasonably priced. Benefits include access to the physical fitness facilities downtown.

Other budget-priced lodging can be found at chains such as **Days Inn, Motel 6, Super 8** and **Rodeway Inn.** See LODGING chapter for details.

Metro Colleges and Universities

Each campus has a student center and a director of activities, and most publish calendars and newspapers and sometimes advertise on radio and in newspapers to promote student programs of general interest.

Student travelers in Houston often are welcome to participate in a wide variety of such events. The following is a select list of area campuses. Contact the school for a calendar of student events and activities.

Houston Baptist University (E1), 7502 Fondren Rd.; 713-774-7661. This is a small liberal arts institution on Houston's southwest side. The university welcomes out-of-town students to some planned activities.

Rice University (D2-3), 6100 South Main; 713-527-8101. Opened in 1912 as Rice Institute, this university has a history of quality education with emphasis on science, engineering, and the humanities. Its Mediterranean-style architecture and tree-shaded campus make this an interesting stop whether or not one participates in student events.

San Jacinto College Central Campus (E6), 8060 Spencer Highway, 281-476-1501; **North Campus** (B6), 5800 Uvalde, 281-458-4050; and **South Campus** (F5), 13735 Beamer, 281-484-1900. This is a two-year community college with full academic, vocational and technical programs.

Texas Southern University (D3), 3100 Cleburne; 713-527-7011. This is Texas' largest predominantly black and minority-oriented campus with a wide range of cultural, recreational and entertainment activities.

University of Houston—Central Campus (D4), 4800 Calhoun Blvd.; 713-749-1011. **University of Houston—Clear Lake** (F6), 2700 Bay Area Blvd.; 281-488-7170. **University of Houston—Downtown** (G10), One Main Street; 713-221-8000. This is the city's largest academic institution, with a total enrollment of more than 33,000. Begun as a junior college in

1927, the University of Houston campuses offer a large program of student activities of every description, including NCAA Division I athletics.

University of St. Thomas (D3), 3800 Montrose Blvd.; 713-522-7911. This is Texas' largest Catholic institution and is convenient to downtown. Among its many amenities are mini-concerts at noon, major drama events and programs featuring guest artists.

Popular Student Hangouts

The variety of Houston's student hangouts is incredible. Entertainment at these gathering spots ranges from punk to classical and from country to reggae. And clubs often use food and drink specials, dance lessons and other gimmicks to draw youthful clientele.

Many of these clubs are on the Richmond Strip (D1), which covers an area along Richmond roughly from the 610 Loop to Hillcroft. Some of the traditional watering holes with live entertainment include **Sam's Place,** 5710 Richmond; **Billy Blues Barbecue,** 6025 Richmond; and **City Street,** 5078 Richmond, which features five clubs in one.

While the party-hardy crowd in T-shirts and shorts adore the Richmond Strip, more sophisticated (read that better dressed and with more cash) collegians are flocking to the blossoming downtown club scene. Among the currently hip clubs: **Spy,** 112 Travis; **Swank Lounge,** 910 Prairie; **Mercury Room,** 1008 Prairie; **Lava Lounge,** 112 Milam; **State Bar,** 909 Texas; **Tonic,** 310 Main; and **Dean's,** 316 Main.

Two clubs that regularly feature alternative music and bands that draw large—and mostly male—youths are **Fitzgerald's** (C3), 2706 White Oak; and **Numbers** (F3), 300 Westheimer.

Also see DINING and NIGHTLIFE chapters.

NEW RESIDENTS

AN INTRODUCTION TO HOUSTON LIVING

Much has already been written for the newcomer, but it is our aim to offer additional information and as many referrals as possible so that you may at least have a feeling of familiarity with the terrain and climate.

Geographical profile

Everyone has at least heard of Houston, but many don't know what to expect in the lay of the land.

The city is situated at about 29 degrees latitude—or on a line approximately equal with Cairo, Daytona Beach and New Delhi—and 95 degrees longitude. Houston sprawls across flat coastal prairie and marshes, with many various-sized streams (bayous) and creeks. Much of the northern half of the city is wooded, and the metro area encompasses several lakes, including Lake Houston, Lake Conroe and Clear Lake. The southern half is largely built over saltgrass prairies and marshlands with wooded areas along waterways in the southeastern extremes.

The altitude in Houston ranges from near sea level to 55 feet. This means certain areas are subject to flooding and lie in what is known as the "100-Year Flood Plain."

Houston's year-round temperature averages 68.6 degrees F. The spring and fall are delightful but brief; summers are prolonged with mild to hot weather prevailing from March to November. During much of this time, the humidity presents a problem for many new residents and even some of the old-timers. The solution is air conditioning, and Houstonians burn lots of money on it to stay comfortable.

Thanks to abundant rainfall, Houston is green nearly all year and neighboring farmlands yield bountiful crops of rice, soybeans, grains, cotton and some vegetables. Fruit and flowering trees that do well here include pecan, fig, pear, peach, crepe myrtle, mimosa, Japanese yew, magnolia, Chinese tallow, rain trees and tapioca. Certain hardy species of palm also thrive in this semi-tropical climate. Houston's prevailing soil is thick black clay called "gumbo," although in sections close to the coast it becomes more sandy. Because of contractions and expansions in the soil, there are scattered ground faults that can cause foundation problems. Prospective buyers need to be aware of such problems, or the potential for such problems, when considering a home site.

People Profile

Southern and Southwestern accents still prevail here, but they are joined more and more by the distinct accents of Midwesterners and Easterners who seem to make up the majority of Houston's newcomers. The burgeoning international community, too, adds to this medley of accents, at times creating a real polyglot in malls, markets and other high-traffic places.

Despite—or perhaps because of—the urban growth, Houstonians continue to cling to the traditional Southwestern love for the open spaces. Because the city regularly exercises its legal right to annex unincorporated communities, Houston continues to offer plenty of room for homeowners to maintain yards and gardens. Indeed, you will find few neighborhoods without well-manicured lawns and some degree of landscaping.

The more affluent districts are exemplary of this management of surroundings. In areas such as River Oaks, property restrictions aim specifically at preserving nature and the aesthetic appeal of the neighborhood. The beautiful estates of River Oaks, Memorial and much of the West End lend credence to the passion Houstonians have for the outdoors.

The temperate climate leads many people here to be extremely outdoor conscious. When they are not in their gardens and on their patios, they are likely involved in various other forms of recreational activity. This goes particularly for the young who account for a large portion of the populace.

In Houston, you'll find unprecedented growth and variety among ethnic communities. The racial mix here is 54 percent white, 23 percent Hispanic, 19 percent black and 4 percent Asian or other races. Houston has the nation's sixth-largest Hispanic population, and more than 65 primary languages are spoken in Houston.

Houston Insight

This town is crazy about sports, particularly baseball, basketball and football, but almost any sporting event will draw a crowd. You will find few cities where the rodeo following is as avid as it is here. During the annual Houston Livestock Show & Rodeo, Houstonians nearly go overboard going Texan. And that has nothing to do with what's "in" or with trends in fashion, for just under that skin-deep layer of sophistication simmers a boisterous frontier spirit.

A flair for casual living is sometimes disconcerting to new residents until, they too, finally relinquish their more serious ways, relaxing to let go and enjoy the Houston style. Not peculiar to Houston, but certainly a major social component, is the roundup of patio and pool parties, usually accompanied by outdoor barbecues. Of course, boating, fishing, picnicking and other forms of outdoor recreation are popular weekend pastimes during warmer months and days. In the winter, most folks turn inward to the theater and other cultural activities. The social calendar of Houston's well-to-do is filled with teas, luncheons and garden parties, but in recent years many of these gatherings have taken on a politically correct philanthropic tone.

In all of Texas, folks think nothing of driving long distances, and our sense of mileage and how long it takes to get from point A to point B can be misleading, particularly if you are from the East, where cities are more compact and states are considerably smaller. Immediately, newcomers might be jarred by Houston's addiction to the automobile. The locals click off about 22.3 billion miles a year commuting, and this is usually with only one or two people in a vehicle. You rarely see anyone walking, and it has been said Houstonians are born with wheels instead of legs; the farther from the center of town you go, the more folks you see riding bumper-to-bumper up and down neighborhood arteries. The law of the West seems to prevail in spite of Texas highway signs that remind us to "Drive Friendly." The Southwesterner's usual rugged individualism prompts far too many to make up their own set of rules, and some drivers take to freeway traffic as if they were running a herd of cattle.

Perhaps the most amazing insight for newcomers is that Houston has somehow survived without zoning laws. This is one of the last outposts of "laissez faire," and with a lingering pioneer spirit, just about anything goes, except putting up a bar too close to a church or school. Historically, Houston has shied from, indeed fought, high-handed government interference, both in civic and private business affairs.

Social changes might erode some of this individualism. But new folks like you might be just the thing to keep it alive. Because a big part of Houston style means accepting and appreciating you for being you, welcome!

HOUSTON FACTS

Motor Vehicles

Insurance

Texas law requires drivers to carry "Minimum Liability" insurance, and you must have a **Texas Automobile Insurance Identification Card** in your possession at all times while driving. These cards are issued at the time of purchase of insurance. Such coverage is called 15-30-15 or $15,000 each person bodily injury, $30,000 each accident, and $15,000 on property damage liability. An insurance agent can answer questions about coverage and rates.

Registration and Vehicle Inspection

New residents are required to register their vehicles with the state within 30 days of establishing residency. Before you can obtain registration tags for your automobile you must first acquire a valid **Inspection Sticker.** The Texas Department of Public Safety requires all vehicles to pass inspection once a year through a licensed station. On approval you will be issued a VI-30-A form which you must take, together with car papers from your home state, to the **Harris County Tax Assessor and Collector.** Call 713-224-1919 to determine the office most convenient to you.

You also must have a valid Texas driver's license, a current odometer reading, proof of liability insurance, a sales or tax-use affidavit, and, if importing the vehicle from outside the United States, proper customs documentation before you can get Texas license plates.

Fees for registration and certificate of title must be paid in cash.

When registering your vehicle you are issued front and rear tags. Your new title will be sent in 60 to 90 days. The license fee depends on the weight of your vehicle. In addition, there may also be a new resident fee, and transfer and filing fees.

Reporting of Accidents

In an accident involving another vehicle, if you can move your vehicle, pull over to an emergency lane and exchange insurance identification and other prescribed information.

You have 24 hours to report an accident to the Houston Police Department or to the law enforcement agency in whose jurisdiction the mishap occurs.

If there is bodily injury, remain in place and contact the emergency office of the Houston Police Department, 911 or 713-222-3131; or dial the operator for emergency assistance.

If it appears the other party is intoxicated or abusing drugs or can show no valid driver's license, you must report the incident immediately.

Should you require emergency ambulance service, call the **Houston Fire Department** paramedics division at **911** or **713-222-7643**; or dial the operator for assistance.

Driver's Licenses

Out-of-state drivers have 30 days after establishing residency in which to obtain a Texas driver's license. The basic license to operate a motor vehicle is valid for four years. There are Texas Department of Public Safety licensing offices for testing throughout the city. For license information call 713-681-6187.

Driving Safety Tips

Texas law requires that drivers and front-seat passengers wear seat belts. Infant seats also are required. Just as a matter of safety, not law, children should ride in the back seat and use seat belts.

Keep doors and windows locked at all times. Carjackings are not common, but they do occur. Before exiting your car, look around. Avoid parking in unlighted areas.

When leaving malls and offices, security officers often are available as escorts to parking areas. Just ask.

And we should offer a caution about road rage. With more than 2 million cars maneuvering in Harris County alone, congestion and frustration are inevitable. Unfortunately, road rage—irrational acts of temper and violence on our highways—seems to be a growing problem. It is advisable not to tailgate and use your horn sparingly. Avoid aggressive drivers. If you are being followed or harassed on the roadway, drive to a well-lighted, well-trafficked place such as a gas station or convenience store and call the police.

Banking

Houston is a leading banking center in the Southwest. It is home to more than 570 banks, more than 100 credit unions and no fewer than 700 mortgage banking businesses.

Every conceivable financial service is rendered, catering to all domestic and foreign needs. For answers to specific banking questions go to the bank most convenient to you or call the **Texas Bank Association** in Austin; 512-472-8388.

Here are some of the largest banks and savings and loans:
Bank of America: 713-659-1111; www.bankofamerica.com.
Bank One: 713-659-1111; www.bankone.com.
Bank United: 713-543-2000; www.bankunited.com.
Chase Bank of Texas: 800-235-8522; www.chase.com/tx.
Coastal Bank: 713-435-5500; www.coastalbanc.com.
Comerica Bank: 800-525-8361; www.comerica.com.
Compass Bank: 713-266-7277; www.compassbank.com.
Frost National Bank: 713-652-7600; www.frostbank.com.
Guaranty Federal Bank: 713-658-0885; www.gfbank.com.
Klein Bank: 281-438-4636; www.kleinbank.com.
Prime Bank: 713-209-6000; www.primebanktexas.com.
Washington Mutual: 800-788-7000; www.washingtonmutual.com.
Wells Fargo: 800-869-3557; www.wellsfargo.com.

Chambers of Commerce

Please see MATTERS OF FACT chapter.

Churches, Synagogues, and Temples

Practically every religious denomination is represented in Houston with more than 1,000 churches, synagogues, temples, mosques, and ecumenical chapels. Among the major denominational and ecumenical organizations here are:

Assemblies of God South Texas District Council; 713-455-1221.

Beth Yeshurun (conservative); 713-666-1881.

Church of Jesus Christ of Latter Day Saints—Texas Houston Mission; 281-440-6770.

Eastern Orthodox Church; 713-526-5377.

Episcopal Diocese of Texas; 713-520-6444.

Islamic Society of Greater Houston; 713-524-6615.

Lutheran Council—Houston Area; 713-864-6987.

Methodist Board of Missions of Texas; 713-521-9383.

Presbytery of the New Covenant; 713-524-6632.

Roman Catholic Diocese of Galveston-Houston; 713-659-5461.

Rothko Chapel (ecumenical); 713-524-9839.

Sri Meenakshi Temple (Hindu); 281-489-0358.

St. Basil's Byzantine Rite Center (Ukrainian); 713-697-7109.

Temple Emanu El (Reformed); 713-529-5771.

Texas Baptist Convention; 713-674-9091.

Theosophical Society—Non-Denominational; 713-861-8526.

Union Baptist Association—SBC; 713-957-2000.

United Orthodox Synagogues; 713-723-3850.

Clubs and Associations

Once you've settled down in Houston and want to become involved in any community activity, whether social, educational, recreational, or civic, you might not know where to begin the search. It helps to know your neighbors and your community leaders who can steer you in the right direction with area civic organizations.

There are various art groups in the city such as the **Art League of Houston,** 713-523-9530, and the **Arts Council of Houston,** 713-527-9330.

The **Young Men's Christian Association** (YMCA, 713-659-8501), the **Young Women's Christian Association** (YWCA, 713-868-9922) and their branches are always great places to become involved in dance groups, exercise, sports and other special programs, as is the **Jewish Community Center,** 713-729-3200.

The **Houston Zoo** has opportunities for volunteers. You also may patronize museum organizations or other cultural groups such as the symphony, opera, ballet or the **Houston Friends of Music** (713-285-5400) Or maybe you dig garden clubs such as **River Oaks Garden Club Forum of Civics,** 713-523-2483, and the **Houston Garden Center,** 713-529-5371.

Other fine organizations that would welcome your participation include **Big Brothers/Big Sisters** of Houston, 713-271-5683; **Girl Scouts of America,** 713-292-0300; **Boy Scouts of America,** 713-659-8111; and **Junior Achievement,** 713-682-4500.

Education

Schools, Primary and Secondary

Education is free in Texas for children from kindergarten through the twelfth grade. Most systems have these levels of education: elementary (grades K, 1-6), middle school (grades 6-9), and high school (grades 9/10-12).

Instruction is regulated by state law, which also restricts class sizes. Core curriculum includes classes in reading, language arts, mathematics, science and social studies. Fine arts, physical education, foreign language and technical skills also can be part of the curriculum.

All students must pass several standard aptitude tests such as the Texas Assessment of Academic Skills (TAAS). The Texas Education Agency rates school districts. For information on a particular school system, contact TEA at 512-463-9734 or access www.tea.state.tx.us.

There are 56 school districts partly or entirely within Harris County, with the **Houston Independent School District** accounting for some 212,000 students, the seventh-largest district in the United States with 280 schools.

The HISD has the most extensive magnet school program of any school district in the area. While offering the core curriculum, magnet schools provide special programs that emphasize topics such as math and science or fine arts. Among the magnet programs are the **School for the Performing and Visual Arts,** the **High School for Health Professions,** and the **High School for Law Enforcement and Criminal Justice.**

HISD also provides Vanguard programs for the gifted and remedial classes for the handicapped.

School programs are funded by the state of Texas and, in Houston, by school taxes assessed on property.

Newcomer students must have a birth certificate or the equivalent, doctor's certification of immunization, and a final report card from the last school attended.

For detailed information on **HISD** call 713-892-6390.

Houston boasts more than 150 private schools, one-fourth of which are parochial. Among the major denominational schools are those run by the **Galveston-Houston Catholic Diocese,** 713-659-5461; the **Episcopal Diocese of Texas,** 713-520-6444; and **Lutheran Education Association, 281-464-6155.**

Other large private schools include **Annunciation Orthodox,** 713-620-3611; **Awty International,** 713-686-4850; **Duchesne Academy,** 713-468-8211; **Honor Roll School;** 281-265-7888; **Montessori School of Downtown,** 713-520-6801; **St. Francis Episcopal,** 713-782-0481; **St. Thomas Episcopal,** 713-666-3111; **Second Baptist,** 713-365-2310; and **Village School,** 281-496-7900.

Schools for the deaf and handicapped are **Center for Hearing and Speach,** 713-523-3633; **St. Dominic's Deaf Center,** 713-741-8704; and **Center for the Retarded,** 713-525-8400.

For information on child care contact the **Child Care Council of Greater Houston,** 713-266-6045.

For information on the name and number of the school district that serves your preferred area of relocation, call the closest community chamber of commerce. Then be sure to investigate the school program thoroughly; it can be a major factor in determining where you buy or rent.

Colleges and Universities

Houston is a major center for higher education with 40 colleges and universities in Harris County. Among them:

Rice University is the city's oldest university (founded in 1891) and one of the top private institutions of higher learning in the country. Call 713-527-8101; access www.rice.edu.

The **University of Houston** system is made up of five campuses serving more than 33,000 students. The main campus offers degrees in nearly 300 programs. Call 713-749-1011; access www.uhsa.uh.edu. Other campuses are UH-Downtown, 713-221-8000; UH-Clear Lake, 281-488-7170; UH-Fort Bend, 281-275-3300; and UH-Victoria, 361-570-4848.

Texas Southern University was founded in 1949 to serve the educational needs of black students. Call 713-313-7011; access www.tsu.edu.

University of St. Thomas is a Catholic liberal arts college founded in 1947. Call 713-522-7911; access www.stthom.edu.

Houston Baptist University is on a 100-acre campus in southwest Houston. Call 713-774-7661; www.hbu.edu.

Junior colleges are: **Houston Community College System** (five campuses), 713-718-6000; **Lee College in Baytown**, 281-427-5611; **San Jacinto College** (three campuses), 281-476-1501, www.sjcd.cc.tx.us; and **North Harris-Montgomery County College District**, 281-260-3500.

Houston is famous for a number of major medical schools, most of which are within the vast Texas Medical Center complex. While practically every institution in the center maintains some form of education and training program, the leading colleges and universities are **Baylor College of Medicine, Prairie View A & M School of Nursing, Texas Heart Institute, Texas Institute for Rehabilitation and Research, Texas Research Institute of Mental Sciences, Texas Woman's University, University of Houston College of Pharmacy, University of Texas Health Science Center,** and the **University of Texas System Cancer Center.**

Still other medical schools are on the periphery of the center.

In addition there are several theological schools here such as **Gulf Coast Bible College, St. Mary's Seminary, Southern Bible College,** and **Texas Bible College.**

Extracurricular Educational Programs

At some point in life many would like a refresher course or an opportunity to learn something entirely new, say, art, a foreign language, photography, word processing, or real estate. Various colleges and universities provide such opportunities, as do community centers.

These are available during the fall, spring, and summer for nominal fees. For information call the school of your choice.

In addition, **Leisure Learning** offers more than 400 short courses ranging from arts and crafts, computer training and personal development. The quality of these courses varies wildly, but many are terrific. Call 713-529-4414; access www.llu.com.

Government

City Government

The City of Houston is governed by a mayor and 14 City Council members who, together with a city controller, are elected for two-year terms. Nine of the members represent their own districts; five are council members at-large.

The public is invited to appear before Council with problems, complaints, or other matters, every Wednesday in **Council Chambers at City Hall** (J9), 901 Bagby, starting at 9 am. Each person is allowed from one to three minutes to state a case. You may reserve time by calling 713-247-1840 (City Secretary's Office).

Houston government is officially independent of political party alignment, and city employees have a choice of belonging to a municipal union or not. The police and firemen have stronger union links. But they may not strike.

Labor unions in general are comparatively small here, primarily because Texas still is a "Right to Work State."

County Government

Harris County is governed by a county judge and four commissioners elected by the citizenry every four years. They are all members of the County Commissioners Court.

Congressional Districts

Metropolitan Houston accounts for the following six Congressional districts: Seventh, Eighth, Eighteenth, Twenty-second, Twenty-fifth and Twenty-ninth.

U.S. Senators from Texas

Sen. Phil Gramm, Republican, has an office in Houston at 712 Main, 713-229-2766; and in Washington, 202-224-2934. Internet: www.senate.gov/~gramm.

Sen. Kay Bailey Hutchison, Republican, has an office in Houston at 1919 Smith, 713-653-3456; and in Washington, 202-224-5922. Internet: www.senate.gov/~hutchison.

Both of the Houston offices are downtown.

Health Care

Houston is known the world over for its excellence in health care, medical research and specialization in certain surgical techniques. The

Greater Houston area is served by more than 80 hospitals and medical centers. In addition, there are numerous convalescent homes and children's care institutions.

Several Houston pilot programs have spread throughout the nation. One is the Houston Fire Department paramedic teams with specially built and equipped ambulances. Another is Hermann Hospital's "Life Flight" program, which provides emergency medical transport via helicopters and small jet airplanes.

Among hospitals with 24-hour emergency care are:

Bellaire Medical Center, 713-512-1500.

Texas Children's Hospital, 713-770-5454.

Northside General Hospital, 713-697-7777.

Hermann Hospital, 713-704-4060.

Ben Taub General, 713-793-2000.

Lyndon B. Johnson General, 713-636-5000.

Among hospitals and clinics with full services also are many with established specialties, such as cancer treatment, plastic surgery, treatment of psychiatric disorders, drug and alcohol abuse, children's diseases and rehabilitation.

The following is a select list of hospitals by locale:

Northwest—Vencor Hospital NW, 281-897-8114.

Southeast—Memorial Hospital SE, 281-929-6100; Clear Lake Regional Medical Center, 281-332-2511.

Southwest—Bellaire Medical Center, 713-512-1200; Memorial Hospital SW, 713-776-5000; Twelve Oaks Hospital, 713-623-2500; and Methodist Health Center-Sugar Land, 281-274-7000.

South and Central—Park Plaza Hospital, 713-527-5000; St. Joseph's Hospital, 713-757-1000; Methodist Hospital, 713-790-3311; St. Luke's, 713-791-1000; Hermann, 713-704-4000; and Texas Children's Hospital, 713-770-1000.

FM 1960—Kingwood Medical Center, 281-359-7500; Houston Northwest Medical Center, 281-440-1000.

Information, emergency and referral organizations throughout Houston cover various areas of specialization:

Cancer Information Service, 800-422-6237.

Crisis Hotline, 713-228-1505.

Harris County Hospital District, 713-715-2800.

Harris County Medical Society (doctor referrals), 713-942-7050.

Houston Dental Society, 713-961-4337.

Houston Health Clinics, 713-794-9320.

Poison Control Center, 800-764-7661.

Texas Nurses Association, 713-523-3619.

Health Clubs & Spas

Houstonians enjoy keeping fit. But when temperatures soar, it is sometimes hard to exercise outdoors. That might explain why the city boasts more than 175 health clubs and fitness centers. The city also has seen a boom in day spas, which provide services such as massage, exfoliation and facials.

Some of the larger fitness clubs offer day passes or have reciprocal privileges if you have a membership in another city. For nearest locations, contact:

Bally Total Fitness, 800-695-8111, www.ballyfitness.com;
Q The Sport Club, 800-381-5555, www.qclubs.com;
24 Hour Fitness, 800-204-2400, www.24hourfitness.com.

Other recommended fitness centers:
Fitness Exchange, 4040 Milam; 713-524-9932.
Memorial Athletic Club, 14690 Memorial; 281-497-7570; www.fitmac.com.

Recommended day spas:
Etienne's, 4100 Westheimer; 713-850-8441.
The Greenhouse, 2535 Kirby; 713-529-2444.
Nature's Way, 5000 Westheimer; 713-629-9995.
Tova, 1409 S. Post Oak; 713-439-1414.
Urban Retreat, 2329 San Felipe; 713-523-2300.

Jury Duty

Juries are called on weekdays for civil and criminal cases. The selection is made from the driver's license list.

Persons 65 or older are, if they wish, exempt from serving jury duty. Also a parent with a child under 10, who has no way of leaving the child at home with proper supervision, is exempted. Other possible exemptions include those attending school (at any level), and the infirm. Persons may call in and request an "excuse slip" and such requests are handled individually. It is illegal to not respond to a jury summons. Information: 713-755-6395.

Legal Services

For reference, the **Harris County Bar Association** is available to mediate minor legal disputes; 713-759-1133.

The **Houston Lawyer Referral Service** can assist with the selection of an attorney; 713-237-9429.

Libraries

The administrative offices for the city library system are downtown at the **Central Public Library,** 500 McKinney; 713-247-2222. There are 36 branch libraries. Services include books by mail and bookmobiles. The Central Library has ongoing programs of educational and cultural interest to the community; call for a schedule of events.

In addition **Harris County** maintains 25 libraries with administrative offices at 8080 El Rio; 713-749-9000.

Houston also has three specialized libraries: M.D. Anderson Patient and Family Library, 1515 Holcombe, 713-792-2229; Harris County Law Library, 1019 Congress, 713-755-5183; and Texas Medical Center Library, 1133 M.D. Anderson Blvd., 713-795-4200.

Local Laws

Texas, like every state, has laws special unto itself.

Liquor Laws

Certain establishments have beer-, wine- and champagne-only permits; others are licensed to sell mixed drinks. Most bars operate with full services, including the sale of mixed drinks, and remain open until the absolute curfew, which is 2 am daily. No business may begin selling alcoholic beverages on Sundays until after noon. Those places without late-hour permits must stop serving at 1 am on weekends and by midnight weekdays. Bars with beer-, wine-, and champagne-only permits usually sell "set ups," and customers may bring hard liquor in their own bottle, but it must be concealed in a "brown bag" and poured personally.

Certain areas in and around the city are "dry" by choice and no alcoholic beverages are sold whatsoever.

Package stores are open from 10 am to 9 pm daily, except on Sundays and certain holidays such as Christmas. When Christmas and New Year's days fall on Sunday, then liquor stores must remain closed for the following Monday.

The minimum legal age to order, buy, possess, or consume any alcoholic beverage in Texas is 21.

Newspapers and Publications

Houston has one major daily newspaper plus numerous weekly and monthly publications serving various neighborhoods, the city and the metro region plus special interest groups.

The major local newspaper is the **Houston Chronicle** (I10), 801 Texas Ave.; 713-220-7171, with weekday, Saturday and Sunday editions.

The leading weekly is the tabloid **Houston Business Journal;** 713-688-8811. Another popular weekly tabloid is **Houston Press;** 713-624-1400. This alternative newspaper has strong entertainment coverage.

The *Greensheet* is Houston's most widely circulated free "want ads" paper; 713-655-3300.

There are two black-oriented newspapers: The *Forward Times*, 713-526-4727, and the **Informer,** 713-218-7400.

Two leading Spanish-language publications are **El Dia,** 713-772-8900, and **La Voz,** 713-644-7449.

Serving Houston's Asian community are the **Chinese Daily News,** 713-472-4001, and the **Korean Journal,** 713-467-4266.

The Greater Houston Partnership compiles a **Houston Area Media Guide** to local and neighborhood publications; 713-844-9366.

Pets

The law requires that pets be properly licensed and vaccinated against rabies. Leash laws are in effect in Houston, and if violated the owner is subject to fine.

For information, contact the **Harris County Rabies Control Center,** 281-999-3191, and the **City of Houston** for more specifics on owning pets, 713-238-9600.

The **Society for Prevention of Cruelty to Animals** is at 900 Portway; 713-869-7722.

The **Houston Humane Society** is at 14700 Almeda; 713-433-6421.

Public Services

City

Houston's utilities are supplied by **Reliant Energy HL&P** (electricity), 713-207-777; **Reliant Energy Entex** (gas), 713-659-2111; **City of Houston Public Works and Engineering** (water and sewer), 713-224-2500; **Southwestern Bell Telephone Company,** 800-464-7928; **City of Houston Utility Division** (water service), 713-371-1400; and **City of Houston Solid Waste Management Department** (garbage and trash pick-up), 713-837-9100.

There are private companies serving some outlying areas.

Deposits are required of newcomers with no former record of service, and there is a start-up fee as well. These vary according to each individual case. An advance notice is required to start services.

Free garbage pick-up is twice weekly in Houston. For information on recycling or disposal of hazardous material, call 713-837-9130.

Most garbage collections are curbside, or, in some neighborhoods, in alleys. New residents should call to find out which are the pick-up days for their area. Residents outside the city of Houston usually get water and sewer services by contract with independent districts.

Taxes

City/State

Many newcomers are happy to learn Texas has no state, county, or city income tax. Sales taxes are 8.25 percent, from which most food and prescription drugs are exempt. One percent of that sales tax goes to the Metropolitan Transit Authority. Of the remaining monies, 6.25 percent goes to the state and 1 percent to the city.

The city tax rate on land and real estate is 67 cents per $100 value. The city also collects taxes for the Houston Independent School District and that rate is 47 cents per $100. For further information call the **City Tax Department** at 713-892-7700.

County

At this writing, the county property tax rate on land and real estate is 64.17 cents per $100, with the owner paying 100% of assessed valuation. For further information call the **Tax Assessor and Collector's office**; 713-224-1919.

Legally declared homesteads qualify for exemptions of about 20 percent of assessed valuation.

TV and Radio

Please see MATTERS OF FACT chapter.

Volunteering

If you have a special gift and a sense of service, opportunities to serve abound in Houston.

You may consider the following suggested areas in which to volunteer your services:

Big Brothers and Big Sisters of Greater Houston; 713-271-5683.
Harris County Heritage Society Preservation Alliance; 713-655-1912.
Greater Houston Chapter of the American Red Cross; 713-526-8300.
United Way of the Texas Gulf Coast; 713-685-2300.

With Houston's large medical center complex, hospitals are always in need of various volunteer services. If you have a special gift in foreign languages, numerous patients from around the world come to Houston for treatment and you might consider translation/interpretation services.

Consider being an usher in one of the city's theaters or training to become a docent or guide in a museum, visitor attraction, or nature center.

If you are sincerely interested in volunteering, it won't be long before you find your niche.

Voting

Citizens 18 years and older may apply for a voter's registration card. Voting rights become effective 30 days after receipt of the application by the county clerk's office. Once a valid card is received, it remains permanent, but a change of domicile must be reported; a new certificate is then issued. A new certificate is automatically issued every two years if the voter does not become disqualified. Voters are disqualified when they move and leave no forwarding address.

You can get a voter registration application at public libraries, post offices and Department of Public Safety locations. For information, contact the **Secretary of State's Voter Registration Hot line** at 800-252-8683.

The **League of Women Voters** also is most helpful, producing a voter's guide and other information prior to elections; 713-784-2923.

HOUSTON REAL ESTATE
An Overview

There are more than 500 subdivisions with building activity in Houston, the majority being in the outlying areas and in particular the west, southwest and northwest regions extending out some 20-plus miles into other counties in the metro region.

The median home price in 1999 ran $108,349.

Throughout the city and in surrounding metropolitan areas the buyer will find a variety of homes, in style and in size, and the prices range accordingly. Most new homes are a combination of wood and brick, and the majority are on concrete slabs and have central air conditioning and heating. Sizes generally range from 1,200 square feet up.

Information and Referrals

There is a host of civic and private sources with information, leads, consultation services, and referrals, some free and some by fee. But first we would like to mention that many Houston hotels and motor hotels may offer special "relocation rates" for newcomers who wisely take their time to shop around and investigate before making the plunge into buying a home. Contact individual hotels or motels for details.

Other good sources of information on Houston are:

The **Better Business Bureau**; 713-868-9500.

Greater Houston Partnership (chamber of commerce facts and newcomer data); 713-844-3600.

CSC Credit Services; 281-878-1900.

Federal Housing Administration/U.S. Dept. of Housing & Urban Development; 800-569-4297; www.hud.gov.

Greater Houston Builders Association (information on builders); 713-975-6400.

Greater Houston Convention & Visitors Bureau (lodging and other general information on Houston); 713-437-5200.

Harris County Flood Control (information on flood plain); 713-684-4000.

Houston Apartment Association (information on types of apartments available); 713-933-2224.

Houston Association of Realtors (information on realtors); 713-629-1900.

Houston Air Quality Control; 713-640-4200.

Houston Public Library (general information); 713-236-1313.

Texas Department of Human Services (information on licensed care facilities); 713-767-2600.

Texas Attorney General (Consumer Protection Division); 713-223-5886.

United Way (information and referral services); 713-685-2300.

Veterans Affairs Department (benefits and assistance); 800-827-1000; www.hic.net/houston.va.

Buying and Renting

Apart from the desirability in a home and its cost, the new home buyer should make a close study of several variables before entering into a contract to purchase. Important considerations include the proximity of the place of employment; the disposition of the school district, and the availability of college prep programs, higher education, and libraries; the tax structure; the type of insurance required; the existence of deed restrictions; land level and soil conditions; and the availability of shops, churches, schools and public transportation.

With more than 2,300 apartment communities, the renter in Houston will find everything from garage apartments to luxury townhouses. Some older neighborhoods have duplexes and four-plexes with efficiency apartments in back. In addition, in areas such as Montrose and the Heights, where many old houses have been torn down to make way for apartment complexes and townhouses, there are numerous attractive patio dwellings with clubs and recreational facilities.

Most recently, young professionals are flocking to the new deluxe apartment complexes being built near downtown and to luxury loft apartments renovated from downtown buildings and warehouses.

The overall average rent in Houston ranges around $598 per month for a two-bedroom/one bath, good-quality apartment.

Regional and Neighborhood Profiles ———

The following is an analysis for familiarization with certain sections of metropolitan Houston. But this section in no way pretends to fully define the vast environs of Houston with its hundreds of new subdivisions plus older neighborhoods. For a comprehensive understanding of what the city has to offer, read all available newcomer material, the newspapers and magazines oriented toward Houston living, and, of course, confer with your realtor or an independent locator service firm.

In order to understand the layout of Houston, imagine, if you will, one loop circling the city at a radius of approximately six miles from the Central Business District. This is Interstate 610, referred to as "the Loop." For the purpose of locating and referencing, specific points are either "inside the Loop" or "outside the Loop."

Southwest Region—Inside the Loop

This vast region, inside and outside the Loop, encompasses an area from near downtown all the way out west some 20-30 miles into Fort Bend County, and includes many separate villages and incorporated communities. The southwest sector has long been among the most active areas of the city for the development of planned communities and subdivisions, particularly at its southwestern extremity bordering Fort Bend County.

Neartown and **Montrose** are the areas closest in to downtown.

Bordered by I-45 to the north and U.S. 59 to the south, Neartown has only in recent years become a desirable place to live. The new luxury apartments in this area appeal to the young professionals who are rejuvenating Houston's downtown.

In Montrose, there are many older homes dating back some 60 years with an enormous mix of single-family dwellings, townhouses, condos, and two-story brick duplexes, four-plexes, and garage apartments for rent. This area has been under continuous restoration for the past 20-30 years with many young couples and singles moving in to refurbish and expand existing structures. It offers unique urban home sites in neighborhoods interspersed with a potpourri of commercial interests. It is a highly mobile area with many tree-lined streets, and its inhabitants cover a wide range of the social strata.

West of Montrose lies **River Oaks,** Houston's bastion of wealthy citizens, whose mansions rival anything in Beverly Hills. A board of directors maintains stringent deed restrictions governing everything from the height of a hedge to putting up signs. The area is dense with foliage, and the winding streets are lined with huge old oaks and magnolias. It generally parallels the path of Buffalo Bayou. At the outset, River Oaks was carefully planned for the preservation of the natural environment and to protect it against commercial encroachment or other threats to residential planning.

Residents of the neighborhood enjoy elite social and fine recreational outlets as found in the River Oaks Country Club. Relative security is enforced by an auxiliary police force.

Across the Bayou and Memorial Drive is the old **West End.** In the early 1980s, this was a mixed-use neighborhood with warehouses and a smattering of World War II-era bungalows. Snapping up the cheap lots, artists created unique work/living spaces featuring tin roofs and industrial architecture that blended into the neighborhood. At the turn of the century, the West End's proximity to downtown and Memorial Park has made it a most desirable address and has prompted the building of scores of towering townhouses.

Just north of River Oaks and on the eastern edge of the city's largest park, **Memorial,** are several smaller quiet neighborhoods dating from the post-World War II era. Such are **Crestwood** and **Glencove,** with family dwellings nestled in the beautiful park surroundings.

These sections have small shopping outlets nearby, plus the ease of a fast commute into downtown.

Southward across the Southwest Freeway are still other fine old neighborhoods such as **Southampton** and the area known as **Rice University Village** or, more often and more simply, the Village.

Southampton is especially majestic, with massive oaks spreading across quiet streets with esplanades and large estates featuring formal gardens and pools.

The homes in the Village area are somewhat smaller but still offer a mix of lovely two-story dwellings with a variety of architectural styles. They range from modest one-story frame family homes to two-story brick executive-type structures.

The area is especially popular with students and faculty at nearby Rice University and professionals and staff at the Texas Medical Center. The Village has one of Houston's most compelling commercial centers with many unique boutiques, cafés, stores, and galleries.

The city of Houston has grown to envelop a number of smaller, incorporated communities, and two of them fall within the boundaries of this region, both inside and outside the Loop.

Typically, **West University Place** is a quiet, older residential district, well-planned and minus much traffic beyond a couple of key arteries. Most of the homes are one- and two-story handsome frame and brick structures with well-manicured lawns, as are the homes in the adjoining **South Side Place.**

The **City of Bellaire** straddles the Loop, and it, too, is an old residential community with many modest frame homes and some brick. As in other areas, Bellaire is becoming popular with young move-ins who prefer to take a house in need of repairs and remodel according to their own designs. Many others have bought, demolished, and rebuilt just because they like the location. Some have bought multiple adjacent lots to site one house.

South of these communities is a section of one of the loveliest swaths of home sites found in the city, extending as far west as Braeburn Valley.

Brays Bayou winds east and west across the southern half of Houston, and along its entire course stand numerous beautiful home sites, some dating from World War II.

In this region are **Braes Heights** and **Link Wood** with small but gracious homes on lovely grounds. The majority are of brick, and the styles range from California Ranch to Spanish stucco. The banks of the bayou are popular with joggers and bicyclists in the neighborhood, and residents are close to such commercial complexes as Meyerland and Meyer Park.

To the east of these sections across Main Street is the famous Reliant Park/Astrodomain complex, the northern edge of which nearly reaches the Texas Medical Center.

Just north of the Medical Center and Hermann Park is an area known as **The Binz.** Preservationists have been buying the older homes and small apartment complexes of The Binz for restoration and conversion.

Just across Main Street from The Binz is another of the oldest and wealthiest sections of town called **Shadyside.** It was planned about the same time as River Oaks, and some of Houston's most famous families dwell here within the confines of a high brick wall that serves as a buffer against traffic along Main.

Shadyside borders Rice University, and property owners maintain their own private streets with alleys of old oaks.

Southwest Region—Outside the Loop

Toward the south **Willowbend** and **Westbury** both lean heavily to strictly single-level homes of brick and frame combined. A few townhouses are beginning to crop up in the area, but it still is geared to single-family living with scattered shopping centers.

Farther south and southwest of Westbury are several incorporated towns crossing over the Harris County line and extending into Fort Bend County.

Among them are older communities such as **Missouri City** and **Stafford** with many single-family modest frame homes. Farther out, however, some 20-plus miles from the center of town, are beautifully planned communities in the area of **Sugar Land.**

Sugar Creek, for example, is one of the most prestigious area communities outside the Loop. Here the homes are built around the Riverbend Country Club golf course and many face canals running through the district. The average home is two floors with loft and some have as many as 11 principal rooms. The styles range from Tudor to Colonial and most are of brick or stonework, with handsome galleries and patios.

Next to this is **Venetian Estates,** another desirable area with waterfront homes. Some date back 20 years, but there has been considerable newer building activity, too.

This path of immense new subdivisions continues north, following the route of Highway 6, and includes an array of home sites and developments such as **Towne West** just outside the Houston city limits, **Sugar Mill** which is in Sugar Land, **Wilcrest Park,** and **Alief,** most of which enjoy settings with plenty of open space, perhaps even a vegetable farm nearby. Homes in such areas are mostly brick and frame combinations, two-story. Throughout the area are new shopping centers, schools, apartments and townhouses, usually built along commercial strips.

Sharpstown, one of the first planned areas in Houston, covers many thousands of acres, many of them taken up with such commercial developments as malls, hotels and motels, and restaurants. While there are plenty of single-family homes ranging from modest frame/brick to executive, most of this area is made up of apartment complexes, patio homes, and condos.

Near and just west of Sharpstown Center, stores and signs proclaim the influential influx of Asians into the community. Even some street signs are bilingual English-Chinese.

One of the longest streets in Houston is Westheimer Road, which becomes Highway 1093 and extends all the way from Montrose, through The Galleria/Post Oak area, and way out west some 20 or more miles before poking into the rural farm and ranch areas.

Parallel to its course on both sides are pockets of middle-class to upper-middle-class residential areas from just outside the Loop west through **Tanglewilde, Woodlake Forest, Rivercrest, Briargrove Park, Southlake,** and **Ashford West.**

These and many other neighborhoods share numerous commercial centers, with a vast array of shops including The Galleria, restaurants, nightclubs, hotels, and small businesses.

Rivercrest offers valuable wooded home sites for the likes of highly paid executives; **Woodlake's** townhome developments lean more to younger career types.

Except enclaves restricted to single-family dwellings, the bulk of the Westheimer corridor is devoted to large apartment complexes and townhouses.

The northern tier between the Westheimer Strip and the Katy Freeway is the beginning of a wooded area that constitutes much of Houston's northwest and northeastern quadrants. Here you will see villages with a bayou or creek running through them and hundreds of houses hidden in dense thickets that are home to many small animals as well.

The principal artery cutting a winding path through this section is **Memorial Drive,** which begins on the edge of downtown and continues west all the way to State Highway 6, sometimes known as the Outer Belt, looping around the southwest and northwest region where it then becomes FM 1960.

Starting closer to town at the western edge of Memorial Park are beautifully wooded sections known as **Post Oak, Briar Grove,** and

Tanglewood, which are just south of Memorial along an extension called Woodway.

Many of the expansive homes on winding streets along Buffalo Bayou in the **Post Oak** have an almost rural setting, with fine ranch-style houses on spacious grounds covered with pines. Most are brick and many date back to the '60s and '70s. Going west into **Briarcroft** and **Briargrove,** the homes are closer together and on smaller lots but still are beautiful brick, one- and two-story dwellings. Abutting all of this are many new high-rise condos, huge townhouse developments, and apartment complexes, particularly along **Fountainview.** Some quiet streets lead onto cul-de-sacs.

North and west of Briargrove is a handful of private villages that have grown up around the Memorial/Buffalo Bayou corridor, including **Hunter's Creek, Piney Point, Bunker Hill, Hedwig** and **Willowick,** which is next to the Houston Country Club. The area offers many tennis, racquetball, golf, and swimming facilities, while, of course, many of the beautiful estates have private pools.

These villages boast tall pines and even wildlife. Some of the homes rival those in River Oaks with a wide assortment of architectural styles. They are largely highly restricted areas, and many lots cover half an acre, which adds to the rustic flavor of the communities.

Between **Hunter's Creek** and the Loop are the older homes that grew up along Memorial, many of them hidden away in dense foliage and thickets along cul-de-sac streets. Subdivisions in this area tend to be strictly private with guarded gates and high brick walls.

West of the villages the trees are smaller and there is less natural foliage, but the sites are still beautiful, neighbors to a large selection of townhomes such as in the Woodlake area.

Northwest Region—Inside the Loop

This area is wooded and lined with bayous. It features some of the oldest and most historic neighborhoods in Houston, more recently joined by apartment complexes. One particularly noteworthy section, called **The Heights,** has numerous old frame Victorian-type homes and cottages, drawing floods of restoration-minded young couples and other folks.

Nearby, the **Sabine** district also has many old frame, two-story houses with a turn-of-the-century look. Many are undergoing restoration by new owners.

The **Woodland Heights,** along White Oak Bayou, is made up largely of single-family brick and frame homes dating back to the 1930s. Family home sites mix with rentals in duplexes, apartments, and condos.

Northwest Region—Outside the Loop

This immense region also has proved to be one of the fastest growing in all of Houston, both commercially and residentially. It extends 20 to 30 miles out, all the way west to Cypress, north to Tomball, and to Conroe in Montgomery County. The major freeway artery cutting through the region is Highway 290 to Austin, and on each side are many subdivisions both old and new. Much of the region is dense with tall pines and big thickets, more so closer to metro Houston's northern extremes.

Closer in toward the Loop are fine old residential districts dating back to post-World War II such as **Garden Oaks** and **Oak Forest** with many one- and two-story frame and brick homes along tree-lined streets. Some of the houses in these areas are executive level, and residents find convenience in major shopping malls and other commercial centers nearby.

The districts are divided by large business center strips along such thoroughfares as North Shepherd, Ella Boulevard, and T.C. Jester Boulevard.

Farther west is **Spring Branch,** which contains a couple of incorporated villages just north of I-10 West. Affordable homes and apartments abound.

At the western extreme of this region are vast new sub-divisions from the Addicks area 20 miles out to Katy. These farm and ranch land communities are springing up all over the prairies with corn fields and gullies in between. Close by are Lakeside Airfield and the mammoth Bear Creek Park at the Addicks Reservoir. The majority are brick or a combination of frame and brick. In addition to the many fine new homes, there are new townhouse and apartment complexes with units for rent and for sale.

North around FM 529 some of the largest subdivision developments have grown under the banners of **Copperfield** and **Colonies.** The area is pocketed with office parks and strip developments along FM 1960.

Area recreation facilities include the prestigious Champions Golf Club. There are great executive homes in the **Champions** area, some facing right onto parkways and with lovely wooded gardens.

Keeping up with this growth are shopping malls and high- fashion stores. Here, too, are plenty of townhomes for sale and rent.

The majority of the executive homes off FM 1960, or Bammel Road as it's known at this point, are of a wide variety of styles and materials, mostly two-story and invariably with well-cared-for lawns and gardens, many with pools in the back.

In the **Cypress** area, there are fine colonies such as **Steeplechase.**

In addition, in subdivisions such as the newer **Hastings Green,** homes are affordable and the majority are single-family units, but multiple-family dwellings are being built here.

North into the **Tomball** area are homes ranging from modest tract houses to large-acreage estates. Tomball boasts clean air, plenty of wooded areas, a golf club, shopping, and a small-town atmosphere.

Continuing north and just west of I-45 North are the resort living areas around **Conroe,** namely **April Sound,** a private community; **Walden,** with its excellent golf facilities and yacht club; and others capitalizing on the waterfront lots and wooded acreage all around Lake Conroe, one of Houston's most popular recreation spots.

There are many resort homes as well as plenty of rustic-type condos.

Finally, 27 miles northwest of downtown Houston is the famous celebrity golf course and conference center called **The Woodlands,** around which is growing a planned community on some 23,000 acres of forest land. Here you will find a wide range of homes and affordable lots. Residents commute to Houston via van pools, cars and park-and-ride buses.

Northeast Region—Inside the Loop

This is a comparatively small area and principally made up of old neighborhoods with many frame houses widely mixed with commercial enterprises ranging from warehouse districts to shopping parks. The area closest to I-45 North around **Moody Park** can be pleasant with residential areas dating from pre-World War II. Most of the homes are one-story, single-family frames with some apartment complexes mixed in. This region heavily intersperses residential, industrial and major rail transportation sites.

Northeast Region—Outside the Loop

This region extends north and east into Montgomery and Liberty counties, and much of the territory is covered with tall pines because it abuts the southern fringe of the East Texas piney woods. In addition, many canals and bayous, plus Lake Houston and the San Jacinto River, water the area. It encompasses Bush Intercontinental Airport at the western edge and includes such incorporated towns as Humble and Spring.

The area just south of the airport includes older sub-divisions such as **Aldine** with its own independent school district, **Western Homes,** and **Woodsdale.** Between these large subdivision areas and the airport is the H and H Guest Ranch and Country Club set in forest bordering Intercontinental.

North of the airport are **Westfield** and **Spring.** Significant strip development along this corridor follows I-45 North all the way to Conroe, which straddles our regional divide.

Old Town Spring reflects the early days of this rural community. The area is full of Victorian-style houses. Nearby are newer developments such as **Inverness Forest. Spring** has an independent school district and is served by North Harris County College. Shopping centers and other commercial developments are nearby along the I-45 corridor.

To the east and just outside Bush Intercontinental is the old town of **Humble,** site of one of Texas' greatest oil discoveries, whence eventually Exxon flowed.

While this area blooms with new shopping malls, apartments and condos, it maintains its small-town flavor. It, too, has an independent school district serving planned communities farther north. **Kingwood** is one of those fast-growing residential communities with close to a dozen villages along forested trails. Homes range from modest to upper level.

Another such community is **Atascosita,** a community synonymous with golf, tennis and other great recreational features on Lake Houston. There are fine resort homes in sections such as Atascosita Shores.

Southeast Region—Inside the Loop

Much of this region is devoted to industry and is populated by families of workers in the surrounding refineries, chemical plants, and other installations that compose the mighty industrial districts of Houston and Pasadena. Nearly all of the sector between I-10 east and I-45 south is such big business. Few of the once-lovely old East End neighborhoods remain intact.

Areas such as **Pecan Park, Mason Park, Forest Park,** and **Idlewood** are especially scenic, with Brays Bayou winding through and lots of quiet, tree-lined residential streets.

There still are one- and two-story 1940s brick homes in good condition, and at the center is the lovely wooded area around Gus Wortham Golf Course.

South of the Gulf Freeway is **Riverside Terrace** with both Texas Southern University and the University of Houston at its door. It borders still another recreational facility at MacGregor Park.

North and South **MacGregor Way** and their environs boast some of the most lavish old mansions in Houston. This scenic wooded setting follows the path of Brays Bayou. Farther south these sections become **Forest Place** and **MacGregor Terrace** toward the Loop.

Southeast Region—Outside the Loop

Most of this land is coastal prairie and marshland. Numerous waterways include scenic bayous with moss-covered trees; the Houston Ship Channel lined with heavy industry; the San Jacinto River, which is popular with fishermen and skiers; and Clear Lake, with manmade canals in neighboring subdivisions. Homeowners park their boats at the front door.

Just outside the Loop, **Park Place** and **Glenbrook Valley** typify modest residential areas developed during and right after World War II. They remain peaceful neighborhoods with tree-lined streets and primarily frame and some brick two- and three-bedroom homes. **Park Place** borders Pine Gully and Glenbrook Golf Course.

To the south is ever-expanding Hobby Airport with small industrial strips, hotels, restaurants and shopping centers along Mykawa and Almeda-Genoa roads.

From the Gulf Freeway East is the **City of South Houston,** another World War II-era product, a bedroom community with modest frame homes and small shopping and business centers. It is close to Houston's Ellington Field.

Pasadena is another pre-existing city Houston has virtually surrounded. It retains its own school district, city government, law enforcement, shopping venues, and a general hospital. It lies in the heart of the industrial quadrant, where a number of similar small cities are home to refinery workers and their families—**Deer Park, Galena Park** and **Jacinto City.**

Just to the east of San Jacinto Battleground, across the channel is **Baytown.** Formerly called Goose Creek, this city derives its economic backbone from such big industries as Exxon and Chevron. The community offers some pleasant residential areas, with urban amenities in a small-town atmosphere. It is the home of Lee College.

South of Baytown and following Galveston Bay into Galveston County, small villages intersperse with incorporated towns: **La Porte, League City, Dickinson, Webster. Texas City** is at the tip of the mainland some 45 miles from Houston.

The area known as **Clear Lake** grew with the establishment of the Johnson Space Center, when hundreds of related industries moved in with NASA. This catalyzed the region as a preferred residential area catering to employees of the center and of other area businesses. Principal streets through the district are El Dorado, Bay Area Boulevard and NASA Road 1. The latter slices through the center of such towns as **Webster, Nassau Bay, El Lago,** and other resort-type communities that offer a wide range of middle- to upper-income brick homes, many in forested bayou settings, others on lakefront property.

The entire area has stimulated bordering towns such as **League City.** Marinas and apartment and townhouse complexes have sprung up along with business and single-family dwellings. The University of Houston—Clear Lake campus provides higher education to the communities in this area, as does the College of the Mainland.

La Porte is an old community with many small frame houses dating back more than 60 years. Its coastline, however, is still a popular resort area with some large homes and mansions along winding, wooded streets on Galveston Bay.

Just south is a string of villages with weekend homes and cottages, along with plenty of shopping to support the recreational business. Many Houstonians buy property in **Bayview, Bacliff,** and **San Leon,** and commute to work in Houston.

Galveston Island is our last outpost in this vast region, 50 miles from downtown Houston. Long deemed a resort and port, Galveston boasts many new developments in condos, townhouses, and restorations of old historical homes—all becoming immensely popular among Houstonians commuting to work in the big city and living by the sea. Much growth has been along Seawall Boulevard and toward the western tip of the island.

We have taken you in whirlwind fashion over many miles of metropolitan Houston, barely skimming over all the options available to new residents. But as stated at the outset, our intent is to offer you an overview of the area and a glimpse of neighborhood profiles. Such information should at least help you nail down a starting point in your search for new quarters, whether you are buying or renting.

Whatever your needs, whatever your income bracket, and whatever your preference, Houston can deliver practically anything but mountains and snow.

HOME AND GARDEN SOURCES & SERVICES

It pays to shop around, but for starters—the author's or editor's choices:

Air Conditioning Repairs— Bissonnet Air & Heat, 5901 Allday; 713-667-8942.

Alterations (clothing)—Ann's Tailor and Alterations, 2380 W. Alabama; 713-524-8090.

Appliances—Conn's, 2901 N. Shepherd; 713-864-5490. Other locations.

Automobile Repairs—Auto Tech, 7521 Pagewood; 713-781-9071.

Building Materials (old and new)— Home Depot, 5445 W. Loop South; 713-662-3950. Other locations.

Carpet & Rug Cleaning—Alpha Chem Dry; 713-522-5339.

Caterers—Tony's At Home, 3009 Post Oak; 713-622-3009.

Cleaning (clothes)—Craig's, 3520 So. Shepherd; 713-528-3016. Other locations. Pick up & delivery service.

Computer Repair—Electronic Service Center, 3506 Chimney Rock; 713-784-2291.

Concrete—Classic Paving, 6355 Westheimer; 713-850-6375.

Delivery Service—Hot Shot, 701 Shepherd; 713-869-7575.

Doors (residential)—Campbridge Doors & Windows, 12999 Murphy; 281-530-8100.

Doors (garage)—Overhead Door Co., 11533 S. Main; 713-667-1757.

Draperies—Laura's, 6135 Kirby; 713-520-7100.

Electrical Repair—Read Electric, 4704 Dickson; 713-523-5707.

Fencing—Houston Fence Company, 13300 Murphy Road; 281-499-2516.

Fireplace (sales and installation)— Fire Place Man, 5902 Southwest Freeway; 713-740-9001.

Foundation Repair—Atlas, 2830 Renshaw; 713-641-4844.

Furniture Cleaning—Coit, 9001 Spring Branch; 713-461-6171.

Furniture Rentals—Hoffer, 3118 Hillcroft; 713-780-4636

Gas Leaks (repairs)—Entex—emergency only, 713-659-3552.

Glass (car and home)—Binswanger Glass Co., 3402 N. Shepherd; 713-862-8874. Other locations.

Gutter (installation, repair and cleaning)—Vogler, 705 Shepherd; 713-861-1154.

Hardware—Bering's, 6102 Westheimer; 713-785-6400. Other locations.

Hardware (decorative)—Expo Design Center, 7600 Westheimer; 713-781-6662. Other locations.

Interior Design—American Society of Interior Designers, 5120 Woodway; 713-626-2743.

Internet Provider—PDQ Net, 1330 Post Oak; 713-830-3100.

Kennel—Pet Hotel, 5602 Royalton; 888-367-7387.

Keys/Locksmith—Precision Locksmith, 2226 Richmond; 713-521-3822.

Lamp Repairs—A&O Lamp Co., 3936 Bellaire; 713-660-0686.

Landscaping (design)—McDugald-Steele Landscape Architects, 849 W. Twenty-sixth; 713-868-8060.

Landscaping (equipment)—University Lawnmower Center, 2419 South Blvd.; 713-526-0333.

Landscaping (maintenance)—A J's Landscaping, 1223 W. Twenty-first; 713-864-9713.

Leather Cleaning—Sims, 9623 Hillcroft; 713-721-3100.

Lights (service trouble)—Reliant Energy HL&P; 713-228-7400.

Luggage Repairs—Bag 'n Baggage, 3900 Polk; 713-223-2181.

Mail Services—Pack N Send, 6200 Richmond; 713-266-1450.

Paintings Restoration—St. Mark Fine Arts Conservation, 1612 W. Alabama; 713-526-2302.

Party Rentals—Aztec, 3641 Westheimer; 713-552-9933.

Party Supplies—Arne's, 2830 Hicks; 713-869-8321.

Pest Control—Alamo; 4103 S. Main; 281-261-0052.

Photography Lab—Wolf Camera, 2612 S. Shepherd; 713-627-2689. Other locations.

Picture Frames (sales and repairs)—Allart Framing & Gallery, 2635 Revere; 713-3631.

Plumbing—Santhoff Plumbing, 6330 Alder; 713-665-4997.

Printing (copies, binding, business center)—Kinko's, 2455 Rice Blvd.; 713-521-9465. Other locations.

Recreational Vehicle Supplies—RV Suppliers, 6220 N. Shepherd; 713-691-3780.

Rentals (tools, machines, cleaning equipment, etc.)—A to Z Rentals, 1301 W. Alabama; 713-523-4459. Other locations.

Roofing—Mullins, 5706 Seymour; 281-442-6881.

Security Systems—San Jac Security, 415 Atascocita; 281-446-7500.

Shelving—Container Store, 2511 Post Oak; 713-960-1722.

Shoe Repairs—Houston Shoe Hospital, 5215 Kirby; 713-528-6268. Other locations.

Stained Glass (custom-made and repairs)—Glassworks, 2503 Montrose; 713-524-8455.

Stationery—Iconography, 2552 University; 713-529-2630.

Stereo—All Star Audio/Video, 10615 Katy Freeway.; 713-464-0014.

Storage—Mini-Storage Off Memorial, 160 Birdsall; 713-864-5757.

Swimming Pools (design, construction and maintenance)—Pool Innovations, 12919 Southwest Freeway; 281-240-7946.

Telephone (service trouble)—Southwestern Bell; 800-246-8464.

Veterinarian (emergency clinic)—Gulf Coast Veterinary Specialists, 1111 W. Loop South; 713-693-1111.

GALVESTON

GALVESTON PAST

Not only is Galveston one of Texas' oldest cities, it is among the most colorful with a long history of exploration, buccaneer days, wars, fortunes made and fortunes lost, natural disasters and the struggle to remain in the competitive mainstream of major ports.

The City of Galveston was founded in 1838, but its trail through history really started in 1528, when Spanish explorer Cabeza de Vaca arrived.

Less than 40 years after the first voyage of Columbus to the New World, de Vaca became the first white man to set foot on Texas soil. Galveston Island at the time was a favorite location for a tribe of Indians known as Karankawas, who lived primarily in nomadic fashion along the Texas Gulf Coast, existing on fish and small game. Little is known about the Karankawa people, but there is no doubt the cannibalistic rituals attributed to this much-maligned tribe were exaggerated in early historic accounts.

French and Spanish Claims

Later, Cavalier Sieur de la Salle came to the Texas coast and he gave the island its first name, San Luis, in honor of his French sovereign. The name is still in use today for a bay opening at the west end of Galveston.

By 1777, Texas and Mexico had come under Spanish rule and it was Count Bernardo de Galvez, viceroy of Mexico under Spanish dominion, who ordered the first survey of Galveston Bay. The island's name changed to Galvez in his honor, and it eventually metamorphosed into "Galveston."

The island was then largely ignored until a Frenchman named Louis-Michel Aury was made resident commissioner by rebel Jose Manuel de Herrera, who proclaimed the land for the non-existent Mexican Republic. Aury, who was involved in contraband and slave smuggling, left the island temporarily on an unsuccessful mission to

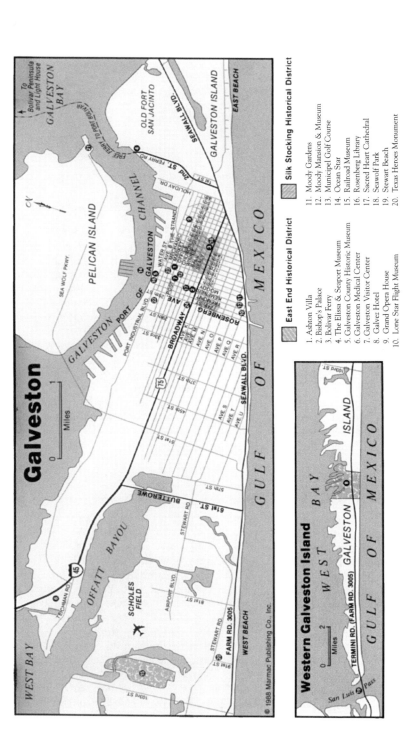

Galveston

0 — 1 Miles

© 1988 Marmac Publishing Co., Inc.

Western Galveston Island

0 — 2 Miles

East End Historical District

Silk Stocking Historical District

1. Ashton Villa
2. Bishop's Palace
3. Bolivar Ferry
4. The Elissa & Seaport Museum
5. Galveston County Historic Museum
6. Galveston Medical Center
7. Galveston Visitor Center
8. Galvez Hotel
9. Grand Opera House
10. Lone Star Flight Museum

11. Moody Gardens
12. Moody Mansion & Museum
13. Municipel Golf Course
14. Ocean Star
15. Railroad Museum
16. Rosenberg Library
17. Sacred Heart Cathedral
18. Seawolf Park
19. Stewart Beach
20. Texas Heroes Monument

help free Mexico from Spain. On his return, he found that a rival band of bounty hunters had taken over.

A Pirate Rules

Jean Lafitte, one of history's most famous pirates and a man whose name has become synonymous with Galveston, perhaps even more than Galvez himself, made this his island domain. He was named governor by the Mexican Patriot Government and called his little kingdom "Campeche." An imposing but suave man, feared by seafarers and statesmen alike, Lafitte attracted a large settlement of buccaneers who went along with Mexico's idea of sweeping the Gulf clear of Spanish ships.

Earlier, an English officer had approached Lafitte to take up arms against the United States at the Battle of New Orleans. But instead Lafitte befriended Gen. Andrew Jackson and, overnight, became a hero of the War of 1812. He was left then to rule Galveston with an iron fist. He ran raids on sea traffic and, according to legend, built up a cache of gold and silver that many today believe is still buried somewhere around Galveston.

Lafitte vowed to Jackson he would commit no act of piracy against U.S. vessels, but several secret raids by some of his men eventually led the United States to demand that he abandon Campeche forever. With this downfall, he ordered his settlement burned to the ground, then quietly put out to sea with his chosen freebooters. Finally, in broken health, he died in Venezuela, according to legend.

Galveston Comes into Its Own

The Galveston of more recent times had its beginning on the heels of Texas' winning independence from Mexico. In 1836, the same year that the Allen brothers founded Houston, a French-Canadian named Michel Menard bought a league of land from the new republic for $50,000. Two years later he formed a partnership to organize the Galveston City Company and immediately opened a port facility with private wharfing.

During the early days of the Texas Republic, Galveston conducted a fair amount of trade, shipping hides, cotton, wool, and cattle, and bringing in foodstuffs and other goods needed by the Southwestern colonists. Following Texas' annexation by the United States and the subsequent war with Mexico, Galveston continued as a leading port, and the largest and richest city in the state.

By 1850 it was known as the "commercial and cultural emporium of the Southwest." Cotton was king and many a fortune was made with cotton presses, storage and shipping.

Texas by then was a full-fledged slave state and, despite strong opposition from Gov. Sam Houston, who was deposed because of his refusal to sign allegiance to the Confederacy, Texans voted to secede from the Union. From the outbreak of the Civil War, Galveston was blockaded by the Federals, and the most important engagement in Texas took place when the U.S. Navy captured Galveston. It was later regained by Confederate troops out of Houston, who used vessels fortified with cotton bales to block enemy fire.

Later during the Spanish-American War, when it was feared Galveston might again come under siege, earthen-camouflaged gun mounts were set up along the seawall. They were fired only in practice, but the mounds remain as points of interest, and they are part of the landscape design of today's San Luis resort hotel.

Galveston freely concentrated on port development and other industrial efforts until 1900, when one of the most destructive natural disasters in American history struck.

Galveston's Nemesis

The calamity came suddenly in September.

Despite warnings of an approaching storm, Galvestonians, who were accustomed to such tropical invasions, went on about their business with little heed to the rising tides and increasing winds.

A few cautious souls headed for higher ground in Houston, but the majority retired as usual, only to be awakened early on Sept. 8, trapped by two gigantic forces converging on Galveston; one, a West Indian hurricane out of the Gulf, and the other, a northeasterly gale descending from the bay, driving a wall of water 15 feet high across the island.

When the waters finally met, a swirling sea inundated the island. Before the storms subsided, Galveston was nearly wiped off the map. More than 6,000 people perished in just a matter of hours.

An outpouring of aid from around the world relieved the suffering and immense damage to a degree, but it was years before Galveston recovered completely. At least the storms prompted the city to build a 12-mile-long, 17-foot-high seawall along the Gulf, and workers literally raised the island grade level by up to 12 feet, using tons of landfill. It was quite an engineering feat for those days.

Recovery

While Galveston was rebuilding, Houston surged ahead with its port development and wrenched the title of No. 1 shipping center in Texas. But then Galveston was resourceful and rebuilt itself into importance in world trade as well as other realms. Its list of firsts in Texas history and the great contibutions by the citizenry could not be erased by a few strokes of ill fortune.

GALVESTON TODAY

This island is a natural sandy barrier about 32 miles long, following the curve of the mainland. It is accessible by a causeway across the bay off I-45 from Houston, by a bridge over San Luis Pass at the western tip, and by ferry at the eastern end from Bolivar Peninsula or Highway 87.

With a population just shy of 60,000, the island covers an area of 264 square miles, including water. Like Houston, Galveston enjoys or endures a sub-tropical climate, but temperatures here tend to range 10 degrees warmer in winter and 10 degrees cooler in summer.

The coastal, sandy loam soil is fertile ground for tropical vegetation and produces a substantial annual income from rice, soybeans, and grain sorghums plus good grazing land for cattle.

In business, Galveston ranks high among world cotton centers with immense storage facilities and mammoth presses.

Resort City and Educational Center ———

Long a resort city attracting millions of tourists annually, Galveston also was once on the international gambling circuit with beautiful casinos, nightclubs offering star-studded entertainment, and slot machines on every corner.

Many thought the closing of the last illegal gambling halls in 1957 would be the final death knell for Galveston, but since that time it made still another comeback as an important center for medical research and education.

Galveston opened the first medical school in Texas, an ornate red-brick structure locals call "Old Red." That school is still in use, and around it is built a vast medical center complex with the University of Texas Medical Branch and the world-famous Shrine Burn Center.

Galveston also boasts of other educational institutions, including Galveston College, the National Maritime Research Center and the Texas A&M Maritime University. Galveston also is home to Texas' first library, the Rosenberg.

While its deep-water port is best known for cotton shipping, Galveston also moves considerable tonnage in oil, petrochemicals, grain, sand, gravel and other commodities.

It is ideally situated for studies in oceanography and, of course, the fishing industry. Visitors may catch a glimpse of some of Galveston's famous "mosquito shrimp fleet" tied up along the piers on the bay side of the island.

But surely the industry most closely identified with Galveston is tourism, for it continues to grow as a mainstay in the city's overall economy. Tourism and its related industries have mushroomed throughout Galveston, expanding its repertoire to appeal to all tastes and ages in all seasons.

The fine lodging establishments include some of the most unusual and historic in Texas. Diners can catch the super seafood here. Browsers can go nuts in shops, boutiques, and stores offering a range of goods from seashells to Steuben.

From its grand and glorious days as an early cultural center of the Southwest, Galveston carries that tradition forward with the 1894 Galveston Opera House restored to offer stellar entertainment; outdoor symphonies; fine art and antiques exhibits; and galleries for arts and crafts.

The city is a natural for sports enthusiasts who enjoy biking, hiking, horseback riding, tennis, golf, soccer and, of course, watersports galore. Visitors may enjoy a family bike ride or skating along the famous seawall, surf or swim in the tepid Gulf waters, or fish from long, low jetties. Party boats are available for bay or deep-sea fishing jaunts, and there are several excellent charters.

Galveston's rich history comes to life on guided tours of old mansions or on trolley rides through the historical districts.

However you choose to see Galveston—by private auto, by boat, on guided tours or afoot—there are many facets and many frames.

We invite you to peruse the following checklist of things to see and do on Texas' most exciting resort island.

LODGING

There are numerous hotels and motels of all sizes and priced to fit most any budget. Our recommendations are merely a selection. We've also included several bed and breakfast inns, which are becoming increasingly popular with Houstonians looking for a quick romantic getaway.

We do suggest you make reservations well in advance if you are planning to visit here during the summer months or special events. Consult a travel agent or call the hotel to inquire about seasonal rates, weekend packages and special promotions. Rates can vary considerably. The price categories we have affixed here reflect average summer rates and can be considerably less during the winter—except during Mardi Gras and other special events.

E—Expensive, $100 and up for a double.
M—Moderate, $75-100 for a double.
I—Inexpensive, less than $75 for a double.

Away at Sea Inn, 1127 Church; 800-762-1668. *M-E*. Located in the East End Historical District, this charming inn has three carefully appointed rooms. No televisions or telephones.

The Flagship Hotel, 2501 Seawall Blvd.; 800-392-6542; www.flag-shiphotel.com. *M-E*. The only one of its kind in the nation, this hotel is built on a million-dollar, 1,100-foot pier over the Gulf, with seven stories and 220 rooms, offering a spectacular view of the surf. Guests can fish from the hotel's T-head pier. Popular for honeymooners and wedding receptions.

Gaido's Seaside Inn, 3828 Seawall Blvd.; 800-525-0064; galveston.com/gaidos. *I-M*. Popular family-operated motel. Boasts 102 comfortable rooms. Pool. Best feature: Its neighbor is the venerable Gaido's seafood restaurant.

Harbor House, Pier 21; 800-874-3721; www.harborhousepier21.com. *M-E*. Constructed to look like a waterfront warehouse, this dockside inn's 42 rooms all provide views of Galveston Harbor. Located within walking distance of museums, shops and restaurants.

Holiday Inn on the Beach, 5002 Seawall Blvd.; 800-452-6002; www.holidayinnonthebeach.com. *M-E*. An eight-story hotel overlooking the Gulf offers 178 rooms, landscaped pool area, restaurant, cocktail lounge. Suites available.

Hotel Galvez, 2024 Seawall Blvd.; 800-392-4285. *E*. The terrace lounge of the grand and historical old Galvez provides a marvelous view of the Gulf. Outdoor pool. Sports and recreational outlets nearby. Some of its 228 rooms are small.

La Quinta Motor Inn, 1402 Seawall Blvd.; 409-763-1224; www.laquinta.com. *I-M*. Overlooks the Gulf of Mexico. Has 115 rooms and suites. Restaurants nearby. Pool. One-half mile from Stewart Beach.

Mermaid & the Dolphin, 1103 Thirty-third St.; 888-922-1866; www.galveston.com/mermaid. *E*. Six antique-filled rooms in an opulent 1866 Greek Revival mansion. Outdoor spa, sundeck and conservatory.

Moody Gardens Hotel, Seven Hope Blvd.; 888-388-8484; www.moodygardens.org. *E*. Lushly landscaped grounds and its proximity to Moody Gardens attractions add to the appeal of this 300-room convention hotel. Full-service spa.

The San Luis Resort & Conference Center, Fifty-third and Seawall Blvd.; 800-445-0090; www.sanluisresort.com. *E*. This four-diamond hotel offers 243 rooms, all with balconies overlooking the Gulf. Also a tropical garden with heated pool, swim-up bar and waterfall. Its

The Galvez of Galveston Island

Courtesy of Dale Young

new spa offers a full menu of body treatments. Fine dining room and lounge.

Stacia-Leigh, Pier 22 at Harborside Drive, 409-750-8858. *E.* Galveston's most unusual accommodations are found aboard a 1906 schooner permanently docked at lively Fisherman's Wharf and just steps from the Strand historic district. Eleven guestrooms and TV lounge.

Tremont House, 2300 Ship's Mechanic Row; 800-874-2300. *E.* Delightful rooms and suites in the heart of the historical area. Hotel has full-service dining room. Surrounded by excellent shopping and dining. Enjoy cocktails on the hotel's rooftop patio.

DINING

With tourism its top industry, Galveston offers a wide range of dining options, ranging from delis to fine dining. Here are some of Galveston's most famous and best restaurants:

Rates are based on appetizer, entree, and dessert, no beverage.

E—Expensive, $25 plus per person.
M—Moderate, $10-$25 per person.
I—Inexpensive, less than $10 per person.

Clary's Restaurant, 8509 Teichman Rd.; 800-278-0771; www.galveston.com/clarys. *E.* A favorite with the locals and many Houstonians who drive down for fine fresh seafood. Small dining room, attentive service. Good gumbo, and oysters and crab (in season). Also steaks. Lunch and dinner. Closed Mondays. Reservations and jackets for men recommended.

El Jardin Café, 413 Twenty-fourth St.; 409-763-9289. *I.* Off the tourist path, this homey spot serves up arguably the best Mexican food on the island. But unless you have an iron stomach, lay off the homemade green sauce.

Fish Tales, 25th and Seawall; 409-762-8545. *M.* This casual eatery has Gulf views and a terrific second-floor dining deck. Fried and grilled seafood specialties. Lunch and dinner daily.

Gaido's Seafood Restaurant, 3800 Seawall Blvd.; 409-762-9625; www.galveston.com/gaidos. *E.* A tradition in good seafood and fresh Gulf fish. A large family restaurant overlooking the Gulf's rolling surf. Always popular with locals and visitors alike. Specialties include stuffed broiled flounder and, of course, fresh oysters and crab (in season). Open for lunch and dinner daily, except Monday.

Ocean Grill, 2227 Seawall; 409-762-7100; www.galveston.com/oceangrill/. *M.* Fried seafood, grilled chicken and po'boys are the specialties of this casual diner. Located in a former turn-of-the-century bathhouse, this restaurant extends over the Gulf for marvelous al fresco dining.

Old Strand Emporium, 2112 Strand; 713-763-9445. *I.* This is a must stop when strolling The Strand. Picnic tables under the big veranda or tables inside. Terrific deli sandwiches and other unusual treats. A treasure-trove of import items from around the world plus many gifts and souvenirs. Hear the old piano roll and sip a glass of wine while you browse through yesteryear. Very casual. Open daily.

Phoenix Bakery & Coffee House, 220 Tremont; 409-763-4611. *I.* Your best bet for breakfast with terrific beignets, bagels and bacon-and-egg burritos. Light lunches.

Strand Brewery, 101 Twenty-third St.; 409-763-4500. M Handcrafted beers and sandwiches. The roasted garlic and spinach pizza never disappoints. Lunch and dinner daily. Go casual.

SIGHTS TO SEE
AND MUCH TO DO

Historical Districts

Many of Galveston's favorite attractions can be found in its three historic districts, which include:

The **East End:** bounded by market, Broadway, Nineteenth, and Eleventh;

the **Silk Stocking** district: south of Broadway, between Twenty-third and Twenty-sixth;

and **The Strand:** Strand and Ship's Mechanic streets between Twentieth and Twenty-fifth (Rosenberg).

Founded in 1871, the **Galveston Historical Society** (409-765-7834; www.galvestonhistory.org) is the oldest historical preservation group in the state. The society operates nine museums and historic sites, and oversees programs that encourage the restoration of historic commercial and residential properties.

Many of the historic homes date back more than 140 years and range in style from Moorish to Queen Anne. In addition to hundreds of homes, there are magnificent commercial structures with ornate iron facades, also dating to the early 1800s.

Early immigrants to Galveston built churches along the grand European style and particularly the **East End** contains beautiful examples reflecting various styles popular at different stages of island development. Historic churches include **St. Mary's Cathedral,** which was the first Catholic cathedral in Texas (1848), Twenty-first and Church; **First Presbyterian Church** (circa 1840), Nineteenth and Ave F;

Trinity Episcopal Church (1857), Twenty-second and Winnie; and **St. Joseph's Church,** built by German immigrants in 1859.

But the most outstanding church on the Galveston skyline is the **Sacred Heart Church and School** at Broadway and Fourteenth, across from the Bishop's Palace. It is painted stark white with onion-shaped cupolas in the Moorish style.

Along **The Strand** exciting shops, boutiques and other retail outlets intersperse with artists' studios and apartments. This gaslight-punctuated street of living history sparkles with activity in cafes, galleries, specialty stores, bars and even an old-fashioned candy factory, where you may indulge in an ice-cream soda and witness candy creations in progress.

Attractions

With its variety of historical sites, entertainment districts and inviting beaches, Galveston has long been Houston's playground. Island maps and other helpful materials can be obtained at the Galveston Island Convention & Visitors Bureau's Visitor Center, (2428 Seawall Blvd., 888-425-4753; www.galvestontourism.com) or at the Ashton Villa, (see below) which is home to the Galveston Historical Society's Heritage Visitors Center. Both centers are open daily and can provide up-to-date information on attractions and tours.

1859 Ashton Villa, 2328 Broadway; 409-762-3933. *CH.* Located on Galveston's "mansion row," this historic Italian home pre-dates the Civil War and has withstood the ravages of both man and nature. An excellent film prefaces the tour with good insight into the city's history, including the wrath of the 1900 storm and the incredible rebuilding efforts that followed. Open 10 am-4 pm Mon-Sat.; 10 am-5 pm Sun.

Bishop's Palace, 1402 Broadway; 409-762-2475. *CH.* Begun in 1886 and completed in 1893, the Bishop's Palace was erected by U.S. Congressman Walter Gresham at a mere cost of only $250,000 in those modest times. Designed by the well-known Nicholas Clayton, the palace features many mantels from around the world, one of which is lined with pure silver. The house was later purchased by the Catholic Church to serve as a bishop's residence.

It is listed both in the Library of Congress and on the American Institute of Architecture roster of the most architecturally significant 100 homes in the United States. Open 10 am-5 pm Mon-Sat, noon-5 pm Sun during the summer; noon-4 pm in winter.

Bolivar Peninsula—Ferry Boats and Lighthouse, at the end of Ferry Rd. (Second St.) from Seawall Boulevard. *NCH.* A fleet of free, state-run ferries continuously plies the three-mile crossing over the channel to the Bolivar Peninsula onto Highway 87, providing a fun experience for the entire family.

You may leave your car and stroll the deck for an occasional glimpse of playful dolphins, a good view of Pelican Island, and a survey of the merchant ship activity in the Port of Galveston.

At Point Bolivar there is an abandoned lighthouse that is one of the few of its era still intact. Built in 1872, it miraculously survived the great 1900 hurricane that swept over the peninsula with massive tides and gales.

Galveston Arts Center, 2127 Strand; 409-763-2403. This airy center displays and sells the works of local artists. It also sponsors the popular Galveston ArtWalks, which are held on Saturdays every six weeks. Downtown galleries and studios hold a community-wide open house with refreshments, entertainment, and free trolley transport. The Arts Center is open 10 am-5 pm Mon-Sat; noon-5 pm Sun.

Galveston County Historical Museum, 2219 Market; 409-766-2340. NCH. This understated museum is housed in the handsome 1919 City National Building. Among its treasures are exhibits on the 1900 storm, the 1947 Texas City disaster, and the origins of Juneteenth. Open 10 am-4 pm Mon-Sat; noon-4 pm Sun.

Galveston Island State Park, at 13 Mile Road and FM 3005 on West End of island; 409-737-1222. CH. Situated among the natural dunes, bay marshes and along clean sandy beaches, this 2,000-acre park is popular with campers and nature lovers. This vast park reaches from the bay to the Gulf beaches. At its center is a self-guided nature trail and the multimillion-dollar **Mary Moody Northen Amphitheatre.** Open daily.

Grand 1894 Opera House, 2020 Post Office St.; 409-765-1894; www.thegrand.com. Restored by the Galveston County Cultural Arts Council, this European-style opera house, built in 1894, spotlighted many of the world's great artists over the years. Lillian Russell, Sara Bernhardt and Otis Skinner all performed here. Year-round schedule includes ballet, opera, symphony, musicals, comedy acts and pop concerts. Open for free, self-guided tours daily.

The Great Storm, Pier 21; 409-763-8808. CH. This multimedia documentary uses eye-witness accounts, historic photographs and dramatic lighting and sound to tell the story of the deadliest natural disaster in U.S. history. This attraction is key to understanding the historical significance of all existing buildings and homes built before 1900. Open 11 am-6 pm Sun-Thu; 11 am-8 pm Fri-Sat.

Historic homes account for many of the more than 550 landmarks listed on the National Register of Historic Places. The Galveston Historical Society maintains two for tours:

The **Menard Home,** 1605 33rd St.; 409-762-3933. CH. Federal and

American Empire antiques fill this gorgeous Greek Revival mansion, which was built by a city founder in 1838. It is Galveston's oldest home. Open noon-4 pm Fri-Sun.

The **Samuel May Williams Home,** 3601 Avenue P; 409-762-3933. CH. The house built in 1839 offers an unusual architectural mix of Creole plantation house and New England sea captain's home. Open noon-4 pm Fri-Sun.

Lone Star Flight Museum, 2002 Terminal Dr.; 409-740-7722; www.lsfm.org. CH. More than 40 restored aircraft, most in working condition, are on exhibit. Among the aircraft on display are World War II fighters, bombers and cargo carriers.

The museum also houses the **Texas Aviation Hall of Fame,** whose inductees include long-distance flier Wiley Post, astronaut Alan Bean and Tom Landry. The latter is the late coach of the Dallas Cowboys, who also was a U.S. Army Air Force pilot with 30 bombing missions to his credit. Open 10 am-5 pm daily.

Mardi Gras Museum, 23rd and Strand; 409-763-1133. CH. This colorful museum pays tribute to the island's biggest party. Elaborate costumes and historic memorabilia are on display. Open noon-6 pm Fri-Sat.

Moody Gardens, One Hope Blvd.; 800-582-4673; www.moodygardens.org. CH. This lushly landscaped recreational and educational complex with its three striking 10-story pyramids began as just a barn and riding arena where children with head injuries rode horses as part of their therapy. The Moody Foundation still carries out that important work today but the complex has grown to include a hotel and convention center, an education center, green houses for medicinal plant programs and several attractions of tourist appeal. Among the latter:

Rainforest Pyramid explores the tropical ecosystems of Africa, Asia and the Americas. See vibrantly colored birds, hundreds of brilliant butterflies and scores of active bats.

Discovery Pyramid focuses on space exploration and includes a mock-up of the International Space Station.

Aquarium Pyramid offers close-up views of the diverse marine life found in the Caribbean, Pacific and Atlantic waters. Touch tanks add to the kid appeal.

Palm Beach draws in families with its white sand, water lagoons, relaxing spas and water slides. Paddleboats, sand volleyball courts, concession stands and lockers.

Colonel Paddlewheel Boat is an 800-passenger reproduction of an 1800s paddlewheeler. Hour-long cruises depart several times daily.

IMAX 3D Theater shows a variety of in-your-face 3D films on its six-story screen.

Moody Gardens is open daily. Hours vary by season.

Moody Mansion and Museum, 2618 Broadway; 409-762-7668. CH. Hand-carved woods, coffered ceilings and stained glass add to the luster of this elegant 42-room mansion, which was built in 1894. The ballroom is decorated as it was in 1991, when a young Mary Moody celebrated her social debut. Open 10 am-4 pm Mon-Sat; 1 pm-4:30 pm Sun.

Ocean Star Museum, Pier 20; 409-766-7827. CH. Learn about the day-to-day business of operating an offshore drilling rig at this unique museum located over the water at Galveston Harbor. Open 10 am-4 pm daily.

Rosenberg Library, 2310 Sealy; 409-763-8854. NCH. Galveston gave Texas its first free library. The Rosenberg was a gift to the state from philanthropist Henry Rosenberg who emigrated from Switzerland to Galveston in 1843. Among his other gifts was the imposing **Texas Heroes Monument** that still dominates the traffic island at Broadway and Rosenberg. This library is noted for its collection of rare books and artifacts, including original letters of Jean Lafitte, Sam Houston and Stephen F. Austin, among others. It also features a fine art collection and special exhibits. Open 9 am-9 pm Mon-Thu; 9 am-6 pm Fri-Sat; 1 pm-5 pm Sun.

Seawolf Park. Take Seawolf Parkway from Fifty-first and Broadway to Pelican Island, the other island off Galveston; 409-744-5738. CH. During the 1800s, Pelican was Texas' version of Ellis Island in New York. Thousands of immigrant families were detained here for quarantine before being admitted to the United States and moving on to settle in their new homeland.

World War II-vintage vessels and other military equipment now have a permanent home in the park. You may peer through the periscope of the USS *Cavalla*, a submarine distinguished in battle against the Japanese navy, or learn how the USS *Stewart* destroyer came to serve under both the U.S. and the Japanese flags. CH.

Then take to the T-head for fishing in the fertile waters of the bay or simply relax, picnicking at a three-level modern pavilion from which point you can sight the *Selma* or what remains of a World War I concrete vessel that sank here long ago.

Open daily dawn to dusk.

The Railroad Museum, Twenty-fifth at Strand; 409-765-5700; www.tamug.tamu.edu/rrmuseum. CH. Located in the restored art-deco Galveston Union Depot, this museum focuses on the golden era of railroads. At the back of the museum is a large collection of vintage rail cars. Open 10 am-4 pm daily.

Texas Seaport Museum, Pier 21, 409-763-1877; www.phoenix.net/~tsm/. CH. An immigration data base that allows visitors to search for relatives that arrived in the United States via

Galveston is among the interactive exhibits at this museum, which is a project of the Galveston Historical Foundation.

A highlight of a visit here is a tour of the **Tall Ship Elissa,** which is docked adjacent to the harbor-side museum. The four-masted schooner was built in Scotland in 1877 and is one of the world's few remaining tall ship square-riggers. Elissa has served under five different flags and has called on many of the exotic ports of the world. Open 10 am-5 pm daily.

Tours

Galveston offers not only many sights to see, but also many ways to see them. Pick whichever way best suits your time, taste and temperament, but know that really getting into the heart and soul of Galveston means striking out in your most comfortably sturdy walking shoes.

From Houston there are several Galveston tour possibilities. Look at the Tours section of the TRANSPORTATION chapter. Most of the firms offer full-day Galveston excursions that will cover all the highlights. CH.

We offer our own version of an overview of the island in the SELF-GUIDED TOUR below if you prefer to see Galveston in the familiar comfort of your own vehicle.

When in Galveston, consider:

Galveston Island Trolleys run on two fixed loops. One loops around downtown; the other makes a loop from the Seawall to The Strand Historic District. The trolleys run continually daily. Main pick-up points are 2100 Seawall and 2016 Strand. Information: 409-762-2950. CH.

Galveston Sightseeing Train has been taking visitors on 1 1/2 hour tours of the island since 1962. The 17-mile narrated tour motors past dozens of historic sites, including Ashton Villa, the Bishop's Palace and the remains of Fort Crockett. Boards at Seawall at Twenty-first Street. Operates daily, weather permitting. Hours vary by season. Information: 409-765-9564. CH.

Galveston Island Duck Tours combine a land tour of historic sites with a quick excursion on Offats Bayou using a special vehicle that runs on land and in water. The 90-minute tours feature fun narration. Boards at Seawall at Twenty-first Street. Operates daily, weather permitting. Hours vary by season. Information: 409-621-4771. CH.

Galveston Harbour Tours provides an assortment of bird-watching, dolphin-watching and other nature tours. It also runs frequent tours of the Galveston seaport, where visitors can see docks loaded with sugar, bananas and cotton. Boards at Pier 22. Information: 409-765-1700. CH.

SHOPPING

The Strand has a most interesting assortment of boutiques, art galleries, a fine old jewelry and gift store, arts and crafts shops, clothing, cards, gourmet foods, and antiques.

Postoffice Street, just a short walk from and parallel to The Strand, is the latest historic district to be redeveloped. It bulges with art galleries, antique stores and eateries.

Seawall Boulevard is lined with shops—some on piers—for souvenirs, seashells, T-shirts and all the traditional coastal resort items.

SPECIAL EVENTS

Its temperate climate and tourism focus gives Galveston plenty of reason to celebrate. You'll find festivals and special events scheduled all year. We have selected just a few of the major annual items to give you an idea of the range of festivals by seasons.

For event dates and details, contact the Galveston Island Convention & Visitors Bureau's Visitor Center at 888-425-4753, or access www.galvestontourism.com.

Mardi Gras. February. Twelve days of festivities that include elaborate parades, street dances, masked balls and concerts.

Beach Party Weekend. April. This 20-year-old event is a spring break tradition that attracts more than 120,000 black collegians each year.

Kite Fest. April. Colorful kites guided by professional teams fill the air over East Beach during this two-day, kid-friendly event.

Galveston Historic Homes Tour. Early May. A marvelous opportunity for an inside look at historical homes not generally open to the public.

AIA Sandcastle Competition. Early June. Teams of architects and engineers compete for the Golden Bucket Award for sculptures built of Galveston beach sand.

Caribbean Carnival. June. The music, dance and cuisine of the Caribbean are spotlighted at this event held on Pier 21.

Fourth of July. Moody Gardens stages a watermelon festival and old-fashioned Ice Cream Crank Off.

Harborfest. October. The Port of Galveston is the focus of this dockside festival that features boat tours, musical entertainment, and naval demonstrations.

Parade of Lights. November. Dozens of colorfully lighted boats, many toting sea-going Santas, parade through Galveston Harbor.

Dickens on The Strand. Early December. Merrye Olde England and the days of Charles Dickens come alive with parades, performing artists, food booths and fun for all ages—all on one of Galveston's most historical streets. *CH*.

SELF-GUIDED TOUR

If you are coming from Houston stay on I-45 South (Gulf Freeway), which, after crossing the causeway, becomes Broadway. Even if you are already on the island, start at the foot of Broadway near the causeway. This will give you a comprehensive overview of Galveston.

From this tour, then, you tailor the time at each point according to your interest. Depending on the waiting time for the ferry, and the volume of traffic on Broadway and along the seawall, this tour should take five or six hours, including a stop for lunch or dinner.

Along Broadway

As soon as you get off the causeway the first thing to catch your eye, if they are in bloom, will be the oleanders along the esplanade. This is the Galveston city flower and they provide a profusion of color during the summer.

A short distance ahead, as you come to the Port Industrial Boulevard exit, you'll see to your right the *Galveston Daily News* on a slight knoll. The News is the oldest daily newspaper in Texas.

Between Forty-third and Forty-first streets on your right is Galveston's cemetery, which was founded in 1839. Among the buried here are leaders of the Republic of Texas, Confederate soldiers and a few victims of the Great Storm. Although more than 6,000 people died as a result of the 1900 hurricane, few received proper burials because of the sheer number of fatalities.

Moving along Broadway to its intersection with Twenty-fifth Street, you will see a tall bronze statue on a handsome pedestal with four panels depicting the highlights of the Texas Revolution. Galveston philanthropist Henry Rosenberg gave it to the state to commemorate the heroes of the Battle of San Jacinto which, just a few miles inland, won Texas' independence from Mexico in 1836. In the next block past the statue you will begin to see beautiful old mansions on your left. Galveston is filled with nineteenth-century architectural wonders as evidenced by these homes. At Twenty-fourth Street, one block past the statue, is Ashton Villa, a Mediterranean-style Italianate home with wrought-iron balcony, dating from 1859. Today it is a museum depicting the lifestyle of Galvestonians at the turn of the century.

Bishop's Palace is next at Fourteenth Street across from Sacred Heart Cathedral, which is a key landmark on Galveston's historical skyline. The palace was built in 1886 by U.S. Congressman Walter Gresham, and, in architectural significance, ranks among the top 100 homes in the United States.

The church features Moorish architecture accented with beautiful stained-glass windows.

Continue to the end of Broadway and turn left onto Seawall Blvd. Proceed two more stoplights to Ferry Road (Second Street), which leads to the free, state-run ferry boats to Highway 87 on the Bolivar Peninsula.

Take the Ferry to Bolivar

Turn left at Ferry Road and go to the end to board the ferry. The actual crossing of the three-mile-wide channel to the peninsula takes about 20 minutes. A good view of Pelican Island is one advantage; a chance to see dolphins cavort alongside the moving vessel is another. (Note: Hours-long waits to board the ferry are not uncommon on busy summer weekends. Watch for signs warning of lengthy waits.)

At Bolivar there is an abandoned 1872 lighthouse, one of few in Texas left intact. You may turn around at the lighthouse for the return trip, but if you need film or other sundries first, continue just past the lighthouse to Fisherman's Cove on the right.

Back on the island, take Ferry Road 14 blocks and turn right onto the Strand.

The Strand

On the left is a cluster of buildings that constitute the Galveston Medical Center, including the University of Texas Medical Branch and the Shrine Burn Center.

You are now approaching the section of The Strand that is most historic and which has been under massive and continuous restoration by the Galveston Historical Foundation since before the 1976 U.S. bicentennial celebration.

When you get to Nineteenth Street we suggest you find a parking spot and stretch your legs a bit, for this is an ideal place to start a stroll along The Strand. Stop by the clearly marked Visitor Information Center at 2016 Strand. Besides providing helpful and informative brochures, the staff can assist with all types of recreational referrals. We will proceed only a short distance from here to give you an idea of what to expect in the area.

The Old Strand Emporium exemplifies early Galveston commercial interiors and houses a yesteryear shop with a deli. Walk past the Emporium to the corner, **cross the street and turn right.** Here is the entrance to one of the most fascinating stores anywhere: Col. Bubbies Surplus Senter, a warehouse crammed with military gear from around the world.

Now continue to the dead end of this street to Fisherman's Wharf at Pier 22. An old seafood market is now a restaurant with views of Galveston's busy ship channel. Just to the right of Pier 22 is the entrance for tours aboard the *Elissa*. The restored square-rigged merchant ship that called at Galveston during the 1800s permanently berths here as a maritime museum.

Next door is Pier 21, a retail and entertainment complex with two good seafood restaurants and The Great Storm, a multimedia theater that presents an outstanding program on the 1900 hurricane several times daily.

The Pier area and The Strand offer dining options ranging from the elegant to the egalitarian. This would be a good place for lunch, dinner or just a snack.

Now head back to your car and proceed on down The Strand to the end at Twenty-fifth Street, also known as Rosenberg.

The large art-deco building you see there is the Shearn Moody Plaza, formerly the Gulf, Colorado and Santa Fe Terminal. It houses a railroad museum. Innovative audio systems and vintage railroad cars make this an interesting stop.

East End

To continue on, **turn left on Twenty-fifth and go five blocks to Winnie Street. Turn left** and just ahead you will see a couple of old churches with striking stained-glass windows. Winnie is one of several interesting streets in this historical East End. You will see many homes with "gingerbread" facades, wrought-iron fences, galleries, turrets, towers and gables.

Continue on Winnie to nineteenth Street and turn right. Then go two blocks to Sealy and turn left. This is one of the most charming streets in all of Galveston. Just as you turn, notice the Gothic house on the left with its intricate woodcarving. On the right, at Seventeenth Street, another unique edifice mixes Moorish style with Gothic design.

When you get to Fourteenth (Christopher Columbus), take a left and go to Market Street. There, turn left again, and on the right at Fifteenth, note the white frame home with columns and ornate front. This home has a state historical marker, as do so many of its neighbors.

At Nineteenth Street, the modern building (Galveston's tallest) on the right is the headquarters of American National Insurance Company, one of the largest insurance firms in Texas. At one time, the company publicly displayed the insurance policies they issued on the infamous 1930s criminals, Bonnie Parker and Clyde Barrow.

Turn left onto Nineteenth, go one block to Post Office Street, then turn left again.

Note the red brick and tile home at the corner of Sixteenth, unusual for this area because most houses are of wood frame construction. Built in 1887 in the Richardsonian Romanesque style, it offered refuge for some 200 people during the 1900 hurricane.

To Seawall Boulevard

Follow this street now all the way to University, turn right there and get into the middle lane. Pass the light at Broadway and turn right onto Seawall Boulevard.

Stewart Beach Park will now be on the left. This is a popular summer beach and it offers a number of conveniences including bathhouse, snack stands, gift shop, lifeguard stations, umbrellas and chaises for rent, and children's playground with rides and games. It also is alcohol-free, which means it is illegal to possess any alcoholic beverage.

The Seawall, 12 miles long and 17 feet high, was built following the devastating 1900 storm to protect property along the beachfront. It is lined with cafes, hotels, motels, restaurants, souvenir shops and commercial piers that, in Galveston's heyday, swarmed with gambling activity.

If you missed the Visitor Information Center on The Strand, you have another information resource at another Galveston Island Convention & Visitors Bureau center at Twenty-first St. (Moody) and Seawall.

Across the street from the Galveston Information Center you will see the restored Hotel Galvez, circa 1911, on your right.

The Flagship, just ahead, is a newer landmark property, unique in that it is the only hotel in the nation built completely over a body of water.

If you arrive at this point late in the afternoon or early evening, consider a stop at Gaido's for a late lunch or dinner. This is the city's oldest family-operated restaurant (see DINING above).

When you are ready to move along **continue down Seawall Boulevard.** Note a couple of artillery bunkers in the area of Forty-fifth St. These are left over from the Fort Crockett installation built for coastal defense in 1897.

To get to Galveston Island State Park this is the route you would take on to Highway 3005, but **to return to downtown simply head back in the direction you came.**

If you are returning to Houston go back about two miles until you get to Sixty-first Street and turn left. Pass a small Serbian cemetery on your right, continue to Broadway. Turn left onto Broadway, which will take you back to the causeway, which becomes I-45 North into Houston.

BITS AND PIECES

Intrigued by tall Texas tales, a German film company came here some years ago to research a documentary titled "Only in Houston." They found that many of the facts were harder to believe than the fictions.

The truth in telling true Texas tales is that even the most righteous tend to, shall we say, elasticize. There are several what you might term types of truth in Texas: True truth. Sorta true truth. And baldface untruth too good to shoot down with the other two.

Many Texas legends have been passed down for generations, expanding en route from past to present with romantic embellishments or other fanciful exaggerations.

So, partly for edification, but mostly for fun, here are a few that have become as much a part of this part of Texas as bayous and oil.

Each item is marked with an asterisk or two. One * means solid to semisolid truth; two ** means that, like freshly drilled oil, there might be a little gas in it.

*The Battle of San Jacinto was one of the briefest in world history. No one knows for sure, but it took the Texans either 18 or 19 minutes to rout the Mexican forces and midwife the independence of Texas as a republic.

**The song, "Yellow Rose of Texas," was written in honor of the Texas heroine, an octoroon named Emily, who, shall we say, distracted Mexican general Santa Anna sufficiently to enable Gen. Sam Houston to launch his victorious surprise attack at San Jacinto.

**The Episcopal Diocese of Texas might be the only church anywhere that has a pair of Texas Longhorns on its official seal. It reportedly commemorates the day of groundbreaking for Houston's Christ Church Cathedral when a Longhorn heifer broke away from a Texas Avenue cattle drive and scampered right through the formal gathering. Church leaders took it as a good omen.

*In a dubious achievement, Houston surpassed Los Angeles in 1999 for the first time as the city with the nation's worst smog.

*Houston has more than 1 million trees on public rights-of-way and is one of few major cities still celebrating Arbor Day by dispensing free trees to citizens.

*One of the most expensive pieces of land in Houston history was a half block purchased by the Woolworth Company. The price paid: $3,050,000, or about $2,000 a front inch. This is significant when you consider that the initial league of land for the city cost only around $9,000.

*President John F. Kennedy spent the last night of his life, Thursday, Nov. 21, 1963, dining in Houston at the Rice Hotel. The next day, he was assassinated in Dallas.

**Hermann Square in front of City Hall was a gift to Houston from philanthropist George Hermann, with the stipulation that it always would remain a refuge park for transients and the like. He had trouble getting his hands back to work in the cotton fields after a weekend binge downtown that usually wound up with a night in jail. So he bought a parcel of land with firm instructions that his help should head for the square to avoid encounters with the law. If they got drunk they could sleep it off in the park and make it back in time for muster on Monday morning.

*Houston is the egg roll capital of the world. The nation's top two egg roll makers—Minh Foods and Chung Gourmet Foods—are based in Houston and combined they hand roll more than 750,000 egg rolls each day.

*The flagship of the Texas Navy is the battleship USS *Texas*, permanently moored as a museum near the San Jacinto Battleground.

*Buffalo Bayou was once a source of drinking water for Houstonians. Later it was dubbed "The worst polluted such body of water in the nation." More recently Houston has cleaned it up and some aquatic life has returned to the murky waters.

*In 1882, Houston became one of the first two cities to build an electric power plant. The other, shockingly enough, was New York.

*Gail Borden, the inventor of the process for condensing milk, was hired by the Allen brothers to produce the original plan for Houston streets. Texas Avenue was the only street he made 100 feet across . . . that was to accommodate 14 head of Longhorn cattle, horntip-to-horntip, during cattle drives.

*The Kellum-Noble house in Sam Houston Historical Park, besides being the oldest home on its original site, has been put to sundry uses. It was at one time a private elementary school and the city's first zoo.

*The Rice-Nichols-Cherry house, also in Sam Houston Park, was being demolished when one Emma Richardson Cherry came along and took a fancy to the front door. Unable to convince the crew to sell the door by itself, she bought the whole house for $25. Who says those weren't the good old days?

*The founders of Houston advertised their new town as being a most salubrious place to live . . . they failed to mention that so many were dying from yellow fever and cholera the city was almost abandoned.

*Houston was the United States' fastest-growing city in the twentieth century. Using U.S. Census Bureau data, a researcher for the Houston Business Journal tracked the growth of the 100 most populous U.S. cities from 1900 to 2000. In 1900, 44,633 people lived in Houston; the 2000 population was an estimated 1,816,522. Houston's population grew almost 4,000 percent during that time. In terms of population rankings, the city went from Eighty-fifth to fourth.

*The first word spoken from the surface of the moon when the first astronauts landed in July 1969 was "Houston."

*Houston is called "Bayou City" with good reason. There are 26 major streams, plus a list of smaller bayous long enough to fill four type-written pages, crisscrossing the metropolitan area.

**Stories relate how President Sam Houston entertained his cabinet and foreign ministers grandly in the city's first hotel, The Mansion. Imagine the president at that time spending $6 on a pair of fowl, $1 a pound for butter, and $3 for a dozen eggs, not to mention the price he must have paid for champagne.

*The downtown block where the old Rice Hotel stands is full of history. It was once site of the capitol of the Republic.

*Saucy news: Among the nation's 10 largest cities, Houston has the most barbecue joints. The Yellow Pages list 103 barbecue spots in Houston. The closest is Chicago with 59.

*Houstonians are intensely loyal to their own. In World War II, when the cruiser *Houston* sank in the Java Sea, a thousand crew members were lost. Shortly thereafter, during a rousing demonstration of patriotism, 1,189 young men were sworn in en masse at Main and Lamar to serve aboard the new cruiser *Houston*. A granite historical marker was placed at the site.

*The oldest commercial structure on its original site is a pub at 813 Congress. It once adjoined an Indian trading post owned by a John Kennedy, who ran a stage coach inn upstairs where, reportedly, Sam Houston once slept.

*Late U.S.President Lyndon B. Johnson taught school here in the old San Jacinto Senior High School, now located at 1300 Holman and San Jacinto. His home here was at 435 Hawthorne.

*Clark Gable lived here while he was studying elocution and his home was at the southeast corner of Whitney and Hyde Park.

*The late billionaire Howard Hughes was brought up in Houston. His home is now part of the University of St. Thomas complex at 3921 Yoakum. He is buried in Houston's Glenwood Cemetery.

*Houstonians love dining out. They eat out an average of 4.9 times a week, which is more than any other U.S. city.

**When a famous Houston oil baron passed on some years ago his widow decided to have their mansion torn down. The demolition squad uncovered a secret underground cache with some $10,000 in silver coins that no one, including his wife, knew was there. He used to throw such coins to the poor on his way to work, driving a different Cadillac for each day of the week.

**It is said that the two spots in the nation with the strongest ultra-violet rays are at Salton Sea, California, and Houston/Galveston. Bring your strongest sunscreen.

*Houston's temperate climate and seemingly endless sunshine has earned it promise as the "The Third Coast" of filmmaking. Among the movies and television shows shot (at least in part) here are *The Evening Star, Apollo 13, Armageddon, Local Hero, Reality Bites, Robocop 2, Urban Cowboy, Rushmore* and *Tin Cup*.

*U.S. public television began here in 1953, when the University of Houston's KUHT-TV Channel 8 went on the air as the nation's first public TV station.

*Galveston-based American National Insurance Company once issued policies covering the lives of the infamous 1930s criminal couple Bonnie & Clyde, who died together in a hail of police gunfire. The policies, which have been on display at the firm's headquarters, named Bonnie Parker's and Clyde Barrow's respective mothers as beneficiary.

*Glen McCarthy, a famous Houston wildcatter from early oil-boom days, built his own Texas-size playhouse, which he named the Shamrock Hotel. It sat stark on a bald prairie out on South Main, and to be sure it acquired an indelible identification, he staged a week-long party for openers. To liven up the show he brought in a trainload of Hollywood celebrities. He staged water-ski shows in the Texas-size swimming pool. The hotel has since been razed.

**Flash! It used to take steamboats seven hours to go 50 miles between Galveston and Houston via Buffalo Bayou . . . now you can make a little better time (less than an hour) if you drive via the Gulf Freeway—unless you go during rush hour, in which case you might well be better off back on the bayou!

**Cultural note: Iced tea is widely considered the "National" Drink of Texas, and Blue Bell brand Homemade Vanilla flavor ice cream is just as widely considered the "National" Ice Cream of Houston.

*The Rockets, in June 1994, became the first Houston team to win a major sports championship. They made Houston beam by taking the NBA crown again in 1995. But it is the heroics of the Comets that, arguably, will go down as Houston's greatest sports triumph. The Comets earned the championship titles each year in the first four seasons of the Women's National Basketball Association play beginning in 1997.

INDEX

250